Reaching English Language Learners in Every Classroom

Energizers for Teaching and Learning

Debbie Arechiga

EYE ON EDUCATION

Eye On Education
6 Depot Way West, Suite 106
Larchmont, NY 10538
(914) 833-0551
(914) 833-0761 Fax
www.eyeoneducation.com

Library of Congress Cataloging-in-Publication Data

Arechiga, Debbie.
Reaching English language learners in every classroom : energizers for teaching and
learning / Debbie Arechiga.
        p.   cm.
Includes bibliographical references.
ISBN 978-1-59667-219-2
1. English language—Study and teaching—Foreign speakers.
2. English teachers—Training of.
I. Title.
PE1128.A2A64 2012
428.0071—dc23   2012004967

Sponsoring Editor: Robert Sickles
Production Editor: Lauren Davis
Copyeditor: Andrew Miller
Designer and Compositor: Matthew Williams, click! Publishing Services
Cover Designer: Dave Strauss, 3FoldDesign

Also Available from EYE ON EDUCATION

Multicultural Partnerships:
Involve All Families
Darcy J. Hutchins, Marsha D. Greenfeld, Joyce L. Epstein,
Mavis G. Sanders, and Claudia L. Galindo

Engaging the Families of ELLs:
Ideas, Resources, and Activities
Renee Rubin, Michelle H. Abrego, and John A. Sutterby

Literacy from A to Z
Barbara R. Blackburn

Building a Culture of Literacy Month-by-Month
Hilarie Davis

Active Literacy Across the Curriculum
Heidi Hayes Jacobs

CALLing All Foreign Language Teachers:
Computer-Assisted Language Learning in the Classroom
Tony Erben and Iona Sarieva

100 Games and Activities for the Introductory Foreign Language Classroom
Thierry Boucquey

Activities, Games, and Assessment Strategies
for the Foreign Language Classroom
Amy Buttner

A Good Start:
147 Warm-Up Activities for Spanish Class
Rebekah Stathakis

Improving Foreign Language Speaking through Formative Assessment
Harry Grover Tuttle and Alan Robert Tuttle

Steve, you are my rock.
Chad, Kyle, and Carly, you are the future.
Dr. Esposito, you are an inspiration.
Joan, your words dance off the page.
Mom, you are my first teacher.

Meet the Author

Debbie Arechiga has been working as a literacy consultant in schools across the country since 2005, striving to equip teachers with effective strategies that she often demonstrates in their own classrooms. She returns regularly to several school districts with high percentages of children of poverty and children learning a second language. The rapid and sustained literacy progress made by these students has been recognized as a turning point for some of these schools, yielding better instruction and significantly improved test results.

Twenty years as a classroom teacher, teacher mentor, and staff developer in Tucson, Arizona, laid the groundwork for Debbie to become an independent consultant with her own company, Tools for Literacy. She also earned a masters degree in the art of teaching from Grand Canyon University in 2004. Debbie has conducted teacher training seminars on a wide range of topics and has presented at national conferences.

Focusing on English language learners is something Debbie has in common with her husband Steve, an elementary school teacher in Tucson. They also share the lively adventure of raising three kids and two dogs. Debbie makes room in her schedule to play tennis as often as possible and participates in a city league, finding that—much like teaching—it keeps her on her toes both mentally and physically.

Contact Information:
Debbie Arechiga, author and literacy consultant
E-mail: tools4literacy@comcast.net
Web site: www.toolsforliteracy.com
Become a fan: www.facebook.com/toolsforliteracy

Table of Contents

Introduction

My path to teaching started when I began first grade. I found great joy in gathering all my friends in my garage so I could set up "school" and be their teacher; it was in that garage that I envisioned the possibilities of what I loved to do and wanted to become. From those early years, there was never a question as to my career choice. I found a passion: something to nourish my soul, energize my thoughts, and challenge my capabilities. When I began my teaching career, I wanted my students to experience the gifts of a quality education that had moved my life forward. The doors to literacy had been opened for me, and I was determined to open those doors for my students.

Through many challenging, yet rewarding years in the classroom, I discovered some valuable tools of the trade that propelled me forward as an educator and kept me searching to learn more about my craft. While the road was never easy, it was always worthwhile, because for every student who left my room as a reader and writer, I knew the doors had opened wide for their future.

Over the last several years, I've had the wonderful opportunity to share the tools gained during my years in the classroom with teachers and students all over the country. While there isn't a magic potion or perfect program that will reach all your students, there *are* mental aptitudes and attitudes that will sustain you and enlarge your skills as you pursue your educator's path. This book is my gift to teachers committed to reaching and teaching *all* students, and giving them the gift of literacy. Enjoy the journey!

Debbie Arechiga
"A teacher's teacher" (the best compliment I ever received)
Literacy consultant, teaching coach, author

How to Read This Book

· ·

This book will make the most sense if you read the chapters sequentially. Each chapter has both call-outs of key ideas in the margin and summary points at the end. If you prefer, you can scan those features to get the gist of each chapter's content. Chapter 1 presents an overview of the national landscape as it pertains to educating our English language learners (ELLs). It reviews statistics on the rising numbers of ELL students in our schools and the types of programs currently in place across the country. It also introduces a few representative ELL students, briefly telling their individual stories. Chapter 2 encourages you to build and/or renew certain attitudes and aptitudes that will help sustain your commitment and expectations as you work in linguistically diverse classrooms. I call these attitudes the **mental Energizers**. Chapter 3 outlines a literacy framework supportive of ELLs that includes the following components:

♦ Daily opportunities to hear and engage with the language of texts, or the **interactive read-aloud**
♦ Multiple extended opportunities to read text at independent reading levels, or **time with text**
♦ **Phonics and spelling** to provide students with the surface scaffolding necessary to read and write with fluency and understanding
♦ **Guided comprehension**—explicit instruction in how to navigate or think through a piece of text
♦ Daily opportunities to mirror the process of reading through **writing**

This literacy framework will be addressed in greater detail, with supportive strategies, in another book, which will function as an extension of this text. The classroom vignette at the end of chapter 3 will take you inside a literacy lesson in which you will be introduced to the **strategic Energizers**. Chapters 4–8 explore in detail how the strategic Energizers provide the essential teaching elements that empower instruction and promote student learning. The Energizers are not a literacy framework, but rather teaching approaches that enliven and enrich that framework. (A complete guide to the Energizers can be found on page 101.) In each of these chapters you will find numerous tools (or strategies) that you can implement in your classroom right away. You will also get an inside view of these Energizers in action by reading the classroom vignettes. The closing chapter provides a synthesis of the ideas presented in order to both propel your own learning and your success with your students. The planning template available as a download will help you plan and implement the type of energized instruction presented herein.

But enough reading *about* the book; it's time to dig in. . . .

Free Download

· ·

A free Planning Guide for Energizers template is available to accompany this book. You can download it from Eye On Education's Web site as an Adobe Acrobat file. Permission has been granted to purchasers of this book to download this template and print it.

You can access this download by visiting Eye On Education's Web site: www.eyeoneducation.com. From the home page, click on FREE, and then click on Supplemental Downloads. Alternatively, you can search or browse our Web site to find this book, and then click on "Log in to Access Supplemental Downloads." Your book-buyer access code is **REL-7219-2**.

1 English Language Learners and Schools at the Epicenter of Change

· ·

"[R]ecord numbers of immigrants . . . put classrooms on the front lines of America's battles over whether and how to assimilate the newcomers" (Thompson, 2009).

"[P]ublic schools are at the epicenter of this change, and educators are on the front line in figuring out how to respond" (Noguera, 1999).

U.S. population trends have shifted dramatically over the last forty years, and public school enrollments are reflecting that change. The country—and our schools—are now more ethnically, culturally, and religiously diverse than ever before (Campbell, 2006). The old biracial (black/white) paradigm in the United States has evolved into a multiracial collage (Clark, 1999). And an extraordinary result of this growing diversity is just around the corner: the national adjustment to what has been called "the new majority" of minorities (Campbell, 2006).

"Change is inevitable" goes the old saw. But perhaps no change could seem more fundamental and life-altering to many Americans than a shift in ethnic majority. In the very near future, there will be no such thing as a single majority group in the United States. All ethnic groups, including European Americans (whites), will be numeric minorities. This change has already occurred in several states and school districts (Campbell, 2006).

"Because there is no majority group, what does the term *minority* mean?" asks one writer. This seemingly simple question goes to the heart of the emotional and political concerns commonly voiced today. No doubt American communities and schools will be working out answers for the next several decades. The writer who asked the question offered this response: "Clearly, we all need to learn to get along." Again, this concept seems elementary in the face of immensely complex issues, yet it's hard to argue with its truthfulness.

The country—and our schools—are now more ethnically, culturally, and religiously diverse than ever before.

"Getting along" is a concept that children understand. Perhaps that's partly why, as the writer notes, "historically the public schools are one of the few institutions where this cooperation has been taught" (Campbell, 2006).

The public school has always served as the primary institution responsible for the integration of immigrant children into the American mainstream. That role continues today, with particular emphasis on the obligation of schools to ensure that all students learn English (Noguera, 1999). If schools and their communities are at the focal point of social change and political controversy today, they're also at a point of great opportunity. One observer notes that "competing principles have coexisted throughout our history[:] The ideology of exclusion and dominance . . . [and] the ideology of inclusion and equality" (Thompson, 2009). Today, and in the coming years, one of our most important roles as educators will be to help our students choose inclusion and equality.

> *In addition to the obligation to ensure that all students learn English, an important role for educators will be to help students choose inclusion and equality.*

The change seems so sudden; how did it happen?

The changes that we're feeling so keenly today began in 1965, when the Immigration and Nationality Act was amended to repeal long-standing quotas based on national origin. The law also gave preference to people with certain specialized skills and to reuniting family members separated by former immigration restrictions. As surprising as it seems today, those who drafted the new provisions didn't expect a significant increase in immigration. But more immigrants poured into the United States than at any other time in history (Hirschman, 2006). The U.S. Census Bureau figures tell the story: 35.7 million foreign-born people lived in the United States in 2005, up from 24.5 million just ten years earlier (Maxwell, 2009). This influx is in addition to ten million newcomers in the 1980s and seven million in the 1970s (Capps et al., 2007). Nearly half these immigrants came from Mexico, the Caribbean, and Central America, while approximately 15 percent arrived from Asia. Less than 20 percent came from Europe and Canada; 80 percent became members of U.S. minority groups (Kenny, 2008).

The year 1965 not only ushered in a surge of immigration, but it also ended the baby boom. Following World War II, from 1946 to 1964, the birthrate averaged more than three children per woman. Most of these women were non-Hispanic whites. As the birth rates of baby boomers fell steadily, births to new immigrants increased rapidly (Mather, 2009). In 2009 whites had approximately one birth for every death, while Hispanics had about nine births for every death: Hispanic births represented more than half of the total gain in U.S. population during 2009 (Yen, 2008). The birthrate of all other minority groups has also exceeded that of whites (U.S Diplomatic Mission to Germany, 2010). According to the Census Bureau, minorities, collectively, will comprise more than 50 percent of the population by 2042 (up from 34 percent in 2008). Minority children will become the majority even sooner—by 2023 (Goldman, 2008). According to the Census Bureau, minority children will become the majority by 2023.

The history of the United States has always been a story of immigrants. That story is continuing with a greater-than-ever emphasis on diversity. Those who acknowledge that diversity is here to stay can help accommodate and even benefit from the change. Driven by competition and the need for profit, many businesses have made significant adaptations to appeal to a multicultural customer base. As early as the 1970s, Ma Bell, which has since become Verizon (as well as many other phone companies), began providing services in several languages other than English. A company spokesperson commented, "Back then, it was survival mode. Today, there's a business reason to do it." That business reason is its U.S. customer base, which is 11.2 percent Hispanic and 6.7 percent Asian, while multilingual customers are increasing at 9 percent each year. In addition, Verizon stores whose employees speak languages other than English are 20 percent more profitable than other stores. Verizon's vice president for workplace culture, diversity, and compliance explained that these results don't just happen: "You have to be as intentional and determined about diversity as any other business imperative" (DiversityInc., 2008). *Intentional and determined about diversity*—this phrase expresses succinctly the outlook that will enable individuals, communities, government agencies, schools, and other organizations to make adjustments that will move productive change forward. It's a motto we should all consider adopting.

Becoming intentional and determined about diversity will help schools and other organizations make adjustments that will move productive change forward.

Historically, immigration and political controversy go hand in hand

Despite the fact that all U.S. residents other than Native Americans were new immigrants at some point in their family's history, immigration has always been a contentious political issue. There's a long-standing pattern of immigrants already assimilated into U.S. life resisting newer immigrants for fear that the newcomers will pose an economic threat (taking over jobs, overusing public services, etc.) and be culturally or religiously incompatible.

Perhaps one of the reasons that immigration has always been a political hot button is that *assimilation* doesn't mean that the status quo remains unchanged. Instead, as researcher Hirschman (2006) declares, "The 'new immigrants' [of the early twentieth century] have remade American society in their image." Because immigrants of that era settled in cities and provided labor for a newly industrialized economy, they ushered in "a more cosmopolitan America that places Catholicism and Judaism on a par with Protestant denominations." According to Hirschman, the most important legacy of these Eastern and Southern European immigrants is that they paved the way for the New Deal (1930s), the Great Society (1960s), and the current wave of immigration from Asia and Latin America. In the process of joining American society, the immigrants of the early twentieth century changed that society markedly—and there's no question that our newest immigrants will effect equally transformative changes. "Immigrants always change the United States as much as the United States changes them" (Kenny, 2008).

The most notable difference between our present immigrants and those from prior eras is that the great majority of today's newcomers are people of color. Their numbers are radically altering the ethnic and racial mix in many communities and will continue to do so. Unlike the German, Italian, Irish, Polish, and Jewish immigrants whose arrival was once vigorously resisted, Hispanics, Asians, and other people of color cannot eventually become "full-fledged white Americans" (Noguera, 2009). Clearly, the issue of racial equality is going to be more significant than ever before in American life.

While immigrants of the past settled mainly in large cities on the East and West Coasts, today they are going wherever they can find a demand for their labor, including suburbs, small towns, and rural areas. Ethnic diversity is often a new experience for these communities. In some locations, the immigrants have reinvigorated an area's economic future; in others, they have been less than welcome. In either situation, the status quo changes, and residents must adjust (Noguera, 2009).

Assimilation doesn't mean that the status quo remains unchanged. To a significant degree, immigrants have always reshaped the social landscape.

The great majority of today's newcomers are people of color, which makes the issue of racial equality more significant than ever before.

In many Hispanic families, successive generations are not experiencing the increased economic opportunities and achievements that have traditionally brought former immigrants into the middle class. Although Hispanic immigrants are usually employed, they are commonly relegated to low-paying jobs due to their lack of skills and education, and to date many of their children and grandchildren have not broken out of this cycle. This is a significant and troubling reversal of the usual pattern of upward mobility for immigrants (Noguera, 2009).

Many new immigrant families are not achieving upward mobility in successive generations.

Given the hurdles confronting our most recent newcomers and their communities, it's easy to wonder, "Will the social fabric stretch or tear?" A study of the intense immigration pressures in California concluded that society *can* stretch, so long as it receives plenty of help from local and state governments (Clark, 1999). And, we might add, plenty of help from schools, which have always served as "primary institutions of socialization and support for immigrant children" (Noguera, 2009).

"Politics is never far from the schoolhouse door." (Thompson, 2009)

It should be no surprise that the general controversy over immigration is making itself felt in our schools. In areas of the country that have experienced a large increase (in some cases as high as 200 to 300 percent) of students with limited English proficiency, education costs have escalated. Communities, rather than states, must bear these costs, a fact that can foster resentment locally, especially when taxes are raised and services are impacted. School district boundaries have been contested in an effort to exclude immigrants or minimize their enrollment, and some parents argue that the attention teachers give to immigrants diminishes the educational quality of the other students. In response to intense public demand for English-only instruction, some states or school districts have curtailed bilingual programs (Thompson, 2009).

Racial and ethnic issues in our schools are reshaping themselves as student demographics change. While white students are now more likely to be exposed to minority students (as of the 2005–2006 school year, only one out of five white students attended a nearly all-white school), black and Hispanic students have become more segregated. In 2005–2006, almost one-third of blacks and Hispanics attended schools in which the student body was comprised almost entirely of minorities (Fry, 2007). In fact, as of 2009, Hispanic students were more likely than any other ethnic group to attend schools segregated by both race and social class. Their high school dropout rates are the highest of any group; their college attendance rates are the lowest. Competition between low-income Hispanics and African Americans for jobs, services, and influence in neighborhood schools has even caused an escalation of tension and violence in some southern California communities (Noguera, 2009).

Although social conditions outside school often foster inequality, schools should function as equalizers of opportunity.

As educators, we need to be aware of these social developments and political issues, not to become overly absorbed in the challenges but rather to enlarge our awareness of the potential of schools to help meet them. "We must recognize that the sources of inequity typically lie outside of schools—in parent education and income, in community access to jobs and resources. . . . Still, the effort to promote equity is consistent with the basic promise of American public education—that schools should function as equalizers of opportunity. . . . The goal of equity remains one that schools must pursue if they are to remain viable as public institutions" (Noguera, 2006).

A commitment to the goal of equity must include a commitment to ensuring that all students master English.

In today's schools, a commitment to the goal of equity has to include a commitment to ensuring that all students master English. More than any other single skill, proficiency in English opens the door to students' academic success and, therefore, to their future opportunities and achievements. English literacy is a goal that everyone—immigrant parents, communities, future employers, and politicians—agrees on.

Proficiency in English opens the door to students' academic success and, therefore, to their future opportunities and achievement.

In a February 2008 webchat sponsored by the U.S. Department of State, New York University history professor Hasia Diner was asked whether she thought English would remain the dominant language in the United States. She responded that a change in the country's monolingualism is hard to imagine because "there is no resistance to English learning by immigrant parents and immigrant communities, and all recognize the power of the one language as the vehicle to foster economic mobility—the point and goal of the massive migrations" (Diner, 2008). All recognize the power of the one language—and all recognize that our schools are the best promoters of language and its power to change lives. To this end, federal regulations require that students with limited English proficiency must be identified and that they must be offered a program designed to help them progress in school (Brown University, 2006).

In the U.S. public schools, there are currently more than five million students who struggle with English and need support to benefit as fully as possible from their educational experience. You may know a few of them. Let's learn more about ELLs and why they're making such an impact on our schools.

Our ELL students: An amazing Technicolor rainbow

The immense immigration flows over the last several decades, coupled with high birthrates among young immigrants, have generated a population of immigrant children who now represent at least one out of every five pre-K–12 students in the United States. Their numbers continue to grow faster than any other group of children in the country. Three in four of these children speak English exclusively or very well, and nearly three in five have at least one parent with good English skills. In every state, children in immigrant families (including those who speak a language other than English at home) are more likely to speak English well than to have limited fluency (Hernandez, Denton, & Macartney, 2007).

Looking at those figures from the other side, one-quarter of immigrant children have limited English proficiency. English language learners include all schoolchildren who speak a language other than English at home and who speak English less than "very well." Many of these children live in households where no one over age thirteen speaks English well. One of the most significant issues regarding ELLs is that their numbers are increasing out of proportion to the growth of the general school population. Between the school years 1998–1999 and 2008–2009, while total pre-K–12 enrollment grew 7.22 percent, ELL enrollment exploded by 51.01 percent. The 5.3 million ELLs enrolled during 2008–2009 comprised approximately 10.8 percent of all pre-K–12 students in public schools (NCELA, 2011). While ELLs in the United States speak over 400 different languages, 80 percent are Spanish speakers (Goldenberg, 2008). According to the Census Bureau's 2006 American Community Survey, Hispanics were the largest minority group in the public schools of 22 states. The Pew Hispanic Center projects that by 2050 there will be more Hispanic

English language learners include all students who speak a language other than English at home and who speak English less than "very well."

children than non-Hispanic white children in the nation's schools (Fry & Gonzales, 2008). Students who speak Asian languages (Vietnamese, Hmong, Chinese, Korean, etc.) are the second-largest group of ELLs, comprising about 8 percent of all ELL students.

The distribution of immigrant children by language and ethnic origin varies greatly from state to state. Figure 1.1 identifies which states have attracted immigrant families from which areas of the world. However, it doesn't come close to portraying the extent of ethnic diversity confronting many states and schools. Students in Tennessee, for example, represent between 115 and 130 native languages in a typical year. The Palm Beach County, Florida, school district serves 173,000 students whose backgrounds include 142 native languages or dialects (14 percent are ELLs). Although the school district of Lewiston, Maine, has only 5,000 students, 850 of them are African refugees, many of whom have never had formal schooling in any language (Cech, 2009). Many states and school districts are experiencing similar scenarios.

Reviewing this kind of data can create the impression that a majority of children in newcomer families are not U.S. citizens. That is not the case: 79 percent of them (i.e., four out of five) were born in the United States. Furthermore, 24 percent of these children are second-generation Americans—that is, one of their parents was also born in the United States. In thirteen states, that proportion is as high as 40 percent. More than two-thirds of immigrant children have parents who have lived in the United States for at least ten years (including the 24 percent whose parents were born here). In other words, at least one parent of most newcomer children has spent a significant amount of time—at least a decade, and often his or her whole life—in the United States (Hernandez et al., 2007). These facts dispel the notion that most ELLs are children of illegal immigrants. The reality is that these children belong here and are our future workforce and parents of the next generation of students.

Immigrant families are no longer "somewhere else"—in the Southwest, or on the coasts. Although that was the case as recently as the early 1990s, these newcomers are now spread broadly across the country. There are only eleven states

Some school districts serve children who speak 100 or more languages.

The great majority of children in newcomer families are U.S. citizens. The reality is that these children belong here and are our future workforce—and the parents of the next generation of students.

FIGURE 1.1. Ethnic Origins of Immigrant Children by State

Ethnic Origin of Immigrant Children	*States With Significant Populations of Immigrant Children of This Ethnic Origin*
Mexico	Mexicans represent 50–81% of immigrant children in 6 Western states (Arizona, California, Colorado, Idaho, Nevada, New Mexico), 3 Southern states (Arkansas, Oklahoma, Texas), and 3 Midwestern states (Illinois, Kansas, Nebraska). They are the largest student minority in at least 10 other states and are likely to number among the immigrant children of every state.
East Asia	East Asians represent the largest proportion of immigrant children in Alaska, Hawaii, Maryland, and Virginia. They also constitute 20% of immigrant children in North Dakota, South Dakota, Washington, and West Virginia.
Caribbean	Children from Caribbean nations represent the largest proportion of immigrant children in Florida, New Jersey, and New York. They also constitute 20% of immigrant children in Connecticut, Massachusetts, and Rhode Island.
Indochina	Indo-Chinese represent the largest proportion of immigrant children in Louisiana and Minnesota. They also constitute 20% of immigrant children in Wisconsin.
Central America	Central Americans represent the largest proportion of immigrant children in the District of Columbia. They also constitute 20% of immigrant children in Louisiana.
West Asia	West Asians represent the largest proportion of immigrant children in Michigan.
Europe, Canada, and Australia	Europeans, Canadians, and Australians represent the largest proportion of immigrant children in 14 states. They also constitute 20% of immigrant children in Alabama, Michigan, and South Carolina.
Africa	Africans represent 11–15% of immigrant children in the District of Columbia, Maine, Maryland, and Minnesota.
Former Soviet Union	Children of former Soviet countries represent 5–8% of immigrant children in North Dakota, Ohio, Oregon, Pennsylvania, South Dakota, and Washington.

Source: Hernandez et al., 2007.

in which immigrant children comprise less than 5 percent of the child population, and they make up at least 10 percent in twenty-two states. While the largest number of immigrant children (largely Hispanics) are in the Southwest, high concentrations are located in many large metropolitan areas. Increasingly, they are moving into suburbs and rural areas (Mather, 2009). A significant number of communities and states have been overwhelmed by the dramatic suddenness of the influx. In the decade between 1994–1995 and 2004–2005, the number of ELLs in fourteen states swelled by 100 to 238 percent. An additional eight states experienced growth of between 292 to 417 percent in their ELLs, while the ELL population in South Carolina expanded 714 percent (NEA policy brief, n.d.). A school superintendent in Arkansas saw his district more than double over the last fifteen years, with ELLs constituting almost the entire increase. Speaking of the district's efforts to cope with the demand, he commented, "We had to start from scratch" (Maxwell, 2009). Many districts could tell similar stories.

Although we use the term *English language learners* to refer to an entire group of students, there is no one-size-fits-all profile for these students. Like all children, ELLs come from diverse socioeconomic backgrounds, and their life experiences differ tremendously. The level of their parents' education varies, as does their length of residence in the United States and their immigration status. They present a wide range of language proficiencies and deficiencies, both in English and their native languages. Some students arrive in the United States with strong academic backgrounds and literacy in their native language. Many others with limited formal schooling have significant gaps in their education. Some ELLs have grown up in the United States but don't speak English at home. Some are literate in their home language; many are not literate in any language at all. ELLs may be strongly connected to their native culture, or they may be fully at home in U.S. culture. Still others may straddle two or more cultures. Some ELLs may respond well to school while others remain disconnected. These distinctions remind us that while all ELLs have a common need to learn English, they will require a variety of pathways and different levels of support to reach that goal (Knowledge Loom, n.d.).

While all ELLs share a need to learn English, they will need a variety of pathways and different levels of support to reach that goal.

Learning English is a pressing need for ELLs, but the process takes time and support. Researchers have identified several levels of language proficiency through which learners gradually progress. These have been referred to as beginning, intermediate, and advanced, and also as preproduction, early production, speech emergence, and intermediate/advanced fluency. Developing oral proficiency can take three to five years, with several more years required to master complex concepts and academic English. ELLs often make steady progress from beginning to intermediate skills and then move less quickly toward higher levels of proficiency. This is significant because the abstract concepts and decontextualized descriptions common to academic language require a sophisticated knowledge of sentence structure, nuance, and vocabulary (Goldenberg, 2008).

Several levels of language proficiency have been identified through which learners gradually progress. They are referred to as beginning, intermediate, and advanced, and also as preproduction, early production, speech emergence, and intermediate/advanced fluency.

Researchers have identified effective approaches for teaching basic reading skills to ELLs in early grades, but there are few conclusive findings about how to teach higher-order skills like comprehension and how to improve ELLs' performance in other academic areas. "The bad news is that we aren't where we're supposed to be. There's a lot we don't know. The good news is that the research is growing," explains Claude Goldenberg, an education professor at Stanford University (Viadero, 2009).

Educators need to find ways to teach higher-order thinking skills like comprehension and how to improve ELLs' performance in other academic areas.

What is the best way to equip our ELLs with the English skills they so urgently need? There are many different ideas about this. There's strong support for offering English-only instruction to ELLs; another view is that ELLs should have the opportunity to learn essential skills and content in their native language. A compromise between these approaches is to teach ELLs primarily in English but provide them with certain materials or directions in their native language. But even such a compromise raises additional issues: how often should native languages be used, and for what purposes? While a great deal of research has been done on supporting ELLs in acquiring English proficiency, no one has yet identified a fully proven strategy. Perhaps because of this, ELLs' instructional settings vary widely (Viadero, 2009). That variety is evident in the range of programs reported by states to the federal government in 2006–2007 as required by the No Child Left Behind Act. Although forty-six states support English-only instruction, many of them also provide other programs.

Number of States	Programs Provided
43	Content-based ESL
42	Pull-out ESL
39	Sheltered English instruction
32	Structured English immersion
31	Dual language
28	Transitional bilingual
23	Two-way immersion
18	Specially designed academic instruction in English
16	Heritage language
15	Developmental bilingual
29	Other programs

Source: Viadero, 2009.

School districts have been very resourceful in responding to ELLs. This is vital because achievement gaps are not only an issue for English learners' future educational and vocational options, but for society as a whole.

In an effort to maximize opportunities for ELLs, some school districts have extended the school year and are offering after-school programs with language and academic elements designed to support ELLs. Longer school days and summer school are also options, as is allowing ELLs extra years in school to fulfill graduation requirements (Goldenberg, 2008). A number of schools have enlarged their role to become "community schools" or "full-service schools," integrating social workers, healthcare professionals, and even adult education into the support they offer students and their families (Noguera, 2009). In these efforts and many others, school districts and teachers are proving very resourceful as they strive to provide opportunities for ELLs. And they need to be, because, to paraphrase Michelin's famous ad, "So much is riding on our tires." "Achievement gaps . . . bode ill for English learners' future educational and vocational options. They also bode ill for society as a whole, since the costs of large-scale underachievement are very high" (Noguera, 2009).

Factors contributing to ELLs having lower levels of achievement include poverty, their parents' level of education and English fluency, extended absences from school, and the complexities of learning English.

In addition to the challenge of learning English, the academic success of ELLs is at risk due to factors unrelated to school. Due to the low-wage jobs held by many immigrants, over one-fifth of immigrant families lived at the poverty level in 2007; nearly one-half had incomes barely above the poverty line, struggling to make ends meet and spending nearly two-thirds of their income on housing and living costs. Children in poor families are at greater risk for dropping out of school and teen pregnancy. Students are also impacted by their parents' level of education and English fluency. In 2007, more than one-quarter of immigrant children lived with parents who hadn't completed high school. In that same year, almost two-thirds of children of Latin American heritage had parents with poor English skills (Mather, 2009). Some ELLs are impacted by extended absences from school. Such absences may be due to migrant workers changing locations seasonally or to families sending a child back to their country of origin for several weeks each year to maintain ties with family members left behind (Noguera, 2009). Not surprisingly, these socioeconomic factors, coupled with the complexities of learning English, result in ELLs having lower levels of academic achievement than other students.

For example, while 31 percent of all eighth graders proved to be proficient on the reading portion of the 2005 National Assessment of Educational Progress, only 4 percent of eighth-grade ELLs attained that level. The gap expands in high school: students who are native English speakers are 79 percent more likely to finish high school than non-native speakers (NCTE, 2008). In fact, researchers have documented a disturbing trend: the longer immigrant adolescents have been in the United States, the more their grade-point averages fall and their dropout rates rise (Girard, 2005).

The longer immigrant adolescents have been in the United States, the more their grade-point averages fall and their dropout rates rise.

As teachers, what do we do with all of this disquieting information? We must neither underestimate the challenge or, more importantly, underestimate ourselves and our students. Schools across the country are responding to the rising numbers of linguistically diverse learners with innovative programs and committed effort, and they are experiencing some notable successes. While it's broadly recognized that most teachers lack training specific to ELLs, it's also been established that teaching basic literacy skills to young ELLs is very much like teaching those skills to students in general. On the other hand, certain instructional accommodations can give ELLs an extra boost in learning (Teale, 2009). The purpose of this book is to provide teachers with perspectives and tools that will equip them to work productively with ELLs.

The purpose of this book is to provide teachers with perspectives and tools that will equip them to work productively with ELLs.

Diversity: Do We See It as a Problem or a Challenge?

Pedro Noguera (1999), an educator who writes frequently about diversity, has thoughtfully observed that there's a significant difference between seeing diversity as a challenge and seeing it as a problem. In talking with journalists and while visiting schools, Noguera has found that the comments he hears about community changes brought about by the arrival of immigrants are "typically phrased as complaints." As we might expect, the issues that arise when new ethnic minorities come into settled communities are often described in such terms as "racial conflict," "prejudice," "intolerance," "threat"—and "problem." The problem with "problem" is that it's inherently negative. Most of us tend to use the word to describe something we'd like to eliminate rather than something we're ready to embrace and learn from.

Ethnic diversity is going to be a permanent fact in communities across the United States, and to uphold it as a problem won't help us resolve the many challenges it presents. A more constructive option is to see diversity as an asset and to find ways in which it can benefit our communities (Noguera, 1999).

Noguera believes that educators can—and must—lead the way in bringing about a change of viewpoint about diversity. Because schools are a public institution where people of all cultures meet, educators are in a position to cultivate these exchanges as positive experiences for students and their families. "As educators, we will be on the frontline of this change, and we have a responsibility to show that change can happen without acrimony and resentment if there is an openness to adapt and to continue to learn" (Noguera, 1999).

Educators can—and must—lead the way to bring about a change in viewpoint. Instead of viewing diversity as a problem, we need to see the ways in which it can benefit our communities.

The ELLs in Our Classrooms Are Individuals, Not Statistics

So who are the ELLs in our classes—not just the statistics, but the children themselves? Let's meet a few of them.

♦   Tadeo, age 8, is one of five children. He was born in Mexico and entered the United States at age three. His mom and dad work at a restaurant. Although Tadeo speaks primarily Spanish at home, he can carry on a conversation in English fairly well at school. He reads with fluency but often struggles with comprehension. His writing skills are at a basic level and he has difficulty finding the right words to communicate his ideas.

He says, "When I write in English, it doesn't come out that good."

♦ Phong, age 5, was born in the United States and speaks fluent Vietnamese and English. His parents came to the United States ten years ago to further their medical careers. Phong learned the English alphabet with relative ease and often writes short messages in Vietnamese to impress his friends. His parents are adamant that Phong learn English well.

♦ Maancy, age 10, came to the United States just nine months ago because her father took a job at a local university. Maancy was born in India and attended school there. She speaks, reads, and writes in Hindi. Her last year in India was spent in a school where English is taught, and since arriving in the United States, Maancy has made rapid strides in her acquisition of both verbal and written English. Maancy struggles with spelling and the pronunciation of some words. She comments, "I like to speak English, but I have to repeat myself many times because people don't always understand me."

When we get to know individual ELL students, we quickly discover that each one has a unique story and his/her own particular language needs.

♦ Najelly, age 6, was born in Guatemala and has lived in the United States for three years. Her parents work in various service jobs but originally migrated to work in agriculture. They have limited formal schooling and are described as functionally illiterate. The language Najelly speaks at home is Spanish. She has struggled to learn the English alphabet but is making progress in both receptive and oral English language development, yet she prefers not to speak because she often feels shy. However, she responds well to music and will always participate in lessons and activities when music is involved.

♦ Natalia, age 9, was born in Mexico and arrived in the States two months ago. Natalia lives with an extended family that includes grandparents, aunts, uncles, and several cousins. There is speculation that her parents are illegal immigrants. It's not clear how much schooling Natalia received in Mexico, and there are significant gaps in her literacy development. She speaks limited English but has some foundational literacy skills in English. She seems very motivated to learn English, pays attention during instruction, and has made several friends. She interacts and participates well during cooperative activities and enjoys learning through visuals.

♦ Aponi, age 5, was born in the United States and lived on an Indian reservation until six months ago. She lives with extended family members. Her dad still lives and works in a casino on the reservation. Aponi is extremely shy and rarely speaks, even in social settings. She appears to have a very limited English vocabulary. However, her writing performance indicates that she is developing a beginning understanding of the alphabetic orthography of the English language. *I pa mi sr*, she wrote ("I play with my sister").

♦ Mohammed, age 9, has been in the United States for one year. In that time he has learned how to ride a bicycle, catch a football, and operate a stove so he can cook his favorite food, macaroni and cheese. He has also grown a few inches since he left his refugee camp in West Africa with his mom and four siblings. He has come a long way in learning to speak, read, and write in English, and he's eager to learn about the world through books. In one year, he is already beginning to read, recognizes many sight words, and has learned a lot about how our English alphabet works for spelling and writing. This has been a challenging but rewarding year for Mohammed in many ways. He misses his friends in West Africa and talks frequently about his dad, who has been missing since their refugee camp was invaded three years ago. He loves his new school friends and participates in many activities at school. He understands his teacher much better now. He can communicate with words and feels that he is understood in return. He teaches his mom and little brother all the new words he learns in school. Mohammed comments that many of his friends "speak other languages just like me—I like that!"

What is clear from these introductions is that ELLs, like all students, are distinct individuals with a range of developmental stages. It's easy to imagine their smiles, their eagerness, and their trust in their teachers. If they were our students, we'd share their excitement over breakthroughs in learning and their concern when they struggle. We'd become invested in their progress and strive to find the best ways to promote it. This is what good teachers have always done, and it's what we need to do now. But because ELLs are bringing new learning challenges into our classrooms, we must develop new attitudes and aptitudes. A good first step is acknowledging that we're capable of making the changes and doing the learning that will help us help our ELLs. The entire nationwide community of educators is in this together, and at this moment all of us are pathfinders.

"All hands on deck!" calls a captain when bringing his ship to its maximum state of readiness in order to face a challenge. All of us, at our most alert and energized, are needed in our schools right now. Committed teachers are a formidable resource. As an Iowa teacher explained when describing his school's progress with ELLs, "Children can learn. We just have to find ways to go ahead and get it done" (Girard, 2005).

Teachers need to respond to the new learning challenges ELLs bring into the classroom by developing new attitudes and aptitudes.

● ● ● ● ● ● ● ● ● ● ● ● ● ● ● ● ●

In Brief

- ◆ Our schools are now more ethnically, culturally, and religiously diverse than ever before. Soon there will be no such thing as a single majority group in the United States.

- ◆ Public schools will continue to serve as the primary institution responsible for the integration of immigrant children and are obliged to ensure that all students learn English. More than any other single skill, proficiency in English opens the door to students' academic success and, therefore, to their future opportunities and achievements.

- ◆ The term *English language learners* (ELLs) encompasses all school children who speak a language other than English at home and who speak English less than "very well." However, there is tremendous diversity within this group, and ELLs will need different pathways and levels of support.

- ◆ The purpose of this book is to provide teachers with perspectives and tools that will equip them to work productively with ELLs. Committed, well-trained teachers are a formidable resource for schools responding to the challenge of providing high-quality learning experiences for all students.

2 Energy for Teaching
The Mental Energizers

. . . .

"[T]he most stunning finding to come out of education research in the past decade [is that] more than any other variable in education—more than schools or curriculum—teachers matter" (Ripley, 2010).

"Teachers possess the power to create conditions that can help students learn a great deal—or keep them from learning much at all" (Palmer, 1998, p. 6)

As teachers, it's a given that we want to do the best job possible. We want our students to make steady progress and become confident, able learners. We strive to utilize the best practices and techniques that can help make this happen. As a profession, we talk at length about what content we should teach, how we can most effectively implement instruction, and why certain issues are essential focal points. Undoubtedly *what*, *how*, and *why* are crucial, but too often we underestimate an equally significant element—*who* (Palmer, 1998 p. 4). Who is teaching? Something like, "Ms. Jones, with a masters degree and six years of experience" is a likely answer, but it's an incomplete one. Ms. Jones brings to the classroom not only her skills and knowledge but also her convictions and attitudes. Even though they're unspoken, her expectations for her students and her estimate of their abilities can have an effect as tangible as her lesson plans. Since our genuine desire is to further our students' development, it's important to remember that our assumptions can "form—or deform—the way [we] relate to [our] students" (Palmer, p. 4). They can also energize our work or leave us feeling defeated and incapable of realizing the good results we hope for.

The convictions, attitudes, and expectations teachers bring to the classroom are as significant as their skills, knowledge, and lesson plans.

Operating from "Powerful Conceptions"

Michael Fullan, an international authority on education reform, noted that "leaders who are effective operate from powerful conceptions, not from a set of techniques. The key, then, is to build up leaders' conceptions of what it means to be a leader . . ." (Sparks, 2003). Do we hold powerful conceptions of what it means to be a teacher? Most teachers do. For starters, most of us came to teaching through an impetus to be of service. Fullan (1993) concurs: "Scratch a good teacher and you will find a moral purpose" (p. 12), such as to contribute to the community or to do something meaningful for others.

So what about our powerful conceptions and moral purpose? Do they matter? Very much so. Fullan suggests that moral purpose is essential in keeping teachers attuned to students' needs, but he notes that "the moral purpose of teaching must be reconceptualized as a change theme" (p. 13). Why? Because "creating a vision forces us to take a stand for a preferred future," (Block, 1987, p. 102), which inevitably includes recognizing whatever is inadequate in the present.

Purpose has to constantly evolve; it has to be progressive to retain its energy. What would moral purpose with a change theme look like? It might imply allowing our sense of personal purpose to be constantly reformed by continual questioning and reflection, "behav[ing] [our] way into new visions and ideas," and moving beyond the often-isolated experience of our own classrooms into active collaboration with other committed educators (Fullan, 1993).

We need to identify our "powerful conceptions" and then challenge ourselves to act on them. A college tennis player who learned the basics of this lesson from her coach wrote about the experience years later: "Lyn's coaching philosophy was simple: 'In order to win, you must prepare to win.' More important than mechanics and physical strength, she stressed mental toughness. Lyn taught me two key lessons: In life, when encompassed with doubt, stand firm and persevere. In tennis, put more balls in play than your opponent" (*Principia Purpose*, 2010, p. 36).

Mental toughness and perseverance are some of "the inner resources that good teaching always requires" (Palmer, 1998). What else could we put on the list? Here are some characteristics of quality teaching to consider, as identified by other educators:

Moral purpose is essential in keeping teachers attuned to student needs but must constantly evolve to retain its energy. Continual questioning, reflecting, and collaborating with others helps teachers find ways to put their beliefs into action.

Mental toughness and perseverance are some of the inner resources that good teaching always requires.

- Good teachers "respect children and their diversity" (Rodgers & Rodgers, 2004, p. x).

- Good teachers "provide a safe environment in which all children feel supported" (Rodgers & Rodgers, 2004, p. x).

- Good teachers "hold high expectations of children's ability to learn" (Rodgers & Rodgers, 2004, p. x).

- Good teachers are careful not to accept a "disease model" as the basis for our assumptions ("your students have the following defects and deficiencies, and it is your job this year to remediate these") but instead work from the "immensely more powerful strength model ('your students have the following strengths and abilities, and it is your job to begin there, and build on those, and take advantage of them, and in the process turn areas of weakness around')" (Wigginton, 1985, p. 223).

- Good teachers "have confidence in their own ability to teach to those [high] expectations" (Rodgers & E. Rodgers, 2004, p. x).

- "The best [teachers] are not intimidated or overwrought when things are not going well. They see such times as opportunities for learning and growth, not as excuses for giving up. They push on, convinced they are smart enough to find a better way, convinced an answer lies out there somewhere (or within themselves)" (Wigginton, 1985, p. 275).

- "Good teachers possess a capacity for connectednesss." (Palmer, 1998, p. 6) They "connect themselves to their students, their students to each other, and everyone to the subject being studied" (p. 27).

- "Good teachers are reflective. . . . Failing to observe what happens in our classes . . . disconnects us from the teaching and learning process" (Palmer, 2009)

- "The best teachers constantly ask themselves questions ('Why am I teaching this course in this way? How could I teach it differently? Would it be any better? How do young people learn best?'), and they constantly reevaluate their performance" (Wigginton, 1985, p. 275)

- "The best teachers I know are always actively involved in the process of becoming better teachers. . . . They grow, and that growth is observable" (p. 275).

Quality teaching is expertise plus the inner resources that breathe life into it.

The "best of ourselves" is our highest motivations and expectations— powerful convictions that we can turn into powerful conceptions as we act on them.

If these ideas resonate with us, it's because they express our own best hopes and ideals as teachers. In every field of endeavor, quality is more than expertise. Quality is expertise plus the inner resources that breathe life into it. Consider what animates us as teachers. "Inner resources" alone will not resolve the educational needs of English language learners, let alone equip them with the language skills so important in opening up their futures. Rather, we need to bring to our classrooms not only our proven expertise but also the very best of ourselves. That best is our highest motivations and expectations, powerful conceptions that we can turn into proven convictions as we act on them. "We must tap the energy that comes from moral purpose," Michael Fullan declares (Sparks, 2003), because it tends to activate us on behalf of issues that make a difference.

Putting our powerful conceptions to work

Our best understandings and their active application keep us in balance.

A military strategist wisely observed that "great ideas need landing gear as well as wings" (Jackson, n.d.). Landing gear allows a plane to come down to earth and to maneuver capably on the ground. Our ideals have to be able to do the same. It's easy to appreciate the "wings" provided by our powerful conceptions—they give us uplift and altitude. Bringing them down to the ground of daily experience tends to make us feel a little less lofty. Our "wheels" may bounce uncomfortably or hit some rough spots on the runway. Daily experience may test our ideals sorely, but that's when we most need them. We can't let our day-to-day challenges diminish our certainty that our students can learn and that we can teach them. Neither can we think that high expectations will automatically produce strong results. Relying on both wings and landing gear—our best understandings and their active application—keeps us in balance. It's notable that when airfields are bombed in warfare, planes are safer in the air than on the ground. Similarly, when we encounter roadblocks and questions, returning to our essential goals and purposes can refresh our perspective and help us reposition ourselves to be more effective.

So, how can we put our mental models to work? I've targeted two mental models that are especially pivotal in working effectively with ELLs. I like to think of them as *mental Energizers* because energy enlivens, stimulates, and empowers us and, most significantly, it gives us the capacity to perform our work. Essentially, these mental Energizers are internal impulses that can fuel our external achievement.

> Mental Energizer #1: Cultivate connections:
>   Connect to kids.
>   Connect to colleagues.
>   Connect to cultures.
> Mental Energizer #2: Elevate your expectations.

The Energizers aren't just one more thing to do. It's true that they require action and even risk-taking, but in the end they'll repay us with increased confidence and efficacy. In 2010, when the Hartford Financial Services Group achieved a landmark 200 years in business, they chose to celebrate not just their longevity but the fact that their reliability gave their customers confidence. They adopted a new motto: "With the Hartford behind you, achieve what's ahead of you." Teachers could paraphrase that as: "With our powerful conceptions and Energizers behind us, we can feel confident tackling the teaching challenges ahead of us." Hartford felt their motto was so significant that their Web site at the time announced that it was much more than a new approach to advertising—it was "reinvented thinking." Reinvented thinking is invigorating. It tends to renew our purpose and vision and bring greater freedom to our work. This is exactly what the Energizers are about.

The mental Energizers are designed to reinvent and invigorate our thinking, purpose, and vision.

Mental Energizer #1: Cultivate connections

Connections fill our lives. By becoming teachers, we gained connections not only to students but also to schools, parents, communities, fellow educators, and professional organizations. Or perhaps we should say we gained these *potential* connections. Meaningful connection requires more than sharing space and crossing paths. It requires engagement. Think about the appliances on your kitchen counter. Many of them are probably plugged into an electrical socket 24/7. But they don't really do anything for you (like make your coffee or brown your toast) until you hit the "on" button and let the current flow. Similarly, saying yes to deeper connections in our teaching life can help keep the live current of ideas flowing through our work. Rather than using up our energy, authentic connections have a way of sustaining us and renewing our vitality.

Three connections we especially need to invigorate are those with our students, our colleagues, and our understanding of culture as a life force.

Three connections we especially need to invigorate are those with our students, our colleagues, and our understanding of culture as a life force. These connections matter. Let's look more closely at how to cultivate them.

Connect to kids

Meaningful connection requires engagement. Authentic connections provide a live current of energy that flows through our teaching and invigorates it.

Children learn through interaction: Assisted performance

Relationship and connection are at the core of effective teaching and learning because social interaction is the basis of learning.

"The interactions that take place between students and teachers and among students are more central to student success than any method for teaching literacy, or science or math" (Cummins, 1996, p. 1). Relationship and connection are at the core of effective teaching and learning because social interaction is the basis of learning. This fundamental premise was uncovered by Lev Vygotsky, a Russian educator and psychologist (1896–1934), by observing the explicit assistance children receive from their parents in various learning situations. He emphasized the "unique form of cooperation between the child and the adult that is the central element of the educational process" (Vygotsky & Reiber, 1993, p. 169). He also noted, "What the child can do in cooperation today he can do alone tomorrow" (Vygotsky, 1962, p. 104). Our ELLs will grow in their language and literacy skills through our expert interactions and awareness of their abilities and needs.

Two intertwined perceptions of learning and teaching are "learning is performance achieved through assistance," and "teaching is assisted performance."

It's common to see parents offer their child whatever help is needed throughout the learning of a particular task or skill (tying shoelaces, brushing teeth, throwing a ball), giving active and sustained support until the child begins to gain proficiency. A parent will often perform a task slowly while a child watches, sometimes even placing their own hands over the child's to guide them in the needed actions. Conversing with and cueing the child, talking out loud about each step of the activity they're sharing, the parent is constantly assessing what the child understands, offering responsive coaching or feedback that gradually leads the child to accomplish the task successfully on his or her own. The collaborative style of give-and-take between parent and child suggests two intertwined perceptions of learning and teaching:

♦ "Learning is performance achieved through assistance."

♦ "Teaching . . . [is] assisted performance" (Mohr & Mohr, 2007, p. 442).

"Vygotsky's work, as interpreted by educators, fosters students' construction of knowledge, rather than simple acceptance or reception of transferred information. Accordingly, the teacher serves as a mediator, using language to support and scaffold student learning within a social relationship" (Mohr & Mohr, 2007, p. 442). This statement summarizes several highpoints of Vygotskian theory and its implications for our connectedness to students:

The teacher serves as a mediator, using language to support and scaffold students' construction of knowledge.

♦ **Students have to construct knowledge.** "The learner is active in the process of taking in information. . . . Learning is the active process of engaging in experience and its internalisation [sic] in terms of thinking" (SACSA, 2001). Researchers and educators now recognize that learning must reach students deeply in order for them to achieve ownership of it. The "telling and testing" teaching approach is inadequate to the task. But another traditional model—apprenticeship—has proved its utility over centuries and remains effective today. Would-be carpenters, masons, and plumbers generally begin as apprentices, working under the direction of others experienced in those fields who help them learn the basics and gradually introduce complexities as the apprentices gain practice and experience. Similarly, in a cognitive apprenticeship, teachers employ modeling, mentoring, coaching, and other methods to help students negotiate language and content as they focus on completing learning tasks. "A cognitive apprenticeship is much like a trade apprenticeship, with learning that occurs as experts and novices interact socially while focused on completing a task" (Dennen, 2004, p. 814). Apprentices learn their trade (or academic skills) one task at a time, gradually becoming versed in the overall process of complex tasks by completing them in smaller, guided steps. In this same way—moving from simplified elements of a concept to more complex levels—students can be guided to construct learning. Learning a new language is a daunting task in and of itself: our ELLs' success will hinge upon

Cognitive apprenticeships include modeling, mentoring, and coaching. Experts and novices interact socially while focusing on completing a task.

our ability to provide explicit modeling and methods that will help them negotiate language and content.

♦ **Good teaching involves active fostering, supporting, and mediating.** If a student can be likened to an apprentice in construction, a teacher might be said to be both architect and general contractor. Architects select and assess building sites, design buildings, and often oversee construction, while contractors are responsible for the means and methods used in the actual construction process (choice of materials, tools, subcontractors, etc.). Teachers assess what their students need to learn and are ready to learn (called by Vygotsky the zone of proximal development), design lessons that will walk students through this learning step by step, and then carry out those lessons, mediating students' "construction work" to offer assistance through explanations, modeling, coaching, and other interventions.

The terms *fostering*, *supporting*, and *mediating* imply close and active participation on the part of the teacher. We could also add the words *collaborating*, *facilitating*, and *coaching*. As one teacher expressed it, "Real teaching is an *elbow-to-elbow, eye-to-eye* thing." And she further explained, "We fulfill our instructional intentions by *doing with*, not *to*" (Cole, 2004, pp. 1–2).

♦ **Learning takes place within a social relationship.** Vygotsky noted that parents worked with their children to co-construct learning. As a prefix, *co-* signifies *with*, *together*, *jointly*—or in other words, in relationship. In fact, Vygotsky went so far as to state that learning happens *only* in relationship. This gives enough weight to learning relationships (both teacher/student and student/student) that we shouldn't simply leave them to chance. The fact that teacher and students share a classroom, and even that many children form strong attachments to their teacher, doesn't necessarily mean that trust, respect, and a commitment to mutual interests have been firmly established. This is critical foundation work and, like learning itself, requires some construction. A classroom can be a daunting place for ELL students if they don't feel a part of the group. We must find ways to lower their anxiety and help them feel comfortable yet connected in their surroundings. One group of teachers in Australia explains that they

Fostering, support, and mediating require close and active participation on the part of the teacher.

"Learning culture" refers to a place where learning is valued and everyone involved is also valued. This is a critical foundation and must be carefully developed.

focus on creating a learning environment that not only emphasizes the importance of learning but also the importance of everyone helping each other to learn (Peters, Cornu, & Collins, 2003, p. 8). They offer a few details about how they encourage this to happen:

- "The teachers introduce the term *respect* to the students, early in the year, unpack it with them, and then follow through to see that it is evident in the classroom" (p. 5). Actions that express respect are specifically recognized and endorsed as they occur.
- Teachers continually encourage mutual respect and cooperation by designing "systems, protocol, codes of practice, expectations—all sorts of things to develop a classroom atmosphere where relationships are good relationships" (p. 5).
- "Students are encouraged to see themselves as part of a team and, therefore, having a part to play in others' learning as well as their own." (p. 8)
- Interdependence and communication are emphasized and are regarded as "essential learnings" (p. 7).

Our most successful interactions with students generally occur when we're as involved in the learning as they are. A 1948 article titled "How do we know a good teacher?" observed that "she is always looking for ways *into* rather than ways *out of* her responsibility as a teacher" (Biber & Snyder, 1948). How do we look for ways into our responsibilities and possibilities as teachers? Isn't it by paying close attention to our students' needs, efforts, and potential? Are we noticing the body language, participation, passivity, or animation of our ELL students while we teach? Do we understand these behaviors as valid signals ELL students are offering us? The momentum of our ELL students—rather than simply the momentum of our lesson—is what we need to watch and adapt to. This is learning to read our students, and becoming systematic about it can enable us to zero in on their strengths and needs.

Our ELLs come to us from a variety of backgrounds and language experiences. Part of cultivating connections with ELL students is knowing how to stretch their capacity for language and learning without overwhelming them. Vygotsky's constructivist approach will help us make instructional decisions that provide just the right assistance to accelerate our ELLs' learning momentum.

Learning to read our ELL students (their body language, participation, passivity, or animation) while we teach enables us to zero in on their strengths and needs.

Our attentive, systematic observations connect us to students and students to learning

Consistent ongoing record keeping lies at the heart of good teaching.

There are many useful ways to make our observations concrete, and they generally involve various kinds of consistent, ongoing record keeping. In a linguistically diverse classroom, it is vital that we have several different methods for knowing our students as learners and tracking their growth. Many teachers maintain folders or portfolios of student work that illustrate a student's progress over time. These might include student reading lists, writing notebooks, reading-response journals, running records, conference notes, anecdotal notes taken while observing students, and so on. All of us can gradually discover and create the record-keeping systems that work best for us so long as they reflect the learning behaviors and experiences of individual students. "Effective, continuous record keeping lies at the heart of our best teaching and learning. Keeping track of our students with classroom observations and systematic notes yields information that cannot possibly be gleaned from a traditional checklist, report card, or standardized test" (Maxim & Lee, 1997). Why does record keeping lie at the heart of good teaching? What kind of extraordinary information can it give us?

Careful monitoring tools such as the running record provide valuable insight into students' strengths and needs and helps to frame ongoing teaching moves.

Consider, for example, the depth of information we can gain through taking a running record of a student's reading. This assessment procedure was developed by Marie Clay and involves watching for a variety of reading behaviors while a student reads aloud, using standardized shorthand codes to jot notes as these behaviors occur. In other words, the teacher is able to take a record of "the smallest details of the reader's attitude, demeanor, accuracy, and understanding" in a particular oral reading experience. This careful monitoring enables the teacher to reflect on that student's "behaviors, responses, competencies, initiatives taken, and understanding of the specific content and task" (Shea, 2000, p. 10). During the early reading stage, ELLs are learning how to integrate all the cueing systems of meaning, structure, and visual cues. A running record provides valuable insight into how their language development is interacting with the reading process. The next step is for the teacher to use these new insights into the student's strengths and needs to frame ongoing teaching moves. Careful observation isn't an end in itself but is valuable only insofar as it informs our teaching. Then it becomes invaluable.

Another practice that can connect us deeply to our students is *kidwatching*, a term coined by Yetta Goodman. Kidwatching involves making "direct, intentional, and systematic observations" of students in all the contexts of school (their individual work and their interactions in the classroom as well as on the playground, in the lunchroom, etc.) and documenting what we see (O'Keefe, 1997). "Kidwatching is learning about children by watching how they learn" (Flint, 2008, p. 77). Our ELL students will show us how they are understanding in both verbal and nonverbal ways. Anecdotal notes, a form of kidwatching, will help us gather valuable information in a variety of settings.

Kidwatching is learning about children by systematically watching how they learn. This practice can connect us deeply to the smallest details of their learning.

Timothy O'Keefe (1997), who employs kidwatching, makes constant anecdotal notes about the participation, attitudes, and behaviors of individual students in a variety of settings. During a writing workshop, he noted: "Sarah—Reader in an author's circle. Not attending much to suggestions. Wants to discuss her own writing more than the author's." While students were engaged in independent reading, O'Keefe recorded the names of books selected by certain students as well as their degree of difficulty. He also made written observations: "Hanah—Quiet, intense, sits by herself, rarely looks up, moved from a group that was a little too loud for her." He also records some of his own coaching comments to students as well as direct quotes from students that are thought-provoking or revealing. He carries a clipboard with a separate piece of paper for each child so that he can make notes at any time. (Other teachers like to use sticky notes on which they can jot notes, later placing them in students' individual folders.) Over time, you'll evolve a method of taking and organizing notes that works best for you. (Always include in each note the student's name, the date, and the nature of the activity you were observing.)

For teachers new to anecdotal note-taking, O'Keefe recommends writing one sentence a day about every child. He encourages teachers to trust their own insights because they are "so much more valid" and informative than test scores or grades. Or you might begin by observing a different student every day for five to ten minutes and documenting in writing what you see. As you become comfortable with this process, you can increase the number of student observations you make each day. "Like learning any skill, learning how to take

Some ways of documenting students' learning include anecdotal notes, notations of miscues and strategies, conferencing with students, and rubrics.

accurate and useful records may at first appear daunting, but [it] become[s] very doable when you allow yourself to progress step by step at your own pace. Be as patient with yourself as you are with learners. Be as persistent as you want learners to be when facing challenging tasks" (Shea, 2000, p. 5). O'Keefe describes this entire process as "taking what we know about students and turning that knowledge into effective instructional invitations. Kidwatching is not something apart from the curriculum but rather what holds it together and pushes it forward."

The goal of observation is to recognize students' needs and direct our teaching to meet them.

A number of books and Internet resources offer checklists and assessment forms that can be useful in detailing various kinds of observations and providing formats for recording them. However, collecting data shouldn't become an end in itself. The goal is to make the kinds of observations that will allow us to recognize our students' learning needs and direct our teaching to meet them. Gathering data may seem clinical, but what we're actually doing is "watch[ing] students day to day and throughout the year [as] they reveal their understanding in words and performances." Our only purpose in this watching is always to "direct [our] teaching to give appropriate support in a timely way" (Shea, 2000, p. 9).

The strength of assessment practices such as running records and kidwatching is that "conclusions are based on numerous planned, purposeful observations and on observed patterns that have occurred time and time again in real situations in the context of normal classroom activities" (Gill, 1999). Our records become useful tools for conferencing with students and parents because they reveal student work very specifically. They offer proof that "step-by-step assessment of children's learning can be the stitch in time that makes the difference for young readers" (Shea, 2000, p. 9).

Staying vigilant for teachable moments

Effective teaching requires constant, alert engagement to be vigilant for teachable moments.

As a teaching coach, I frequently go into classrooms to model lessons. In these situations I'm new to the students, as they are to me, and I have to implement a meaningful lesson while a group of teachers observes. Despite the potential distractions to the students and me, I'm able to establish a strong connection and have a vital teaching encounter. How do I do this? Certainly one of the most important factors is that my attention is highly focused. It's the only way I can engage students effectively under those circumstances—and it's usually the only way any of us are fully effective.

Michael Pressley, a leading literacy scholar who researched effective teaching for more than twenty-five years, identifies other ways in which alert attention enables teachers to effectively connect with students in ways that ensure learning. He isolated three elements that he found to consistently make the difference in the best elementary school teachers:

1. A balance of skills and holistic approaches to literacy instruction
2. The ability to motivate students "almost nonstop"
3. Exceptional control of their classrooms (classroom management)

Pressley (2003) calls these elements Terrific Teaching's Triad. "Great teaching is that simple—and that hard. I can tell you that it is much harder than flying a 747 or being a graduate school professor." He offers examples of what he means by motivating students and managing the classroom. He speaks of how highly effective teachers motivate by using "virtually every minute" to praise students for their work, adapt tasks so that students can better understand them, help students choose books suited to their interests, and so on. He talks about effectively keeping students on task through constant watchfulness (management). We should consider Pressley's findings great news because all of the teacher activities he's commending are essentially the product of paying close attention, which is something all of us can learn increasingly to do.

"But you can't teach at such a high level of energy all day long!" Variations on this comment have been addressed to me by a number of participants in my teacher trainings. Clearly the same outcry might be voiced in regard to Timothy O'Keefe's practice of persistent kidwatching or to Michael Pressley's call for exceptional efforts to motivate students. The real question is whether it's possible to teach at that level of *attention* all day. The answer has to be that it's not only possible, it's necessary. We wouldn't expect to play a winning game of tennis by focusing on only some of the balls in play. We'd be on our toes, knees bent, ready to move quickly in whatever direction the ball was flying. Similarly, it requires constant, alert engagement to recognize where our students are in any given learning experience and then make the teaching moves that will solidify, redirect, or amplify their learning. If this expectation seems excessive or impossible, set a goal of maximizing your attention for one or two lessons each day, gradually extending the focus to the rest of the day. You can judge for yourself whether taking your attention to a new level also takes your teaching there.

As Mike Rose expresses it, "Teaching requires you to be vigilant for the teachable moment, for the idea forming in a kid's head, just at the point of utterance perhaps. It means to be mindful of possibility, to be alert to what a kid might be able to do and to what might spark interest" (Rose & Ayers, 2010, p. 168). Do you hear the echo of Vygotsky here? Perceiving the teachable moment, sensing the idea forming in a student's thought, staying alert to what a student is ready to do—all of this is working within a student's zone of proximal development, which is identifiable only through our close attention.

An unexpected outcome of writing this book was learning new and important lessons about how paying attention tends to support the work of creative problem solving. I thought I knew the shape of the book very well since I based its essential outline and content on my years of teacher-training workshops. But no sooner did I begin to write than I found I was experiencing my workshops in new ways. *Author* proved to be a significant shift in perspective from *trainer*. As a result, my mental antennae were intensely active, searching in every direction, attentive and receptive. Questions, comments, and experiences of workshop participants consistently sparked new ideas, and my interactions suddenly seemed to magnify notions pertinent to the book. The writing didn't always come easily, even with this heightened focus. But I was always aware that the ideas were active and percolating in my thought, and as I learned to wait on the mental processes of assimilation and understanding, the ideas became more concrete and ordered so that I was able to write about them. In fact, the writing sometimes seemed to take on its own momentum, coming quickly and smoothly after periods of struggle and delay. In these instances, it was clear to me that the sudden freedom in the writing grew directly from the attentive (if sometimes laborious) effort I had already invested in the attempt to express my ideas.

Here's the point of this story: We're all challenged by the numbers of students needing extraordinary support in gaining language skills. It's easy to feel overwhelmed by the demand. But if we respond with heightened attention rather than with fear and doubt, our alert observation will inevitably begin to reveal clues about our students and how they respond. Although we're trained professionals, we're also lifelong learners. We don't need to feel helpless in the face of increased demands, but we do need to be willing to enlarge our skills and find ways to accelerate the effectiveness of our work. We're all retooling and learning together. We need to remind ourselves that we're capable of this learning. We need to be eager to embrace it. If we are, we'll find that our willingness and perseverance win a little progress each day—and progress isn't fatiguing but energizing.

Responding with heightened attention rather than with fear and doubt will begin to reveal clues about our students and how they respond.

Most importantly, we must not stop the work of attentive discovery because we feel we're not getting results fast enough or we have so many unanswered questions. Reaching out for new ideas isn't always comfortable or easy, but as we stay attentive and remain patient, we're likely to find that our questions push us toward answers. This is a mental labor of probing, contemplating, attending, caring, and waiting expectantly. It's commonly known as the creative process, and its natural outcome (if we stay with it) tends to be a breakthrough into understanding and expression. Breakthroughs are what we most need in our classrooms right now, and we can midwife these new understandings if we persist.

Connect to colleagues

Collaboration among teachers can create consistency and improve school quality

Most teachers in U.S. schools are accustomed to working autonomously in individual classrooms. While we're subject to curriculum requirements as well as school policies and schedules, we're generally self-directing in regard to classroom routines, the structure of lessons, discipline, and other elements of teaching. Our interaction with our fellow teachers is probably more social than professional in nature. We may recount anecdotes about classroom experiences or describe a student we're concerned about, but this conversation is often more casual than solution-seeking. There may be several teachers in our school whom we respect as educators and whose advice we may even request on occasion. But what would we think about meeting regularly with a group of teachers from our own school to pursue structured studies or activities that encourage professional growth? Is the idea disquieting? Intriguing? Teachers tend to vary widely in their estimation of working together:

♦ "The great teachers I know . . . build relationships among their peers, fighting isolation with as much strength as they can muster, knowing that such networks are their life-support systems as well as their sources for new ideas and input" (Wigginton, 1985, p. 283).

♦ "Planning the science/writing fair was a nice opportunity to work with all of you, but it's done little to make me feel that we're all moving in the same direction or that I should care a lot about what goes on outside my classroom" (Westheimer, 1998).

The interests of schools and students are better served when teachers work together toward professional learning and change.

Whichever of these statements is closer to your own view, you may soon be invited or even expected to participate in some form of collaborative professional development in your own school. That's because it's become increasingly clear that the interests of schools and students are better served when teachers work together toward meaningful professional learning and change (Harris-Rollins, n.d.). With the increasing demands of meeting the needs of a classroom with linguistically diverse learners, professional collaboration provides a catalyst for sharing expertise to better serve the pressing needs of a wide range of students.

The teacher quoted above who didn't see much value in working with other teachers would no doubt be surprised to know that she pinpointed precisely why connections between colleagues are so significant. She didn't see why she should care about school life outside her classroom, yet her students were certainly shaped by their previous year's teacher, as they will be by next year's. It isn't uncommon for a skilled teacher to enable students to make great progress during a school year, only to see that momentum slowed drastically when teachers in succeeding years can't support it. Students can't afford such a loss—particularly ELLs. It is well documented that most ELLs need a minimum of five to seven years to grasp the academic language necessary to achieve a high standard of literacy. Working closely as grade-level teams as well as in vertical teams (cross–grade level) will help our students continue momentum and not lose ground from year to year. "The sense of teacher autonomy must be broadened beyond the individual teacher to the group of teachers who are working, over time, with a given student or set of students" (Richardson, 1998). When teachers work together to identify and gain proficiency in best practices, students in all classrooms benefit, and variations in quality and effectiveness between teachers are reduced (Sparks, 2003).

Another concern voiced by the teacher who found working together "nice" but not much more is that she didn't believe that she and her fellow teachers were moving in the same direction. If teachers don't see the direction of their work as a collective concern, and if they never discuss the issue with each other, why would their work necessarily pursue the same ends? Students' experiences would be more consistent if the emphases and aims of their teachers coordinated and supported one another. Rather than just working within our own classrooms, we actually function within "a community of practice." Seen in this larger context—which is the context impacting our students over time—it follows naturally that "fellow teachers [should] engage, with each other, in critical discussions concerning aims, goals, procedures, and practices" (Richardson, 1998).

Students' experience would be more consistent if the emphases and aims of their teachers coordinated and supported each other.

Becoming more comfortable with collaboration

Various researchers concur that developing substantial collaboration among teachers within a school is "the single most important factor, . . . the most promising strategy for sustained, substantive school improvement" (Harris-Rollins, n.d.). For many of us, this concept of "interactive professionalism," as Michael Fullan characterizes it, represents a significant and perhaps startling change in our job description. As with all change, it requires adjustments. For example, we may need to become more open to risk-taking as we learn to trust fellow teachers and engage in mutual exploration of teaching practices. Certainly we'll have to acknowledge that our sphere of activity and responsibility is larger than our classroom and that all teachers in our school need to be invested in a common purpose and direction (Fullan, 1993, p. 10). We may have

"Interactive professionalism" happens when teachers learn to trust each other and engage in mutual exploration of teaching practices.

to overcome our own resistance to having others know our challenges or even observe our teaching. The school schedule itself may be a hurdle; it may have to be altered to provide time(s) for groups of teachers to come together on a regular basis.

Proponents of teacher collaboration as a means of school improvement recognize that "it is only when the people in this process are considered first, and their needs and wants met, that educational reform has much chance for success" (Norman, 2012). In other words, they understand that teachers may feel reluctant, uncertain, vulnerable in taking these new steps. Certainly it's essential that an "environment of comfort" respect and support be established. Toward this end, participants can work together to establish norms and procedures for their collaboration and decide on the content and focus of particular projects.

A study group can be a good way to begin collaboration because it offers new ideas and perspectives without necessarily requiring self-revelation.

If personal concerns and discomfort are a stumbling block to initiating collaboration with colleagues, these can be minimized by choosing an impersonal first project. A study group can be an excellent format because it offers new ideas and perspectives without necessarily requiring self-revelation. "Professional discourse is one of the most effective ways to create a common vision. Study groups provide ample opportunities for teacher input and discussion because they are designed to be flexible and offer no predetermined outcomes. . . . Teachers engage in a process of exploration and discovery. . . . There are more questions than answers, and the group creates new understanding together. . . . Offering teachers the chance to be inspired by new discoveries is a fundamental part of study groups" (Sweeney, 2005, pp. 21–22). Topics for study groups can be wide-ranging; they can include discussions based on this book, professional journals, ways to develop classroom libraries, how to present poetry or other genres to students, and so on. When it comes to teaching ELLs, there are numerous topics to explore: learning the English print system from an ELL perspective, reading comprehension and the ELL student, and grouping structures to support ELLs in the classroom, to name just a few.

As collaborative activities build trust and prove meaningful, they can become bolder and even more useful. For example, teachers can delve together into best practices, modeling, and coaching. Rather than exposing inadequacy, such exercises can pool the best resources of the group and enhance efficacy. One teacher found it invigorating and instructive to engage with colleagues in mutual observation and constructive problem solving: "Several very real weaknesses I knew I had I admitted from the outset, as did the others, and we worked on those weaknesses as a team—and in many cases fixed them. It can be a great way to teach, as long as those involved aren't too defensive or territorial" (Wigginton, 1985, p. 277).

Collaboration can initiate effective change and notable improvements in student performance

In exploring teaching practices and perspectives with colleagues, we need to be sure we aren't simply reviewing and reconfirming what we already know and do. Not only is such an approach not progressive, it may be retrogressive. Researchers recommend that professional learning groups incorporate into their reading and deliberations quality curriculum materials from external sources, as well as assessment information. Since our goal is to strengthen student learning through improved teaching, we need to look broadly and deeply into issues, require authority for our conclusions (research and proven experience), and measure ideas against standards (Fullan, 1993).

Our goal for collaboration should be to strengthen student learning through improved teaching.

It is important to bring in quality curriculum and assessment information from external sources rather than simply reviewing and reconfirming what we already do.

The potential gains from collaborative investigation and learning among teachers are enormous *if* we require that these activities be sufficiently rigorous to promote genuine advancement. Michael Fullan views teaching as a scientific and intellectual profession as well as a moral one (Sparks, 2003). If we share his perception, we'll commit our group work to inquiry, evaluation, and proof, rather than simply to mutual support. Collaboration approached in this way can effect innovation and change and alter teacher behavior. It should "reshape beliefs, alter mind-sets, or adjust attitudes regarding educational programs and instructional strategies" (Norman, 2012). Some educators believe its ultimate possibility is nothing less than transformation: teachers working together to "reform, reculture, [and] redesign the schools they work in" (Jordan, 2011). The ideas presented in this book set the stage for further inquiry and have the potential to significantly transform our instructional practices for teaching ELLs. (Chapter 9 sets forth some guiding questions to move forward with collaborative investigation.)

Collaborative activities should be rigorous and committed to inquiry, evaluation, and proof rather than simply to mutual support.

Transformation may sound like a daunting goal, but when collaboration is "embed[ded] in the structure and culture of schools . . . [and] focus, parameters, and support" are provided to direct and strengthen it, extraordinary results can be realized (Harris-Rollins, n.d.). The teachers and leaders of Faubion Elementary School, in a semi-industrial area of Portland, Oregon, created transformation. From 2001 to 2005, the scores of their at-risk students on state assessment tests improved by more than 30 percentage points in both reading and math. How did they do it? Through "devotion to assessment as the compass for instruction, and the conviction that teachers must constantly strive to better themselves with help from a community of peers" (Rubenstein, 2006).

It all began more than a decade ago when a district administrator required Title I teachers to create and implement assessments, and Faubion's principal supported the demand by encouraging teachers to collaborate in implementing the new assignment. As teachers worked together in conducting and interpreting regularly scheduled assessments, they discovered that the process enabled them to zero in on specific student needs and create interventions to address them. Fueled by this success, collaborative efforts were expanded. The staff meets every two weeks for two hours to discuss curriculum issues, consider concerns about particular students, or pursue a professional development activity (frequently led by Faubion teachers who have had training in pertinent skills). In regard to these professional development sessions, teachers agree on a focus for the year. Often the topic they choose is determined by student performance. "We figure if they're weak on it, we must be weak on it" (Rubenstein, 2006).

A long-term Faubion teacher acknowledges that it wasn't easy to create this culture in the school. The initial transition to a focus on student assessment and teacher collaboration was disruptive, and some teachers left. The school continues to be confronted with challenges of overcrowding, inadequate equipment and learning materials, and a high incidence of poverty among students. But the mental tone is one of expectation and confidence based on a schoolwide commitment to teamwork and performance. "We have built this sense that we're all in this together," explained one of the teachers. Shared responsibility, mutual investment, innovative practice, the momentum of greater efficacy, student achievement . . .

this is what Faubion teachers built together. What could collaboration build at our own schools?

Connect to cultures

"I don't belong": Many students feel uncomfortable in school setting

"English language learners come to us with much more than a desire to learn English. They come with knowledge of other places, languages, literacies, customs, and cultures. It's important to remember that ELLs' new learning should honor—not devalue—their home language, family, or culture, all critical sources of self-concept" (Knowledge Loom, n.d.). "Honoring, not devaluing" may represent the ideal of how cultural diversity should be embraced in our schools, but all too often the reality is quite different. Many students of color "see nothing familiar in the curriculum or school environment. . . . They feel, 'I don't belong here.' This sense of alienation from school is reflected in the higher dropout rates and lower test scores for language minority students." (Menkart, 1993).

Most of us have known at least a few uncomfortable moments in our lives when we've felt like an outsider. The perception that "I don't belong here" tends to put us off balance and on guard. It's not a frame of thought that's generally conducive to trust, risk-taking, and self-expression. Why might some students of color feel unsafe or adrift in school, and what can we do as teachers to encourage them to feel like valued, worthy, and able learners? How can we help these students know that they not only belong in school but that school belongs to them? We can begin to find answers to these important questions by developing a larger understanding of culture—both the culture of school and the cultures that each of our students brings with them to school. When these two cultures (the school's frame of reference and an individual student's frame of reference) more or less coincide, school feels familiar and students can progress steadily. But when these cultures diverge, as they often do for students of color, ELLs, and others who stand apart from the mainstream, school can seem strange and unsettling. "When students feel connected to school, they identify as learners and they have a far greater chance of becoming successful students. When they feel that they do not belong, identifying as a learner can be more difficult" (Nieto, 2002, pp. 298–299).

ELLs' new learning should honor–not devalue–their home language, family, or culture.

When the culture of school and the culture of our ELLs diverge, identifying as a learner can be more difficult.

Culture determines how we see and understand life

Culture is a term we all use frequently—but perhaps without recognizing how fundamentally it shapes our lives and thoughts. Here are some concepts and definitions of culture:

♦ "Culture [is] the way of life and thought that we construct, negotiate, institutionalize, and, finally, . . . end up calling 'reality' to comfort ourselves." (Bruner, 1996, p .87)

♦ "Culture refers to integrated patterns of human behavior that include the language, thoughts, communication, actions, customs, beliefs, values, and norms of racial, ethnic, religious, or social groups" (Oregon DOE, 2004).

♦ "Culture is the collective programming of the mind which distinguishes the members of one category of people from another." (Hofstede, 1984, p. 51)

♦ "Culture is mankind's primary adaptive mechanism." (Damen, 1987, p. 367)

♦ "For most people, including Americans, culture is an unconscious yet very significant thing in their lives. It lies at the heart of everything they are, think, and do." (Naylor, 1998, p. vii.)

Culture is not confined to ethnicity. Groups who affiliate on the basis of shared experiences and beliefs also create cultures. Cultures have developed around such issues as gender, sexual preference, socioeconomic class, religion, ideology, seniors, homeless people, cancer survivors, military veterans, and so on. Any one individual is likely to participate in several cultures, and each of these cultures then forms elements of his or her identity (Naylor, 1998, p. 8). "Everybody is multicultural. Every person and every human group possess both culture and cultural diversity" (Banks & McGee Banks, 2010, p. 36).

"Once a culture is learned, it becomes the measure of every other culture. Members of the group judge the ideas and actions of other groups based on what they have learned. This is because culture is learned as *truth*. No cultural group teaches its members that someone else's culture is more correct than theirs. When members of different culture groups come in contact with each other, . . . the learned truth of one group competes with that of another group" (Naylor, 1998, p. 8). All our students are coming to school bringing "truths,"

Cultural influences are so fundamental that they must inevitably influence how students perceive their school experience and the truths and realities conveyed there.

"realities," and identities shaped by their various socioeconomic backgrounds, ethnicities, and other group associations. As described by these researchers, cultural influences are so fundamental that they must inevitably impact how students perceive their school experience and the truths and realities conveyed there.

Cultural premises in American public schools tend to be white, middle-class, and Eurocentric

As teachers, we might protest that we wouldn't require any child to reject his own experience and background, his identity and truth. But a closer look at the cultural premises embodied in U.S. schools tells a different story, as described in the following observations from researchers.

♦ "The educational system [is] dominated by the white middle-class standard. . . . Basically, the educational system is oriented to a single cultural group" (Naylor, 1998, p. 100).

♦ "The educational process has allowed those in power to selectively control the flow of knowledge and inculcate into young minds only those 'truths' that solidify and perpetuate their own hegemony [i.e., dominance]" (Howard, 1999, p. 50).

♦ "Education is not neutral. Schools and daycare centers are institutions, and as such, they are part of the social structure that discriminates against individuals. In the classroom, teachers pass on their values to children through their choice of bulletin board displays, toys, activities, celebrations, unit themes, and interaction with the children" (York, 1991, p. 17).

♦ "*Monocultural education* . . . education reflective of only one reality and biased toward the dominant group, . . . is the order of the day in most of our schools. What students learn represents only a fraction of what is available knowledge. . . . Because the viewpoints of so many are left out, monocultural education is at best a partial education. It deprives all students of the diversity that is part of our world" (Nieto, 2002 p. 36).

♦ "There is a wide gap between the democratic ideals in Western nations such as the United States and the daily educational experiences of non-mainstream groups in their schools. Non-mainstream students in the U.S. . . .

often experience discrimination and marginalization in school and society because of their cultural, language, and behavioral differences" (Banks et al., 2007 p. 7).

◆ If these perceptions of school don't mirror our own, it may be because we're part of the 85 percent of K–12 teachers who are white (NCEI, 2005). We're also likely to be middle-class, to have been born in the United States, and to be monolingual English speakers. In that case, our own personal culture would have coincided reasonably well with that of our education. However, if we were among the 40 percent of today's students who are ethnic minorities, our response might have been quite different (Nieto, n.d.).

Children of minority groups often experience a kind of culture shock in school

Our current ELLs and students of color are probably too young to readily put into words whatever perceptions or feelings they may have about school and any discomfort they may feel in our classrooms. But it can be instructive to hear from adults looking back at their school experiences. As you read the remarks below, remember that these speakers are individuals who made it. They seem to feel, however, that they were able to achieve academically in spite of, rather than because of, our educational system, as school didn't really understand or support their experiences.

As literacy teachers, we need to be aware that language is so closely tied to culture that to learn a new language impacts students' sense of identity and cultural connection.

It's particularly notable that the remembered conflicts and self-doubts of these former students focus strongly on their difficulties in learning and using English. Although they ultimately developed a sophisticated command of English, they do not seem to feel the same connection to English as to their original language. As literacy teachers, we need to be aware that language is so closely tied to culture that to learn a new language (and certainly to lose an original language) impacts students' sense of identity and cultural connection. "Language is the primary means by which people acquire their culture. Without language, culture as we know it would simply be impossible. It is within language that all the ideas, rules, behaviors, and products of the culture are encoded" (Naylor, 1998, p. 7). While ELLs need a solid command of English to participate fully in school and in U.S. society, we as teachers must recognize that even if they succeed in mastering English, they may experience certain conflicts about it. This understanding will keep us alert to ways in which we can communicate our interest in their experience and our confidence in their abilities and contributions as members of our classroom.

Here are impressions voiced by several authors, editors, and university professors of Native American, Latino, Asian, and African American heritage about their encounters with U.S. education and culture:

- ◆ "As a child I spoke only one language, Tohono O'odham [a Native American language]. It was a rich, rich language. I had it in myself as a child and held it quietly, close to my chest, as the English language bounced and rattled all around me. I learned the English language and began to move in it with some fluidity. But O'odham connected me back to [family and tribal elders] and the things they knew and left with us to carry on."—*Ofelia Zepeda, university professor* (Santa Ana, 2004, p. xii).

- ◆ "Part of my education consisted of forcing myself to speak differently. I questioned the efficacy of my having spent seven years unlearning modes of speech that virtually all the people with whom I grew up employed as a rule. The notion that one could speak both right and black, could move effortlessly from proper to street discourse, from their to our forms of verbal address, hadn't occurred to me."—*Michael Awkward, author and university professor* (p. 191).

- ◆ "Not speaking well makes for such embarrassing moments. I hardly asked questions. I just didn't want to be misunderstood. Many Spanish-speaking kids mangled things up. That's the way it was with me. I mixed up all the words. Screwed up all the songs."—*Luis Rodriguez, author, founder of organization to support at-risk youth* (p. 26).

- ◆ "It was when I found out I had to talk that school became a misery. I did not speak and felt bad each time that I did not speak. I read aloud in first grade, though, and heard the barest whisper with little squeaks come out of my throat. 'Louder,' said the teacher, who scared the voice away again. The other Chinese girls did not talk either, so I knew the silence had to do with being a Chinese girl."—*Maxine Hong Kingston, author and university professor* (p. 80).

♦ "To speak Spanish, when I entered grade school in 1960, was to be dumb in every sense of that word. We were treated as inferior and we knew it, though we did not know the word *inferior*. Because the language of my family was Spanish and not English, I have always had an ambivalent relationship to the language of my country [i.e., the United States]. The language I am writing in will always be someone else's before it is mine."—*Benjamin Alire Sáenz, author, artist, university professor* (Santa Ana, p. 282).

♦ "Can I invest in and engage my full personhood, with all of my cultural formations, in my class, my work, my school, if teachers and the adults in the building are both attracted to and repulsed by these cultural formations—the way I walk, the way I use language, my relationship to my body, my physicality, and so on? Will I be willing to work hard over time, given the unpredictability of my teachers' responses to my work?"—*Theresa Perry, college professor* (Perry, Steele, & Hilliard, 2003, p. 5).

While our lessons—and school in general—may seem straightforward to us, our ELLs and nonwhite students have to filter them through several layers of cultural differences and language issues.

It's helpful to read these and other accounts of how multilingual and nonwhite individuals experienced school because it gives us a needed window on the emotional and psychological issues engaging our own students. Clearly, much more is going on beneath the surface than we may be seeing or imagining. While our lessons—and school in general—may seem straightforward to us, our ELLs and nonwhite students have to filter them through several layers of cultural differences and language issues as well as their estimate of whether they're included or excluded. Researchers describe how these undercurrents impact students:

♦ "The research shows that many children use their culture and racial identity every day in striving for access in school and life, only to have their race, language, and culture disparaged in the process. When culture is suppressed and denied, students are educationally disempowered" (Hanley, 2009).

♦ "Fashioning a new culture is no easy task [for students]. It involves first the difficult and painful experience of learning to survive in an environment that may have values and behaviors at polar extremes from those in the home. Young people need to choose from an array of values and behaviors, selecting those that fit in the new society and discarding or transforming others. Those whose values and behaviors differ from the mainstream are inevitably involved in this transformation every day" (Nieto, 2004, p. 288).

♦ "Teachers, who are very often unfamiliar with the language and culture of their students, easily succumb to an unspoken misconception: the smartest child is the one who speaks the language and the dialect of the teacher. Teachers accept this false premise, which lowers their expectations for non-English-speaking or non-Standard-English-speaking children. This preconception creates a self-fulfilling prophecy that is extremely difficult for the elementary school student to overcome" (Santa Ana, 2004, p. 4).

♦ "By devaluing the culture of poor and minority children, teachers encourage an ominous choice: identify with family and friends and disavow the school, or embrace school culture and face emotional/social isolation. The result is that many young people opt for family and friends and become unwilling participants in school culture" (Bowman, 1994).

For many of us, the idea that our schools tend to marginalize nonwhite and non-English-speaking children and their cultural heritages may be disquieting, but this fact has been well documented by researchers over several decades. It's likely, too, that we haven't been aware of the degree of inner turmoil experienced by many nonwhite and non-English-speaking students as they try to navigate schooling. On the other hand, most of us are probably familiar with aspects of multicultural education and cultural competence, which have been developed over the past few decades in direct response to issues of inequity in our educational system. Many states and school systems have implemented programs or at least established goals related to cultural awareness. If we truly want to make a difference in the school lives and academic achievement of ELLs and students of color, we need to actively and persistently cultivate cultural competence and incorporate it into our classroom activities and lessons.

When culture is suppressed and denied, students are educationally disempowered.

Teachers, due to their unfamiliarity with the languages and cultures of their students, may tend to lower their expectations for non-English-speaking students.

We need to actively and persistently cultivate cultural competence and incorporate it into our classrooms and lessons.

Challenging our own biases and enlarging our multicultural awareness

So how do we begin? Researcher and teacher Gary Howard (1999) recommends that we begin by cultivating empathy: "Empathy means 'to feel with.' It focuses our attention on the perspective and worldview of another person" (p. 73). For example, the stark experiences of school culture shock described by ethnic students in their own words (as quoted earlier in this section) revealed emotional depths and complexities in those individuals and probably evoked sympathy and concern in us as we read their comments. "Empathy begins with seeing others in their own light rather than through our projections of them in our light. White educators [need] to challenge our assumptions and face the limitations of our own knowledge. We [can ask] ourselves, 'What am I not seeing here? How are my assumptions and behaviors getting in the way of serving American Indian children [or Latinos, Asians, African Americans, or other ethnic groups]? Who can help me overcome the deficiencies in my own perceptions?'" (p. 75). Multicultural educator James Banks expresses it this way: "Teachers have to begin to see that I am the other and the other is me. That the future of immigrant children is my future, that our fates are intimately connected" (Tucker, n.d.).

Gaining an awareness of pervasive educational inequities and learning how to help counter them is a process that takes time, intention, and personal change.

These comments express a great amount of idealism, and most of us may find ourselves readily agreeing with them. However, gaining an awareness of pervasive educational inequities and learning how to help counter them is a process that takes time, intention, and personal change. The Oregon Department of Education (2004) has developed a working definition of cultural competency that describes it as being "based on a commitment to social justice and equity." It acknowledges that it is "a developmental process" because "individuals begin with specific lived experiences and biases, and working to accept multiple world views is a difficult choice and task." As researcher and educator Sonia Nieto (n.d.) notes, "All of us have biases. So we have to look very deeply into ourselves . . . and what we think about the students who are sitting in front of us. Then we have to think about how to deal with those biases in a way that doesn't jeopardize the students we're teaching."

Respect varied ways that students respond in the classroom environment

Unfortunately, the biases that we may be unaware of have caused teachers and schools to negatively estimate the potential of minority students for many years. This practice is so longstanding and widespread that researchers have even given it a term: *cultural deficit theory* (Crochunis, Edrey & Swedlow, 2002). It means that educators have tended to evaluate differences (i.e., divergences from the dominant white culture) as deficits and thus have often relegated minority children to lesser educational experiences. Even today, we may not recognize that different cultural perspectives and child-rearing practices instill different behaviors in children. These can impact many areas of classroom interaction, such as whether it's appropriate for a child to make eye contact or speak freely with adults, how a child tells a story or describes an experience, what style of questioning children are accustomed to from adults, whether children have been taught to value individual achievement or group contribution more highly, whether it's appropriate to demonstrate one's knowledge in front of other people, and more (Owocki & Goodman, 2002, p. 59).

Variations of these and other cultural patterns are likely visible in many of our students. When students don't participate or respond in ways we expect, this does not necessarily indicate a lack of knowledge or ability. Rather, either we or they may not be reading one another's signals correctly. Not understanding that minority children are very capable but may simply express themselves differently, it is all too easy to conclude that they cannot learn or function at the level of most white, middle-class children. "What is, in fact, the result of a [cultural] mismatch is often explained by schools as the limited ability of the children, who end up being categorized as incapable, unintelligent, and lacking potential. In this way, resilient children who are very capable in other settings are often rendered ineffective" (Crochunis et.al, 2002, p. 63).

> Cultural deficit theory *means that educators have tended to evaluate differences as deficits and have often relegated minority children to lesser educational experiences.*

Tap and value the background experiences of all students

The perception that some minority and working-class children are deficient in academic potential often includes the assumption that their homes are incapable of offering them "school-worthy knowledge" (Santa Ana, 2004, p. 154). Researchers Luis Moll and Norma González visited the homes of such students and developed relationships with their parents, discovering in the process that these households had significant "funds of knowledge" that included strategies for survival, occupational skills, and active social networks through which knowledge was transmitted (p. 153). Learning more about students' family experiences can alert us to background knowledge that we can then build on in school. For example, some students have heard many stories passed down to them through oral traditions. Even if their parents never actually read to them, they may have a strong grasp of narrative structure (Crochunis et.al, 2002, p. 36). Other students are sometimes responsible for the care of their siblings or for working in family businesses (p. 44). These experiences indicate knowledge that can be tapped in school. Moll and Gonzalez urge teachers to make home visits in order to learn more about each student's family life so that they can incorporate those "funds of knowledge" into their teaching (Santa Ana, 2004).

Learning more about students' family experiences can alert us to background knowledge that we can then build on in school.

Another option is to ask specific questions of parents when they come to school. At the very least, we need to remember that homes of every culture and socioeconomic class often have a rich store of knowledge and skill that they pass on to their children. Teachers who conducted home research with Moll and González discovered that many families were remarkably resourceful in overcoming difficult circumstances and that parents placed a high priority on educational opportunities for their children (Santa Ana, 2004, p. 155). These home visits challenged the teachers' stereotypes. One teacher commented, "I used to believe that my students had limited opportunities in life and that this was something too big for me to change as a teacher. This fatalistic obsession of mine has slowly melted away as I have gotten to know my students and their families" (pp. 152–154). She comments further that she regards this change of perception as her "most important transformation."

Accept and affirm students' differences

In an effort to be impartial, some teachers strive to not make any distinctions among children in their class. "'I don't see black or white,' a teacher will say, 'I see only *students*'" (Nieto, 2004, p. 138). While this outlook is intended to promote equality, it can inadvertently cause us to measure all students against a single perceived norm and to conclude that those who don't conform to that expectation must have lesser capabilities. On the other hand, if we recognize that there is no such thing as one usual or acceptable pattern of student attitudes and behaviors, we'll be less likely to misinterpret differences as deficiencies. "Learning to *affirm* differences rather than deny them is what a multicultural perspective is about" (pp. 138–139). In line with making a commitment to equity and social justice in education, it's worth thinking about whether tolerance is an adequate goal for cultural responsiveness. Although tolerance has been widely adopted as a basis for many multicultural programs and can certainly have a positive effect on the attitudes of individuals, the popular sense of the word can imply "a grudging but somewhat distasteful acceptance. To tolerate differences means that they are endured, not necessarily embraced" (Nieto, 2002, p. 262). Nieto suggests that we consciously cultivate a progression in outlook as we grow in our understanding and support of multicultural issues: *Acceptance,* a step beyond tolerance, "implies that differences are acknowledged and their importance is neither denied nor belittled" (p. 264). *Respect* surpasses acceptance because it "implies admiration and high esteem for diversity. When differences are respected, they are used as the basis for much of what goes on in schools" (p. 266). *Affirmation, solidarity, and critique* recognize that "if students are to transcend their own cultural experience in order to understand the differences of others, they need to go through a process of reflection and critique of their cultures and those of others" (p. 269).

Learning to affirm differences means acknowledging the differences that children bring to school, admitting the possibility that students' identities may influence how they learn, and that accepting differences also means making provisions for them.

Cultivate our own understandings about different cultures

On a practical level, we can begin to cultivate our own multicultural awareness by reading fiction, poetry, and memoirs by authors from various cultures, seeking out non-American perspectives on historical as well as contemporary events and participating in cross-cultural events. (Many newspapers feature a weekly calendar in which local events are listed; some of these are likely to include festivals, music, speakers, and so on, from various cultural groups.) Museum exhibits, community centers, and topical DVDs can be good sources of learning about cultures.

Many articles and books have been written on multicultural education. Not only do many of these materials include helpful ideas for implementing multicultural classroom activities, but some of them also include historical perspectives on how U.S. monoculture developed as well as experiences and observations of ethnic students. A number of these books include vignettes of how teachers successfully adapted their teaching to build on cultural references familiar to students. Reading and discussing resources on multicultural education would be an excellent project for in-house teacher development or peer support groups.

Multicultural perspectives to be made explicit in our teaching: inclusiveness, multiplicity of viewpoints, and freedom from bias

What makes the multicultural perspective so significant? Ideally, no one is left out, nor is anyone's experience made to look lesser than someone else's. "Multicultural education is by definition inclusive. Because it is *about* all people, it is also *for* all people" (Nieto, 2002, p. 311). A multicultural approach is about much more than cultural affirmation and learning about various cultures. Sonia Nieto cautions that it's simplistic to merely introduce students to "the pleasant aspects of diversity," such as cultural traditions. She refers to this as "holidays and heroes" or the "tourist approach to diversity" (Nieto, n.d.). "Multicultural education is more than holidays and food; it requires critical thinking with attention paid to complexity. All children must be educated about the multiple strands of the past that have created the webs of the present." (Hanley, 2009). In other words, some of the stories, perspectives, contributions and conflicts that have traditionally been excluded in our accounts of U.S. history and culture need to be included. In this way, people and experiences that have been made invisible by lack of acknowledgement become more visible as a legitimate thread in American life.

The presentation of multiple perspectives is a central element of a multicultural approach. "A major problem with a monocultural curriculum is that it gives students only one way of seeing the world. When reality is presented as static, finished, and flat, the underlying tensions, controversies, passions, and problems faced by people throughout history and today disappear. Textbooks in all subject areas exclude information about unpopular perspectives and the perspectives of disempowered groups in our society. A multicultural perspective reflects on multiple and contradictory perspectives to understand reality more fully" (Nieto, 2002, pp. 316–317).

The tendency of textbooks and popular culture to depict and perpetuate only certain facts and stories has led James Banks to conclude that teaching students to think critically about "knowledge construction" should be an essential element of multicultural education. He points out that much generally believed and accepted knowledge is not necessarily "truth" but rather is "constructed" or built on the frames

of reference of the tellers, whose words and terms are often "heavily loaded [with] a lot of values and assumptions" (Banks & Tucker, 1998). In fact, these values and assumptions are so familiar and natural to many teachers that questioning them may feel uncomfortable.

Banks (2006) offers a clear example of a one-sided perspective on history when he discusses the familiar accounts of western expansion in U.S. history. "Concepts such as the 'Westward Movement' need to be reconceptualized and viewed from the perspectives of different cultural and ethnic groups. The Lakota Sioux's homeland was not the West to them; it was the center of the universe. It was not the West for the Alaskans; it was south. It was east for the Japanese and north for the people who lived in Mexico" (p. 155). The deceptively simple characterization of this great population movement as being "westward" in direction reveals that we have given priority to the history of one group, even though many other groups were in the same place at the same time.

Teaching students to think critically about "knowledge construction" is important because much generally believed and accepted knowledge is not necessarily "truth" but rather is "constructed" or built on the frames of reference of the tellers.

It's more authentic to present a topic or information from several viewpoints (i.e., How might characters in a story have different perceptions of a given situation? What different views might have been held by various parties in a historic entanglement? Did the author include these views? If not, why do students think those views might have been excluded?) Then students can be encouraged to consider these perspectives and why they exist, as well as their impact on actions and results. "Students [learn] that there are many sides to every story and that in order to make informed decisions, they need as much information as they can get. Students [can be] encouraged to be critical of every book or piece of information by asking questions such as: Who wrote the book? Who's missing in this story? Why? Using questions such as these as a basis, they are learning that every story has a point of view and that every point of view is at best partial and at worst distorted" (Nieto, 2002, p. 272).

Another core issue of enlarging social justice in education is what Louise Derman-Sparks refers to as an "anti-bias approach." She describes this approach as "value-based: Differences are good; oppressive ideas and behaviors are not. It sets up a creative tension between respecting differences and not accepting unfair beliefs and acts" (Derman-Sparks, 1989, p. x). From a very young age, students can be encouraged to explore similarities and differences among themselves and others. Many books on multicultural education offer a variety of concrete lesson plans that implement this idea at different age levels. Such exercises can help students learn that differences are not wrong or right, better or worse, but simply different ways of being and living. As students learn about "a variety of people in a variety of roles," (Thomson, 1993, p. 133), they develop a broader range of reference and are less susceptible to stereotypes. Actually, a direct exploration of stereotypes can be useful in illustrating to students how ideas that may hold some truth in them can be made very narrow and inaccurate and then be used untruthfully to hurt people. It's also helpful to expose students to nontraditional ideas (some dads take care of children while their mother works, some boys are more interested in art or music than sports, some children don't live with their parents but have other caring environments, etc.).

Julie Olsen Edwards and Louise Derman-Sparks (2010) further recommend that students be taught to recognize injustice, to understand that it's hurtful, and to identify ways to respond to it when they or others are an object of it. "Plan activities that help children learn how to contrast inaccurate, untrue images or ideas with accurate ones. . . . Build children's budding capacities for empathy and fairness. Support critical-thinking activities, which pave the way for their learning to take action to make unfair things fair" (p. 5). In this regard, it's especially important that teachers not be silent or unresponsive when they hear or witness biased remarks or actions. "Biased behaviors among children such as teasing, rejection, and exclusion based on some aspect of a child's identity are a form of aggressive behavior and are just as serious as physical aggression. An anti-bias approach calls on teachers to gently but firmly intervene, support the child who has been hurt by the biased behavior, and help children learn other ways of interacting. Anti-bias education is a necessary partner of conflict resolution education" (pp. 5–6).

In order to realize the potential of a multicultural, anti-bias approach, its perspectives can't simply be relegated to a certain lesson period every week. Real multicultural education is much more than an additional area of study. Infusing multicultural perspectives in all aspects of schooling is a matter of realigning education to better reflect the diversity that already exists in our communities and the larger world. Although it may be a new way of thinking, we must consider

A multicultural approach (1) is about much more than cultural affirmation and learning about other cultures, (2) presents multiple and contradictory perspectives to understand reality more fully, (3) should teach students to think critically about knowledge construction, (4) should have an anti-bias approach, and (5) is more than an additional area of study. It should be evident in all aspects of schooling.

and ultimately embrace the idea of multicultural education as "a philosophy, a way of looking at the world, not simply a program or a class or a teacher" (p. 6).

Classroom materials and activities can reflect multicultural perspectives

Implementing multicultural education is a big task, and no one expects it can happen overnight. A good way to start is to "change 'things' first." For instance, we can remove from our classrooms all materials that present stereotypes and replace them with others that illustrate diversity (York, 1991, p. 32). (Public library resale shops are often excellent resources for obtaining used magazines and other sources of photos and illustrations.) Stereotypical depictions might include a strong focus on white faces or middle-class environments or illustrations of men/women or boys/girls engaged only in traditional gender pursuits. Visuals that contradict biased expectations offer students new options and ways of thinking.

As a guideline, Deborah Menkart (1993) offers a range of categories familiar to children (economic, physical ability, family, race, gender, nationality, cultures, age) and encourages us to identify stereotypes typical of each. Images that capture our common humanity (people of different cultural groups engaged in family activities, working, shopping, playing, etc.) illustrate shared interests and needs that can lessen feelings of distance and strangeness. Menkart notes that one cultural group that has come under close and often negative scrutiny in recent years is Arab Americans. Bulletin board displays and stories about these individuals could serve as a springboard for discussion and classroom activities. Further topical examples suggested by Menkart include the elderly and Native Americans. She draws attention to the inaccuracy of popular views that generally regard older adults as inactive or even frail and Native Americans as left behind by white culture. Again, students need to see images of members of these groups in active, contemporary, meaningful roles because that is a more faithful view of their experiences. As we build a collection of images, we can offer students a broad view of the many ways human beings experience their lives. Lastly, Menkart recommends that images of students and their families be featured in our classrooms. These pictures make it clear that the students are part of school and part of diversity, and developing various displays (including focusing on cultures specific to your students) can be a good opportunity to work together with parents.

Students should see themselves in our classroom materials

The issues discussed in regard to bulletin boards pertain equally to books, newspapers, games, displays, props, music, and other materials used in our classrooms. Many worthwhile books on multicultural education include lists of children's books that emphasize cultural themes, anti-bias issues, children and families around the world (including nontraditional families), and girls and women in self-reliant and capable roles. Selections should include fiction and nonfiction, biography and poetry, and characters should represent a range of ethnicities. Again, the goal is to have children see people like themselves represented broadly in materials they use daily. "The more stories we have, the more we are able to get at the full complexity that accurately represents cultures, and individuals within those cultures" (Aaronsohn, 2000, p. 2).

Promote authentic experiences that cultivate cultural awareness

Along with creating a multicultural environment in the classroom, we need to introduce activities through which a range of ideas can be actively explored with students. It's helpful to review activities suggested by multicultural educators (many lesson plans are available through books and on the Internet). At their best, these authors describe materials needed, the focus of the lesson, how to implement it, and possible questions to introduce for student discussion. Here are a few sample topics from one book: Our Own Families, What Makes a Friend?, A Country Far Away, Skin-Color Comparisons, How a Contemporary Navajo Family Lives, What Families Are Proud Of, and What Are Stepmothers Really Like? (Thomson, 1993, pp. vii–viii). In addition, field trips and guest speakers can bring dimension to multicultural learning. "Guests expand the horizons of the children in concrete ways. They are, in effect, a hands-on learning opportunity" (p. 35), Barbara Thomson suggests inviting guests to speak for about fifteen minutes about their profession, travels, cultural interests, or their experience of prejudice or fighting injustice, and respond to students' questions afterward. Student exchanges with female or minority police officers, firefighters, physicians, and construction workers (whether on field trips or as classroom guests) provide a great opportunity to consider nontraditional roles and learn personal stories about how women chose such paths and overcame obstacles. Male ballet dancers, nurses, and stay-at-home dads can explore the same issues from the masculine standpoint. Local ethnic communities can also be a good resource for finding guests who can share stories and artifacts of interest to students (p. 36).

Involve parents and communicate your goals

Students' parents must be part of multicultural education; at a minimum, they need to be advised of your multicultural activities and goals. This can be accomplished through a newsletter, a phone call, or a meeting. Periodic letters to parents allow teachers to share details of issues students are considering and how they're responding. A newspaper created by students, including articles and illustrations, can be a good tool for reviewing a lesson and communicating with parents (p. 63). When parents can participate directly in school, their activities can have significant meaning for students. "Parents as volunteers, speakers, and field trip helpers are a diversity resource for your students. Children learn a lot when they have contact with different parents. It is also very important for minority children to see minority parents helping in the classroom. Children today cannot possibly have too many experiences in which they see persons similar to themselves in positions of competence and power" (p. 64).

Resistance and commitment

Multicultural topics—and especially anti-bias issues—are sometimes met with resistance. Louise Derman-Sparks and Julie Olson Edwards (2010) alert us that "as children first begin to talk about identity and fairness issues, they may make more, rather than fewer, biased comments than before. But such comments are a natural part of the anti-bias process—it takes many attempts before they learn a new way of thinking about difference" (p. 8). Some parents may not welcome some or all of our anti-bias activities. Derman-Sparks and Edwards note that teachers sometimes find it more difficult to approach adults about these issues than children. As they explain, "This is not surprising. A kind of 'emperor's new clothes' syndrome in our society (i.e., thinking it's better to pretend not to see what is in front of our eyes) keeps many of us silent about anti-bias issues" (p. 9). It's good to be forewarned that we may encounter opposition so that we can respond with respect but without

It's good to be forewarned that we may encounter opposition so that we can respond to a multicultural emphasis with respect without feeling intimated.

feeling intimidated. As Barbara Thomson (1993) reminds us, "Implicit in this [anti-bias] approach is the acceptance of another point of view that is different from yours and from the school's, but nevertheless valid. That kind of attitude keeps communication open" (p. 63).

Our willingness to engage in this sometimes controversial work will depend on our own convictions about its value. "Why do we do anti-bias work? We do it because we live in a world that is not yet a place where all children have equal opportunity to become all they are" (p. 9). If we find ourselves agreeing with this response, we're ready to begin the journey of becoming multicultural educators.

"Put aside your preconceived notions of what multicultural education should be and your worries about implementing it in your program. Open yourself up to your feelings. Take in the information bit by bit. Ask questions, stop for reflection, watch others around you, gather some materials, and create some activities, and talk with children and parents. As you do these things, you will create a greater understanding of yourself, culture, and multicultural curriculum, and you will have begun the steps toward implementing multicultural education in your classroom" (York, 1991, p. 17).

Mental Energizer #2: Elevate your expectations

High expectations lead to stronger academic demands and boost student confidence.

Expectations make a big difference. They can buoy you up or defeat you. In sports, capable teams can fall apart if they're intimidated by a rival they think of as unbeatable. On the other hand, courage and inspiration have been known to sustain hope and effort in dire situations, as it did in 2010 for 33 Chilean miners who were trapped 2,300 feet underground for 69 days. As one of their rescuers observed, "The guys that were down there, I think they never lost their hope. There were critical moments, but at the end they never lost their hope because they had very positive leaders who kept the group unified" (Warren, 2010). In other words, their positive expectations helped to sustain their health and mental equilibrium, even during the first 17 days when they heard nothing from anyone aboveground and had almost nothing to eat.

Expectations are so significant that an entire industry—marketing—has developed to shape and exploit them. Political campaigns, schools, corporations, and retailers all generate slogans, mottoes, and mission statements to express their expectations and garner public support. Our expectations for and assumptions about ELLs impact their success as learners more than all the proven teaching techniques we might employ. "When teachers form low expectations of students based on a perceived lack of intellect or cultural sophistication, these expectations become a kind of self-fulfilling prophecy, and student performance falls" (Crochunis et al., 2002). But ELLs are not remedial students. Falling into the subtle but dangerous perception that ELLs are deficient because they have less command of English tends to diminish our expectations, our demands, and our students' achievement. English proficiency is a tool to be gained, not a barometer of capacity. We need to perceive ELLs as the equals of their English-fluent peers, fully capable of directed effort and higher-order thinking. Our expectations for ELLs should be as high as for any other student, and we should require them to be as accountable as other students as well. Of course, we need to offer ELLs the appropriate support that will allow them to develop and succeed, but the first step is to acknowledge and honor their potential.

We need to perceive ELLs as the equals of their English-fluent peers, fully capable of directed effort and higher-order thinking.

We need to ensure that we do not give our ELLs and other marginalized students less instructional attention than other students. Do we call on them as regularly as other students? Do we provide answers for them too quickly when we would urge other students to work out meanings themselves? (Crochunis et al., 2002). Students have an uncanny ability to pick up on our estimate of them. If we show no real confidence in their capacity to participate in and contribute to learning activities, why should they consider themselves able?

The assumption that ELLs may learn at a slower pace than their native-English-speaking classmates has misled many teachers to excuse ELL students from full participation and even to relegate them to the role of passive observers. "Many well-intentioned teachers seek to assist low-performing ELL and minority students by making the curriculum less cognitively challenging so that students can 'get it.' Sometimes teachers assume that the culturally diverse and poor students don't have the cultural prerequisites that teachers view as precursors to higher-order thinking" (Crochunis et al., 2002). At best, it's a misplaced kindness to shield ELLs from vigorous academic work, and at worst, it can instill in them a

At best, it's a misplaced kindness to shield ELLs from vigorous academic work, and at worst, it can instill in them a learned helplessness that leads to disengagement, self-doubt, and an unwillingness to try.

learned helplessness that leads to disengagement, self-doubt, and an unwillingness to try. Hippocrates, the acknowledged father of modern medicine, is credited with extolling physicians to "first, do no harm." If we permit our ELLs to be non-participants or quasi-participants, we're stunting not only their academic development but also their opportunity to discover and prove their innate capacities for learning and creating. This is a great harm we need to take care not to foster.

Rhona Weinstein (2002), who has done extensive research on the effects of teacher expectations, found through interviews with students that "children learn about their relative smartness largely from the teacher[,] . . . derived from what teachers told them, what teachers did or did not do, and from the structure and content of learning activities" (p. 97). It's particularly thought provoking that teacher feedback was the clue children relied on most strongly regarding their assessment of their own intelligence. "Elementary school children, even young ones, know that teachers, on average, treat high and low achievers differently within the same classroom. High expectations, trust, and opportunity from teachers are linked with doing well in school, whereas scolding, monitoring, and lots of help are associated with poor performance" (p. 110). Research revealed several disturbing facts. First, even very young children display a sophisticated capacity to pick up on signals from teachers about their learning capacity. Second, in classrooms structured to emphasize ability levels, children generally feel that low achievers have little hope of making real progress. Lastly, students' *perceived* differences about their abilities often become *actual* differences in performance (p. 168).

Rather than creating classroom cultures in which performance and comparison divide students (and defeat many of them), we can support the development of all students by focusing instead on learning and individual growth (p. 213). Geneva Gay (2010) urges us to support culturally diverse students through pedagogical actions that will enable them to succeed as learners. She calls this "genuine instructional caring" (p. xxvii). Such caring is possible insofar as we hold "an unshakable belief that marginalized students not only *can* but *will* improve their school achievement under the tutelage of competent and committed teachers who act to ensure that this happens" (pp. 58–59). In other words, we need to combine positive expectations with strong demands. Kleinfeld (1975)

> *Teacher feedback was the clue children relied on most in regard to their assessment of their own intelligence.*

> *"Genuine instructional caring" is characterized by supporting the development of all students by focusing on learning and individual growth.*

> *We need to combine positive expectations with strong demands.*

saw this approach produce good results with Athabaskan Indian and Eskimo students in Alaska, and she described such teachers as "warm demanders." Warm demanders express genuine caring to students, an "unconditional positive regard" which includes a deep certainty that all students can succeed. At the same time, they make a "nonnegotiable demand" for students to exert their best efforts in their academic work (Kleinfeld, 1975, as cited in Bondy & Ross, 2008).

Warm demanders actively build relationships with students. "A smile, a hand on the shoulder, the use of a student's name, or a question that shows you remember something the student has mentioned" are the kinds of personal exchanges that convey awareness and establish trust. At the same time, warm demanders let students know that you expect them to do their best work and to succeed. "It is not uncommon to hear these teachers making declarations to students to the effect that 'there is no excuse for not trying to learn,' 'you will never know what you can do unless you try,' and '*I can't do* is unacceptable in my classroom'" (Gay, 2010, p. 75). To be sure that students can meet these expectations, warm demanders provide appropriate learning supports. These might include offering a variety of materials and activities about a given topic, explaining and reviewing materials thoroughly and as often as needed, breaking down activities or thinking into small steps, and persisting in working with students until they attain understanding. "The teachers who help the most never give up" (p. 75). The findings of Kleinfeld, as reported by Gay, highlight key elements of warm demanding: "academic demands complemented with emotional support and facilitative instruction, a coaching and cajoling rather than a dictatorial style of teaching, and reciprocal responsibility for learning" (p. 56).

Supporting positive behavior is another important element in working toward student success. Behavior is sometimes a significant issue in urban schools in which students are academically disengaged or even resistant. Warm demanders require students to act respectfully toward teachers and classmates. While problems can be frustrating, warm demanders emphasize improvement and resolution. They might employ kidwatching to determine when and why certain behaviors occur. Rather than blame students, they work patiently to redirect students toward cooperation and better choices, praising and supporting every evidence of progress. Warm demanders make their expectations clear to students and keep them consistent. They make both rules and consequences clear, and they follow up on what they say. They remind students of their capabilities often and give frequent feedback and support for good efforts.

Researchers Wilson and Dickson (2001) asked urban high schoolers to describe teachers who helped them to significantly improve their learning. The characteristics named coincide with those of warm demanders: "pushing students to complete assignments, maintaining order[,] being willing to offer help whenever and for however long it was needed, going to great lengths to explain assignments and concepts, varying classroom activities, respecting students and their outside-of-the-school worlds. Students seemed to be saying that they most highly valued teachers who refused to allow them to fail" (p. 3).

Most of us have had the experience of exceeding our own expectations in some situation because someone in our lives (a teacher, parent, coach, employer, or spouse) recognized and encouraged our potential. Unfortunately, many of us have also found ourselves strangely unable to do anything right when we're under the thumb of someone's negative or limited estimation of us. We need to have enough esteem for ELL students to estimate them correctly as able learners. And we need to equip ourselves to help them fulfill that potential. I've had the experience many times of being in classrooms where teachers marvel at what an ELL student achieves in a lesson I model. If you expect it, they will rise to the challenge.

Clearly, ELLs have particular needs that require changes in how we approach instruction. Our own classroom experiences, as well as what we read in education journals and daily news, verify the need for change. The challenge is large, the stakes for our students and society are high, and the demand on us as teachers is to lead the way. Even with the research, instruction, techniques, and examples available (including this book), are these expectations too high?

We tend to measure our expectations against what is usual, and exceeding those expectations therefore seems unusual or out of the question. But consider how every new stage of development requires exceeding the usual. For many years, it was considered impossible, and even physically dangerous, to run a mile in less than 4 minutes. When Roger Bannister

"Warm demanders" (1) express genuine caring, (2) have a deep certainty that all students can succeed, (3) make a nonnegotiable demand for students to exert their best efforts, (4) actively build relationships, (5) provide appropriate learning experiences, (6) require students to act respectfully towards teachers and classmates, (7) have clear and consistent expectations, and (8) refuse to allow students to fail.

accomplished this in 1954, he broke a psychological as well as an athletic barrier. The curious thing about records in sports is that every fastest speed or best performance is always succeeded by a faster or better one. It's notable that in the last 50 years, the record for running a mile has been broken 11 more times, to reach the current best time of 3 minutes, 43.13 seconds, set in 1999 (Ewalt & Rose, 2005). Winning is wonderfully energizing because a winner expects to keep winning. As warm demanders who believe deeply in our students' capacities, we can help them experience the triumph of achieving academic goals and believing in their own large futures.

Every advancement requires the admission that it's possible to exceed old standards. Computers, iPods, cell phones, satellites, digital cameras, and global positioning systems, unheard of just a few decades ago, are now commonplace in our daily lives. All of these developments greatly exceed the expectations of our great grandparents. All of them have changed our estimate of what is usual and essential.

Where do breakthroughs come from? We have to begin by accepting the possibility in thought. Athletes believe they can break records, and then they train to do it. Inventors imagine something never before known and gradually make it reality. As educators, we need to acknowledge that we can learn the languages of cultural awareness, technique, and insight that will enable us to speak in appropriate and useful forms to our ELL students. This acknowledgement sets us on the path to breaking through barriers of traditional teaching. It gives us courage and motivation. This enlarges our expectations and opens the door wide to gaining enlarged expertise, which in turn opens the doors to literacy success for all our students.

As educators, we need to acknowledge that we can learn the languages of cultural awareness, technique, and insight that will enable us to speak in appropriate and useful forms to our ELL students.

High expectations give lift-off to learning

The once-familiar terrain of school is changing and reshaping itself. As educators, we're all faced with insistent demands for learning and adapting. The more things change, the more essential it can be to hold on to what's changeless. This includes the powerful conceptions and fundamental motivations that anchor our teaching. It also includes our commitment to the children we teach. William Ayers proposes eloquently that "children ought to be allowed to stretch

themselves into life buoyed by a sense of being unconditionally welcomed" (Rose & Ayers, p. xiii). Do we genuinely welcome the new majority of minority students? Are we ready to teach to high expectations of their capabilities and to reexamine any preconceptions of "cultural deficits" we might be harboring? Are we willing to undertake the work of understanding the impact of culture on learning and to make appropriate adaptations to our teaching? These are challenging questions that are likely to keep recurring even after we think we've answered them. "The trick is to live with one foot in the world as it is while the other foot strides toward a world that could be but is not yet. Working the contradiction allows you to find the cracks and the crevices within which to build a more effective and at the same time more hopeful teaching life," Ayers suggests (p. 10). He also reminds us, in the spirit of a warm demander, that "the essential and urgent thing is not to let our teaching lives make a mockery of our deepest teaching values" (p. 12).

• • • • • • • • • • • • • • • •

In Brief

Teachers not only bring their skills and knowledge to the classroom, they also bring their convictions and attitudes. Effective teachers operate from powerful conceptions and a sense of moral purpose. Finding ways to put into action the ideas they believe in is empowering.

This chapter discussed ways to energize teachers and to put these powerful conceptions to work effectively in teaching ELLs. These methods are called "mental Energizers" because energy enlivens, stimulates, and empowers us, and gives us the ability to work.

Mental Energizer #1: Cultivate Connections

Meaningful connections require engagement. Three connections we especially need to invigorate are those with our students, our colleagues, and our understanding of culture as a life force.

Connect to kids

♦ Relationships and connection are at the core of effective teaching and learning because social interaction is the basis of learning.

♦ Effective teachers employ modeling, mentoring, and coaching to foster and support learning.

♦ Systematic observations help teachers connect to students and their learning.

♦ Highly focused attention and active engagement help teachers find teachable moments and make strong connections with students in ways that ensure learning.

Connect to colleagues

♦ Establishing an environment of comfort, respect, and support is essential in making connections between colleagues.

♦ Collaboration between teachers can help improve the quality and consistency of students' learning experiences.

♦ Collaborative activities must be sufficiently rigorous to promote genuine advancement. Professional learning groups should examine quality curriculum materials from outside sources, as well as assessment information.

Connect to culture

♦ Monocultural education, biased toward the dominant group, is the order of the day in most of our schools.

♦ Cultural diversity should be honored, not devalued.

♦ Cultural influences are so fundamental that they must inevitably impact how students perceive their school experience and the truths and realities conveyed there.

♦ Some ways educators can ensure that they connect to culture in meaningful, unbiased ways include

   • respecting varied ways students respond in the classroom environment;

   • tapping and valuing the background experiences of all students;

   • accepting and affirming students' differences;

   • cultivating our own understandings about different cultures;

   • encouraging inclusiveness, multiple viewpoints, and freedom from bias;

   • reflecting multicultural perspectives in classroom materials and activities; and

   • involving parents and communicating goals.

Mental Energizer #2: Elevate Expectations

Our expectations for and assumptions about ELLs impact their success as learners more than all the proven teaching techniques we might employ. That is why it is so important to elevate expectations. Our expectations for ELLs should be as high as for any other student.

♦ Acknowledge and honor ELLs' potential.

♦ Provide appropriate support for ELLs to engage in higher-order thinking and vigorous academic work.

♦ Encourage ELLs to be full participants.

♦ Provide genuine instructional caring that focuses on learning and individual growth. Hold an unshakable belief that marginalized students not only can but will improve school achievement.

♦ Become a warm demander by expressing an unconditional positive regard that includes a deep certainty that all students can succeed. At the same time, make a nonnegotiable demand that students exert their best effort.

3 Opening the Doors to Literacy
A Comprehensive Reading and Writing Framework

In schools in the United States, the usual language of instruction is English. And not just plain old everyday English, but academic English. A good grasp of language is a prerequisite for academic learning, so a child's command of conversational English is a significant measure of his or her school readiness. However, as more and more children come to school with underdeveloped language skills, we're having to strengthen their language foundations at the same time we introduce them to an academic curriculum. Low levels of language development tend to have dramatic and long-term impacts on learning, as these findings describe:

- Language-rich first graders know around 20,000 words, while first graders with low English proficiency know only 5,000 (Moats, 1999).
- Students with limited vocabularies don't learn as many new words as those with larger vocabularies. The difference is significant: 2 versus 8 words per day; 750 versus 3,000 words per year (Simmons, Kame'enui, & Baker, 1998).
- The gap in vocabulary not only persists but grows as children go through school (Stanovich, 1986).
- A student's oral vocabulary at the end of first grade can predict his ability to comprehend high school work (Cunningham & Stanovich, 1991).
- Children whose language skills are underdeveloped may learn to read well in the early grades, but these gains are often lost around fourth grade, when texts become more complex and teachers provide fewer contextual supports (Wren, 2001).
- The gap in achievement between English language learners and proficient students is essentially a vocabulary gap (Carlo et al., 2004).

♦   One-quarter of English language learners are not making progress toward learning to speak English well (CivilRights.org, 2009).

These observations tell us that underdeveloped language skills are directly linked to academic underperformance or even failure. Terms like *word poverty* and *vocabulary deficits* have emerged to aptly characterize the problem (Frean, 2009).

What are the best methods for teaching English language learners? How can students learn to read and write in an English-centered curriculum when they don't speak the language well? Why are students not achieving proficiency in the high-stakes reading tests? In my work in schools across the country, I'm bombarded with these queries from administrators and teachers every day. The concern is that a widespread lack of language expertise (too many students not fluent in English and too few teachers experienced in second language acquisition) constitutes such a large and resistant barricade to learning that a successful educational outcome is uncertain.

In an effort to address language issues, many schools adopt reading programs in the hopes that these programs can teach students to read and write. In my experience, these schools often have large numbers of English language learners. Their programs may have quality materials and valuable literacy components, but in the end they tend to fall short of expectations. Why? Because it is the literacy expertise of the teacher—not the literacy program—that is the determining factor for high literacy achievement.

This fundamental truth is supported by the report of the National Literacy Panel on language-minority children and youth released in May 2006. The report acknowledges that "becoming literate in a second language depends on the quality of teaching" (August & Shanahan, 2006).

This is an important reminder of something we know well: teaching can't be reduced to a program or curriculum. Certainly curriculum is enormously significant because it's *what* we teach. But exemplary literacy teaching depends on much more than good lesson plans and high-quality materials. Of equal importance is knowing *how* to implement teaching plans and use materials in purposeful ways because you understand *why*. Your choice of materials and methods should be guided by an in-depth awareness of your learners and of the processes of literacy development.

But above all, the report of the National Literacy Panel is telling us (as have many other sound sources) that good teaching revolves around *who*. Who is teaching? What motivations, expectations, and powerful conceptions underlie our work? Are we willing to stretch ourselves to learn new skills that will meet the literacy needs of English language learners? Who is learning? Do we actively strive to know and value every student? Do we understand something of the emotional as well as technical issues that challenge children who must adopt a second language?

Laura Pappano, whose book *Inside School Turnarounds* (2010) examines the radical transformations of several failing schools, urges us not to focus so narrowly on test results (as important as they are) that we abandon "what makes education great: It's personal." She found that strong bonds between teachers and students are a determining factor in academic achievement. "What changes [students'] paths isn't a formula or a grueling push for a better [school performance] profile. It's a connection, a context, a caring. . . . To raise numbers on the balance sheet, we must raise students up first" (Pappano, 2011b).

Pappano relates that a newly hired, highly effective principal of a floundering school "laid out the reality" at his first staff meeting, asking teachers not to return after the lunch break unless they were ready "to sign on to do what was needed to help kids succeed." Every teacher returned. Not surprisingly, this was one of many turning points for the school. In considering this renewed commitment from his teachers, the principal commented, "I believe they were good teachers. They had lost their confidence. They had lost their spirit" (Pappano, 2011a). This account is clear evidence of the primary significance of who is teaching. In the face of pressing demands from both changing student demographics and accountability standards, we need to consciously decide if we're going to sign on to renew our purpose, enlarge our expertise, and support students tirelessly until we win the literacy battle. We'll probably face this choice many times as we work our way to new answers.

Motivation, commitment, and a keen awareness of our learners are significant elements of effective teaching. Who is teaching is as important as what is being taught, why it's being taught—and how.

This issue of *who* is so central that I spent the first two chapters of this book on it. (Chapter 1 examines who is learning, offering a closer look at the new majority of minority students, and chapter 2 explores the mental and moral touchstones that shape and sustain who is teaching.) While it's natural to want to grab *what* and *how* and jump into instruction, our real launching pads need to be *who* and *why*. Don't miss them if you want to be sure of an adequate foundation for your expanding expertise.

Literacy Is More Than Reading

Literacy means proficiency in reading, writing, speaking, listening, and viewing.

We begin to understand the *why* of literacy instruction only when we recognize what constitutes literacy. Literacy is not just reading. Someone capable of a certain level of reading but unable to express his or her thoughts verbally or in writing is not literate. Literacy is nothing less than proficiency in the full spectrum of reading, writing, speaking, listening, and viewing. Each component of literacy is as important as the others, and each supports the others. Attention to one literacy process strengthens student performance in the others, even as the omission of one diminishes students' opportunities for mastery. Some students make the leap into literacy through writing, others through multiple opportunities with text, and still others through extensive attention to how words work in our language.

All the strands of literacy are essential and reciprocal. Any one of them may be the entryway to literacy for ELLs. The more doorways, the better!

This reciprocity or interplay among reading, writing, speaking, listening, and viewing should be tremendously encouraging for literacy teachers. It means that students can enter the structure of literacy through several doors. While reading may be considered the front door to literacy, some of our students might be more comfortable coming in through the side door of writing or the back doors of listening, speaking, and viewing. Since our goal is to get all students inside, the more doorways, the better. So we must ensure that each of these doors to literacy is open to all students.

Support emerging literacy by maximizing instruction and student participation

Maximizing instructional time is essential for ELLs. We need to make the school day count by keeping students active in a productive sequence of literacy experiences.

The disturbing statistics that open this chapter illustrate that insufficient language skills tend to minimize students' literacy achievements. The obvious rebuttal to minimizing is maximizing. We can significantly increase our ELLs' access to literacy by maximizing the instructional time devoted to literacy and students' practice of literacy skills.

Ideally, students should be actively engaged in various literacy activities for 180 to 220 minutes, spread across the day. That time needs to be on task (reading, writing, speaking, viewing, or actively listening) rather than peripheral (filling out worksheets or spending large amounts of time engaged in activities without instructional guidance or focused purpose). We must scrutinize our literacy programs and/or class routines to recognize how our class time is being spent. For example, many literacy programs allocate 90 minutes each day for reading instruction, but too often a significant amount of that time is spent in activities other than reading and writing. As a general rule, students should spend close to twice the amount of time reading as you spend in preparing them to meet the text and in concluding the lesson. In other words, in a 40-minute lesson, students should spend at least 25 minutes with the text, reading and responding to both teacher and peers.

Students need to be kept active doing literacy. In a reading lesson, they should spend twice as much time reading as their teacher spends introducing and concluding the lesson.

Students are learning only if and when they're cognitively engaged. Therefore, they need to be actively occupied with meaningful literacy tasks that promote a steady momentum of learning. In classrooms that are opening doors for English language learners:

- ♦ All students engage in comprehension every day.
- ♦ All students engage in active word study every day.
- ♦ All students engage in real reading every day.
- ♦ All students engage as writers every day.
- ♦ All students engage in purposeful conversations every day.

This high level of engagement is critical. *To engage* means "to connect." ELLs connect with literacy as they consistently and persistently practice literacy skills. The 2006 report of the National Literacy Panel on language-minority children and youth calls such engagement "a clear advantage. . . . Enhanced teaching of the key components of English literacy provides a clear advantage to English-language learners. More complex, innovative programs typically taught several of these components simultaneously—and these efforts were usually successful in improving literacy for language-minority students" (August & Shanahan, 2006, p. 3).

To engage means "to connect." ELLs connect with literacy only as they consistently engage in the practice of literacy skills.

A comprehensive reading and writing framework

Instructional time and student engagement can be maximized through organization. Organization requires purposeful structure, and schools often adopt literacy programs to provide order and direction for instruction. Without endorsing or critiquing specific literacy programs, it's useful to outline a comprehensive reading and writing framework. Whether or not a school is committed to a particular program, the framework provides a standard for a thorough literacy foundation.

Literacy instruction should infuse the entire school day.

The framework brings all the elements of literacy together in a coordinated, orderly whole that is manageable for teachers and productive for students. It organizes literacy instruction across the day, maximizing time spent in reading, writing, speaking, listening, and viewing.

The word *framework* is important. It implies a supporting structure on which the strategic arrangement of parts can build a whole. What are the components of such a reading and writing framework?

◆ Our English language learners need to hear and engage with the language of texts every day. The *interactive read-aloud* provides this experience.

◆ To complement this process, ELLs need multiple, extended opportunities to spend **time with text**, reading independently at individual reading levels.

◆ Attention to *phonics and spelling* provides students with the surface scaffolding necessary to read and write with fluency and understanding.

◆ Students need explicit instruction in how to navigate or think through a piece of text. This can be accomplished through *guided comprehension.*

◆ Finally, ELLs need daily opportunities to mirror the process of reading through *writing.*

The comprehensive literacy framework consists of interactive read-aloud, time with text, guided comprehension, phonics and spelling (word study), and writing.

The framework is carefully balanced to build, in a variety of ways, speaking, listening, reading, and writing skills. Phonics and spelling underlie reading and writing, and writing, in turn, pushes awareness of word structure and spelling. Lessons in guided comprehension introduce strategies for understanding text, and an understanding of text enables students to be more successful independent readers. All the elements of the framework interconnect and reinforce one another. They can be distinguished from each other but not isolated because all of them need to work together to foster literacy wholeness. With the comprehensive framework, we can be sure we're providing our students with a well-built and enduring structure of skills. Then we won't be merely opening the doors to literacy but welcoming our students inside and making them at home.

A comprehensive approach to teaching literacy gives students ownership of essential skills. As illustrated by Figure 3.1, when students are at home in literacy, the doors are wide open for school success.

Now let's look briefly at each component of the reading and writing framework. These components set the foundation for your literacy instruction across the day. An understanding of these core literacy events will help frame a context for integrating the strategies introduced in the upcoming chapters. Think of this as a flyover—a view of the broad picture that isn't focused on too many details. (A companion book will provide additional strategies for the implementation of this framework as well as more detailed descriptions of each literacy component, including classroom vignettes and strategies for implementation.)

Interactive read-aloud: Letting students hear and respond

The read-aloud has long been heralded as "the single most important activity for building the knowledge required for eventual success in reading (Anderson, Hiebert, Scott, &

FIGURE 3.1. Literacy Opens Doors!

Wilkinson, 1985). The opportunity for strengthening students' background knowledge through a read-aloud is unmatched by any other component of the reading framework. But just reading aloud to students in classrooms with linguistically diverse populations won't yield significant gains in literacy skills. So what specific models and behaviors are needed to support language development while increasing academic literacy? An *interactive* read-aloud gives students the opportunity to hear the language of texts *and* to interact in a way that builds their capacity to think about and respond to their reading. Although this is a group experience, it's not unlike reading to a child on your lap and endeavoring to build a sense of fun and discovery through how you present the story.

Read-alouds are knowledge-builders for our ELLs. Make them interactive so that students are engaged by responding to the reading. When ELLs respond to reading, they're bridging.

Using a book selected for its humor, color, vitality, main character, vocabulary, or any other factors, depending on the desired focus, the teacher can

- ◆ introduce students to the richness of stories, genres, and verbal rhythms that will engage even the most reluctant readers;
- ◆ use stimulating questions that motivate students to become more active learners;
- ◆ raise the complexity of language to a level just above the children's current ability, encouraging students to stretch both vocabulary and meaning; and
- ◆ expand conceptual knowledge by elaborating on what students already know (for example, words like *gleeful*, *exuberant*, and *delighted* help students enlarge what they know about *happy*).

Time with text: Building strong, independent readers

Independent reading time builds velocity, proficiency, interest comprehension, confidence, and motivation.

Independent reading allows students to spend time with books that can refine their individual development as readers. This time is critical for students' development of reading fluency, automaticity in word recognition, and the comprehension processes of a proficient reader. Rereading familiar books builds reading confidence and helps students solidify their learning.

Because choice is important to motivation, the teacher carefully arranges a broad range of reading materials that give students a variety of options. Additionally, students are taught a process for selecting books that supports purposeful engaged reading. While students are reading independently, the teacher confers with a few of them about their books. This one-on-one interaction yields significant learning for students because the teacher analyzes student performance and highlights one teaching point that shifts the learner to higher proficiency.

At the conclusion of students' time with text, there will be opportunities to share their reading in various ways. The teacher selects sharing strategies that promote literate conversation among students. Students discuss their books with partners or in group settings, using their language skills to construct thoughtful responses to the books they're reading.

The ultimate goal of time with text is the development of life-long readers. Spending time with real books that students find appealing builds reading velocity, proficiency, interest and motivation.

Guided comprehension:
Helping students cross bridges of understanding

Daily comprehension instruction helps ELLs cross the bridge from oral language proficiency to academic language proficiency. In the guided comprehension lesson, teachers guide students in applying reading skills and strategies that enable them to gather meaning from print.

Fielding and Pearson (1994) highlight four instructional elements that are strongly related to comprehension outcomes:

1. Large amounts of time for actual text reading
2. Teacher-directed instruction in comprehension strategies
3. Opportunities for peer and collaborative learning
4. Occasions for students to talk to a teacher and to each other about their responses to reading.

ELLs must learn how to gather meaning from print. To do this, they have to cross the bridge from oral to academic language. This transition is fostered as teachers guide students to learn and practice comprehension strategies.

During a guided comprehension lesson, students engage in explicit comprehension instruction, including each of the elements listed above. In every session, the teacher focuses on specific comprehension skills or strategies. Thoughtful consideration in selecting the lesson text(s) ensures that it that will correspond well to the skills the teacher wants to target. Teachers also add value to comprehension instruction by choosing texts that expose students to a variety of materials—both fiction and nonfiction—at varying levels of complexity.

The design of a guided comprehension lesson divides the complex task of reading into before, during, and after segments. English language learners benefit from chunking the

Help ELLs unpack a reading lesson by dividing it into before, during, and after segments. This breaks the text into manageable parts.

instruction in this way, breaking it into manageable, predictable parts.

In the *before* segment of a particular lesson, teachers prepare students to meet the text, building and reviewing pertinent background knowledge and vocabulary. The purpose of the day's reading is explicitly stated several times so that students can approach the reading with clarity and anticipation. You'll often hear teachers say, "When you read today, I want you to figure out . . . ," or, "Today we'll read this book to find the topic and main ideas," or, "Today our purpose for reading is to answer these questions, or talk back to the author."

In the *during* portion of the lesson, students read the text and apply the strategy of the lesson (as presented in the *before* segment). A variety of reading structures are possible and useful. These range from choral reading and echo reading, which offer a high level of support with a segment of text, to partner reading and book club groups, which provide an opportunity for students to work in small groups independently or with the teacher. This diversity of reading structures helps make the text accessible to learners at all levels. Varying instructional levels are appropriately mediated within heterogeneous and collaborative groupings.

Teachers guide ELLs through text in interactive talk that supports thinking about text. And thinking about text is comprehending text. Think-alouds, visuals, and questions offer ELLs direction as they read.

While students are engaged in reading the text, the teacher coaches and monitors them to ensure their success and to keep their thinking on track with the purpose of the lesson. Throughout this time, the teacher is informally assessing students' actions and performance. This ongoing assessment is what guides exemplary teachers as they adjust and extend instruction as needed and determine their next teaching point(s). At all times throughout the lesson—before, during, and after—the teacher is available to guide students through texts in interactive, responsive ways that support the development of thinking about the text. This guidance can take many forms, including questions that direct students to search more deeply in the text or the use of think-alouds and visuals to help students understand and engage with complex thinking.

After the reading, students are gathered together to revisit the purpose of the reading and to glean new understandings of it. For example, students can be asked to produce a written response to demonstrate what they learned about the content, or the teacher can lead the students in a discussion during which they share new thinking or questions about their reading. As teachers guide students to review the lesson, students are again reminded of the new skill or strategy they were working on, and they consider whether they were successful in applying it. It's critically important to help students unpack not only the content of the lesson (e.g., "What new facts or ideas did we learn today?") but also the process of learning (e.g., "What did you learn about yourself as a reader? How did this strategy or skill help you today as a reader?"). In this way, the lesson comes full circle, and students take one more step toward reading competence and independence.

Unpack the process of learning as well as the content. Ask your ELLs, "What new facts did you learn? How did this strategy help you?"

Phonics and spelling: Helping students discover how words are built

Phonics and spelling instruction helps students discover the way words work. Phonics instruction provides students with a set of instructional strategies that focus on the parts of words. It also helps students explore the patterns of letter groups. In spelling, students learn a set of instructional strategies that bring attention to the writing system. Both processes support students' growing word knowledge for reading and writing.

Students spend a few minutes every day in a lively session of chanting, cheering, and writing words they will encounter frequently in both reading and writing. This multisensory engagement makes the words memorable. It strengthens students' visual recognition and accurate spelling of recurring words and builds automaticity. Additionally, students engage in an active phonics lesson that includes the manipulation of letters for word-building and learning about the patterns of the English language. The complementary processes of blending and segmenting are strengthened as students have multiple opportunities to construct and break down words. As students mature, the examination of how words work grows in complexity and sophistication. The connections among spelling, meaning, and vocabulary are explored as students learn about meaningful units of our language, such as prefixes and suffixes.

The goal of any phonics and spelling lesson is to help ELLs become strategic in decoding and spelling new words. ELLs can develop phonemic awareness, phonics, and spelling at the same time they are acquiring conversational fluency in English.

At the close of every lesson, the teacher helps students transfer their new knowledge to words that work the same way as those they just studied. For example, students might read or write new words that build from the same pattern of letters or sounds. Analogy talk is often used to build these bridges: "If you know _____ , then you know _____ " (Cunningham, Cunningham, Moore, & Moore, 2004).

Learning word skills requires repetition and practice. However, practice doesn't need to bore students with endless drills and worksheets. Instruction should be lively, engaging, and purposeful. The goal of any phonics and spelling lesson is for students to become strategic in how they decode new words in reading or spell new words during writing.

"Teach a man to fish and he'll eat for a lifetime," goes an old proverb. Helping students "catch" how words work puts them in command of reading. Phonics and spelling are not the goal of reading, but students' grasp of these skills determines how securely they can set their hook in reading.

Writing: Students constructing their own messages

A student's writing provides a valuable view of how he or she is processing the phonology (sound system), orthography (written system), and syntax (structure) of language. Writing places significant demands on a learner's cognitive capacity. Students have to orchestrate all their alphabet knowledge, letter-sound knowledge, and conventions about print as they construct a message. Our English language learners face unique challenges: sound/symbol dissimilarity or interference, oral vocabulary constraints, and limitations in background knowledge. For this reason, the teacher demonstrates daily by thinking aloud the thought processes that occur during writing. This potent language interchange helps learners observe how writers develop ideas, use planning strategies, and construct a message. "Writing is a craft and is learned best by imitation. Teach your children to write through modeling every day" (Freeman, 2003, p. ix).

Writing requires students to orchestrate all their alphabet knowledge, letter-sound knowledge, and conventions about print. Word banks, think-alouds, idea holders, and sketching help ELLs learn how writers develop ideas and construct messages.

Teachers provide scaffolding by introducing vocabulary that will support the writer during the writing process. This could include building a word bank of transition words students can use to link ideas together or eliciting from students precise words that describe actions (verbs). Listing key words as "idea holders" helps students give structure to their message. This scaffolding of language development is absolutely essential for English language learners.

Several strategies can be used to support developing writers, including shared writing, interactive writing, language experience, and modeled writing. Students spend time imitating the writing process as they talk about their ideas with a writing partner, getting a feel for the words they'll use in their writing. When students begin the drafting process, the teacher confers with students individually, giving each learner what he or she needs to write with increased proficiency. At the conclusion of a writing session, students share their writing with peers and in group settings. When writers have an audience, they construct their ideas with purpose and motivation.

"Good writing . . . is clear thinking made visible" (Bierce, 1905). "There's no substitute for thinking time if you want to do good writing work" (Clements, 2004). Thinking leads to words, and words lead to a message that "speaks" the thinking. Just as we lead our students to think about meaning in text they read, we can lead them to think meaningfully about what they will write. They'll find achievement in seeing their own ideas made visible.

"Good writing . . . is clear thinking made visible."

Supercharging the language arts framework

The framework is a solid language arts platform that will produce good results, especially for students who come to school with a strong grounding in language. But what if this output could be supercharged for students with weaker language skills? What if we could light a flame under time with text sessions, or make phonics and spelling more lively? My work with teachers and students across the country has helped me identify four strategic Energizers, or key strategies, that have impelled substantial literacy progress for English language learners. The strategic Energizers don't replace any elements of the comprehensive framework, but they add thrust to it. Consistent use of the strategic Energizers has been repeatedly proven to ignite comprehension and change low-performing students into solid, motivated achievers.

The Energizers add thrust to literacy instruction and supercharge performance.

Three of the strategic Energizers focus on comprehension. The purpose of our teaching is to open avenues of understanding for our students. We know that language, ideas, and academic content are useful in proportion to a student's grasp of their meaning. The comprehension Energizers explore ways to initiate, promote, and extend students' understanding. We can reach our students and accelerate their growth significantly as we learn to use these tools thoughtfully and creatively. They're not difficult; we simply need to become conscious of their power and put them to work.

Strategic Energizer #1: Keep instruction comprehensible.
Strategic Energizer #2: Build bridges for language and
    learning.
Strategic Energizer #3: Get students talking (active
    engagement).

The key strategies that produce results for ELLs are keeping instruction comprehensible, flooding it with vocabulary, getting students talking, and building bridges for language and learning.

The fourth Strategic Energizer appears to be a content area tool but is really an urgent instructional need across the board. The language proficiency of ELLs is hampered enormously by a lack of vocabulary. Rather than thinking of vocabulary as its own subject or a once-a-day exercise, we need to keep it at the forefront of our teaching, all day, every day. Vocabulary is truly a sink-or-swim issue for ELLs.

Strategic Energizer #4: Flood instruction with vocabulary.

Figure 3.2 offers a helpful way to think of the interplay between a language arts framework and the strategic Energizers. A well-planned, carefully constructed house (like the language arts structure outlined above) has both a framework and an energy system. They're completely interwoven, but they're not the same thing.

Walls, floors, windows, and roof form the body of a house just as reading, writing, speaking, listening, and viewing constitute the body of language arts. Energy—electricity, heating fuel, and plumbing systems—makes a house work; skilled teaching makes a classroom work. Without energy sources, a house is only half useful. The most upscale stove on the market can't cook dinner if it isn't connected to a reliable energy source. Likewise, the latest literacy materials can't guarantee student achievement without instruction approaches that are plugged in to what will best reach the students.

Conversely, the usefulness of energy in a house is dependent on the framework. Many owners of homes built more than seventy years ago discover that the electrical wiring, which was adequate in that era, can't support ceiling fans or the heavy use of electronic equipment. And the entire national energy grid couldn't satisfactorily warm or cool a home that doesn't have a good vent system, even if that house was built yesterday. A framework provides the outlets and systems through which energy can be put to work, while energy gives the framework more action and productivity. The framework of the house and its energy systems are mutually reinforcing

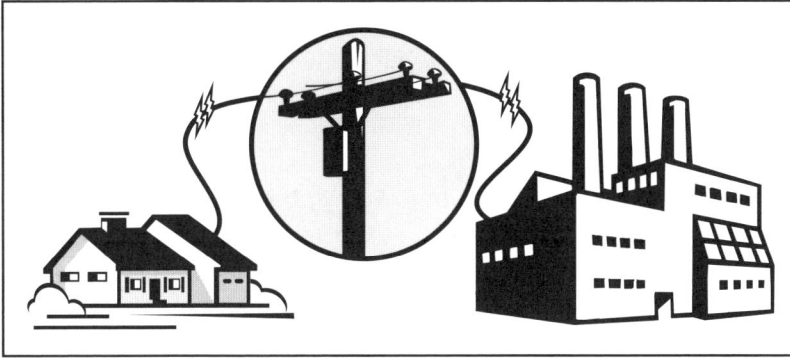

FIGURE 3.2.
Energizers +
Literacy Framework =
Supercharged Results.

and strengthening. So, too, the intertwining of the comprehensive reading and writing framework and the strategic Energizers unfold greater potentials for teachers and students.

Putting the strategic Energizers to work

We'll explore the strategic Energizers thoroughly in chapters 4 through 8. But first, let's see what they look like in action. An elementary teacher asked me to model a guided comprehension lesson in a science unit, and that experience is portrayed by Teacher E in the following scenario.

Teacher X and Teacher E are elementary teachers, and each of their classes includes several ELL students. As you'll quickly see, Teacher E is an energized teacher who conducts an invigorated session, while her colleague Teacher X doesn't quite get the lesson off the ground for some of her students—especially her ELLs.

Both classes are studying the water cycle and weather, and the topic of the current lesson is hurricanes. Central to the lesson is a poem that both Teacher X and Teacher E have selected (Figure 3.3). Both teachers think the poem offers good information and imagery that will be accessible to their classes.

Let's step into these classrooms and watch the lessons in progress. Put yourself in the shoes of the students. Which teaching approach feels energized? Why? How? Let's begin with Teacher X.

TEACHER X

Teacher X: "Yesterday we read about hurricanes. What do you remember about them?"

She calls on a few students and asks them to share their responses. These students offer some general facts about

FIGURE 3.3.
Insane Hurricane

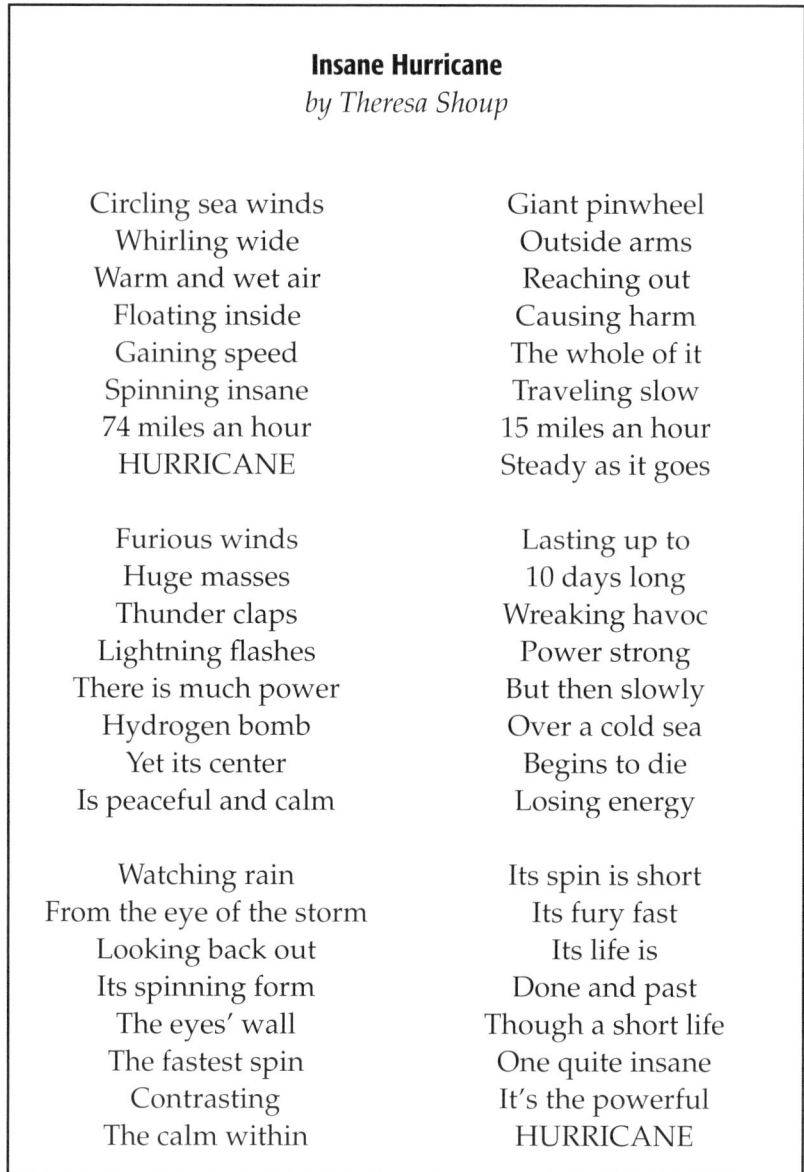

Insane Hurricane
by Theresa Shoup

Circling sea winds
Whirling wide
Warm and wet air
Floating inside
Gaining speed
Spinning insane
74 miles an hour
HURRICANE

Giant pinwheel
Outside arms
Reaching out
Causing harm
The whole of it
Traveling slow
15 miles an hour
Steady as it goes

Furious winds
Huge masses
Thunder claps
Lightning flashes
There is much power
Hydrogen bomb
Yet its center
Is peaceful and calm

Lasting up to
10 days long
Wreaking havoc
Power strong
But then slowly
Over a cold sea
Begins to die
Losing energy

Watching rain
From the eye of the storm
Looking back out
Its spinning form
The eyes' wall
The fastest spin
Contrasting
The calm within

Its spin is short
Its fury fast
Its life is
Done and past
Though a short life
One quite insane
It's the powerful
HURRICANE

(Theresa Shoup uses poetry and song to support education. Her poems, songs, lesson ideas, music, and video offerings can be found at Rhythm-n-Rime.com. Used with permission.)

hurricanes and a few vivid details regarding a recent hurricane in Florida. Teacher X offers some additional details about the impact of Hurricane Katrina (2005) and the need for some people to leave their homes. She explains that a hurricane season occurs every year and that weathermen actually give names to the hurricanes in alphabetical order, such as Agnes, Burt, Claudia, and so on.

Most students seem interested and a few ask questions. One student asks, "Will we ever have a hurricane in our city?" Teacher X explains how their local geography is different from the Florida coast, pointing out some of the basic conditions that generate a hurricane.

Teacher X: "Today you're going to read about how a hurricane is formed and what it can do. Our text includes some words that particularly relate to hurricanes. Let's look at them before we read."

She writes a few words on the board to discuss with her students. She points to the word *hydrogen* on the board.

Teacher X: "Do any of you know what this word means?"

She calls on an eager student who asks, "Does it mean something like water or a gas?" Building on this response, Teacher X explains hydrogen more clearly. Then she writes the word *havoc* on the board. A couple of students immediately put their hands in the air.

Teacher X: "What does 'havoc' mean, Devin?"

"My little brother creates havoc in my house," he offers.

Teacher X: "You mean he makes a mess at your house?"

"Yes!"

Teacher X continues, "You might have seen the word *mass* as part of another word—*massive*. Can someone tell me what it means? . . . Big, yes. A hurricane is bigger than big. It's huge. And it has a lot of energy or power. The body of the storm is called a mass because it's big and powerful." Teacher X turns to the remaining words on the board—*energy*, *whirling*, *contrasting*—and provides brief definitions for them.

"Remember these words, because we'll meet them again in our reading. And as you read, think about how the words we just talked about make pictures in your mind. We've talked before about how words can fire up your imagination, so let's see what this text brings to your thought. Now let's look at the poem."

While Teacher X and her students read the poem, let's see what's happening in Teacher E's room.

TEACHER E Teacher E projects a visual to begin her lesson. It's an Internet image of the recent Florida hurricane, photographed from a satellite. The students are intrigued and want to examine the size and shape of a real hurricane. Teacher E points to parts of the hurricane and names them, using some of the academic terms students will meet in the text (*huge mass*, *eye of the storm*, *eye's wall*, etc.). She asks how a storm could have a wall or an eye.

Get students talking: Whose prior knowledge is voiced most strongly here, Teacher X's or her students'? How much has Teacher X uncovered about what her students already know?

Where is the bridging? Teacher X engages a few students in exploring vocabulary, but she employs no strategy to reveal what all the other students know about these words. Her instruction relies completely on oral transmission of information and offers no alternate avenues for comprehension.

Teacher X relies on previous class experiences with imaging to carry the current assignment. She could better prepare her students by re-teaching and reinforcing what they know.

Keeping it comprehensible: The Internet is a valuable resource for photos and other visuals

Bridging for language: Providing context to set the stage for new vocabulary.

Student talk: *Within the first five minutes of a lesson, students should be engaged in some form of an overt response (e.g., writing, talking, drawing, activating prior learning).*

Student engagement and high expectations: *When teachers provide good models, students naturally learn to support those who aren't as strong in the target language.*

Bridging: *Summarizing discussion points cements learning and serves as a good lead-in to the next stage of the lesson.*

Stay connected: *Teacher E's attentive listening allows her to pick up on student comments and thread them into her teaching.*

Keeping the learning comprehensible *and* **vocabulary flood:** *Explicitly explaining the components of a mental process helps students master it. Naming the process also builds academic vocabulary needed to comprehend at higher levels.*

Active engagement: *The teacher elicits a response from all learners. All students participate actively.*

Teacher E: "Do you think these terms are metaphors? Remember that metaphors describe how one object might be like another. Do you see a wall in this picture? Where is it?"

The students find the hurricane wall and eye in the visual as Teacher E helps them recognize that a wall is like a boundary or edge while an eye can be thought of as the center or middle.

Then she asks the students to share at their table groups what they remember from yesterday's reading about the recent hurricane. As she walks from table to table, she hears students talking not only about the hurricane itself but also about what happened to the people caught in the storm and how scared they must have been.

She has thoughtfully paired five ELL students with others who will help support them during the lesson. She observes the ELLs as she walks around the room. Their English-proficient partners are trying to be careful mentors. She sees one student combining gestures and language as he tries to clarify a concept for his assigned buddy.

Teacher E listens to several student conversations briefly, synthesizing what she's hearing so that she can confirm students' prior knowledge and bridge to the text they'll be reading. She also listens for misconceptions that she can address during the lesson.

Teacher E: "I heard many of you talking about the destructiveness of this hurricane—how the wind knocked down houses and tore off roofs. Many of you were saying that you felt bad for the families. A natural disaster like a hurricane can be very destructive. That's why we have warning systems: so people can leave areas where big storms are going to hit. Today's reading will help you understand better how a hurricane forms, how it moves, and why it has so much force. The author uses powerful words to create a picture in your mind. When you read today, I want you to find words that help you develop a strong image or picture in your mind. Let's take a minute to remind ourselves about imaging."

Teacher E reviews a strategy poster in the classroom:

Imaging
Imaging is creating a picture and a feeling in your mind of what you're reading.

Why do it? Imaging can make a story come alive in your head. It's like making a movie in your mind.

When do we do it? During reading.

How do we do it? Notice descriptive words the author is using.

Teacher E: "We said we're going to notice the author's descriptive words when we read. There are several descriptive words in our

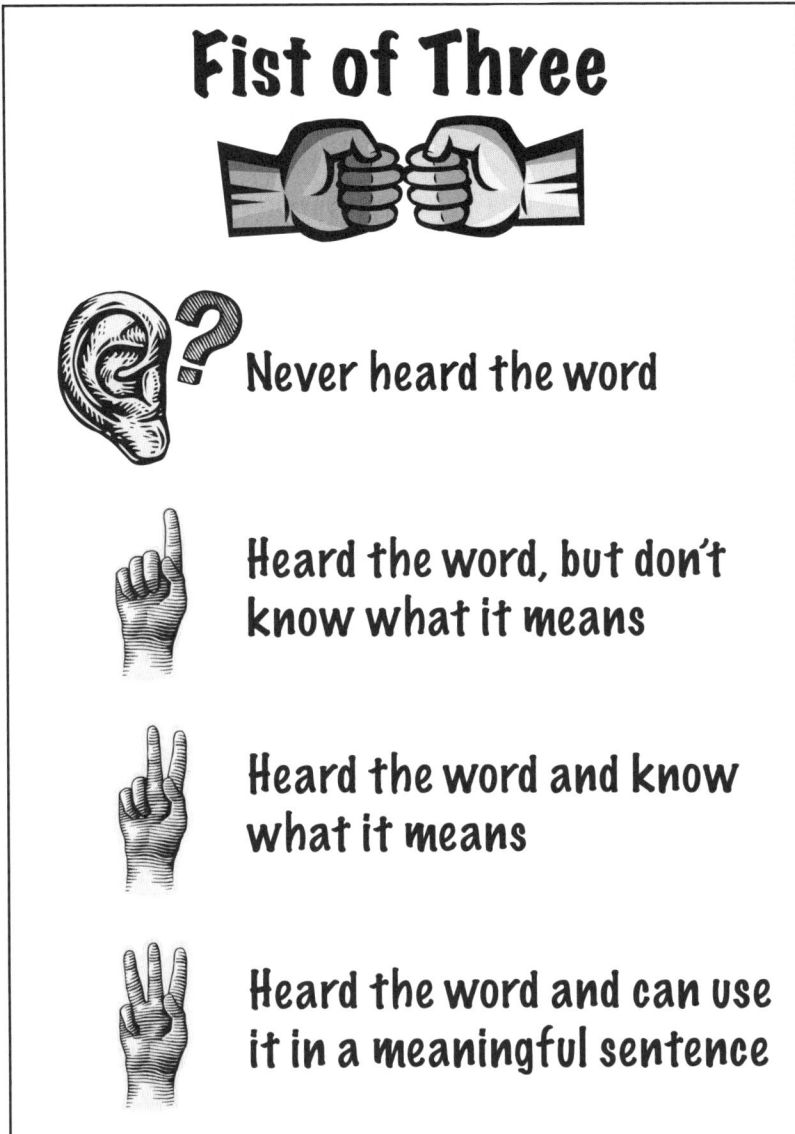

Fist of Three

👂❓ **Never heard the word**

☝️ **Heard the word, but don't know what it means**

✌️ **Heard the word and know what it means**

🤟 **Heard the word and can use it in a meaningful sentence**

FIGURE 3.4.
Fist of Three Chart

text. Let's find out what you know about some of these word meanings by holding up your hands in the fist of three."

Students are reminded of the procedure as Teacher E goes over the chart posted on the board.

Teacher E writes vocabulary words from the text on the board one at a time. As she writes the word *insane*, she says it aloud. The students repeat the word aloud and raise their hands, showing fists or fingers according to their knowledge of the word. (See Figure 3.4.) Teacher E quickly surveys the room, noting the students' responses. She calls on a student with two fingers raised: "Insane is something that is really crazy, like when people don't think very good."

Keeping it comprehensible: *Using an action or gesture when describing word meanings provides an alternate pathway for understanding.*

Vocabulary flood: *Review academic terms needed to build domain knowledge (e.g.,* hydrogen, energy*) as well as words that give precision to what students already know (e.g.,* whirling *is a form of spinning or turning).*

Vocabulary flood: *Pointing out the structure of text helps readers learn specific genres and their academic names.*

Teacher E responds, "You do have a good understanding of this word's meaning. Something or someone that is insane could be described as out of control or crazy."

As she speaks, Teacher E moves her hands in a fast, fluttery motion to help illustrate the sense of agitation or craziness.

Teacher E: "So how could you relate this word to a hurricane?" She calls on a student whose hand is raised.

"A crazy hurricane—it's out of control."

Teacher E affirms the student's response and moves on to the next vocabulary word. She introduces five more words (*whirling, hydrogen, contrasting, wreaking havoc, energy*), continuing to employ the fist of three procedure to monitor students' familiarity with each word and asking students to provide definitions and relate them to the subject of hurricanes.

Teacher E: "Remember what we said about imaging. When we read, we're going to see how these words create images or pictures in our minds."

"Let's take a look at your reading for today. Did the author use whole sentences? No, you're right. She just uses a few words or phrases in short lines, doesn't she? What do we call this kind of text format? Yes, it's a poem."

Teacher X and Teacher E have prepared their students to read the poem about hurricanes. Both teachers understand the value of building on students' prior knowledge. But there's a significant difference in the level of student participation elicited. Teacher X calls on a few students who volunteer to share their knowledge with the entire group and then takes over the discussion, offering additional information. Teacher E asks students to share with one another in table groups while she walks through the room to see who's participating and what knowledge they bring to the subject. *Which teacher is cultivating active student talk? Which one discovers more about her students' prior knowledge of hurricanes and how she needs to support their new learning?* (**Energizer tip:** Student participation allows you to gauge how well students are connecting to a lesson as well as how you might steer instruction to fill in gaps of understanding.)

Teacher E uses a visual to help students understand what a hurricane actually looks like. She also connects the image to academic terms essential to the lesson content. Teacher X relies strictly on oral delivery, requiring students to understand the content through listening or, in the case of a few students, through speaking. *Who is offering multiple channels through which students can comprehend the content?* (**Energizer tip:** It's crucial to maximize opportunities for students to understand the central elements of a lesson.)

Both teachers introduce the same vocabulary before the reading. Teacher E employs a strategy that requires every pupil to respond, while Teacher X calls only on students who think they know a word's meaning. Teacher X provides a written representation of the word and a brief explanation of the word's meaning. Teacher E provides both a written and oral explanation plus nonverbal orientations to some words (such as fluttering her hands to model *crazy*). Additionally, Teacher E's students repeat each word in order to develop a phonological representation that assists in recalling its pronunciation, and they apply the words specifically to the lesson content (e.g., a hurricane might be called "insane" because it's out of control). *Which classroom offers an example of vocabulary instruction that has the potential to last beyond today's lesson?* (**Energizer tip:** To be effective, a vocabulary flood needs to be carefully integrated into the lesson and include student participation.)

TEACHER X — **Teacher X** passes out copies of the hurricane poem to her students. As she moves through the room, she asks certain students to partner with her six ELLs and two special ed students. This assures her that someone will read the poem to the ELL and special ed students if they have difficulty on their own. As the students read, Teacher X walks around and helps a few students decipher some of the words.

One student raises his hand. "What's a pinwheel?"

Teacher X: "Have you ever played with a pinwheel? It's a toy with bright-colored 'fingers' of paper or plastic that spins at the end of a stick, a little bit like a wheel. If you hold a pinwheel up in the air, the breeze will turn it. The stronger the breeze, the faster it turns."

As she talks, she holds one index finger straight like a stick, spinning her other index finger against it. She explains that a hurricane spins like a pinwheel but faster and stronger. None of the other students ask Teacher X about the word *pinwheel*, and she doesn't share this discussion with them.

As she sees students look up from their reading, Teacher X asks them to reread the poem, this time thinking about the pictures that grow in their minds because of what the poem is telling them. Several minutes later, she pulls the group together and asks what they're envisioning. One student says he can picture being in a hurricane

Low expectations: *Teacher X may be fostering passivity in ELL students if she frequently has other students read to them.*

Minimal bridging: *Teacher X offers minimal support to her students during reading. She explains to one student what a pinwheel is (even using gestures to amplify), but doesn't offer this information to the rest of the class.*

Missed opportunity for bridging: *Is it enough to simply ask students to describe mental images from the poem? How could she draw them out more? Notice that her response to the student who fears the hurricane's fast spin doesn't explicitly help him form a mental image, which is what she wants to foster.*

with everything blowing around wildly. Another student offers, "I feel scared when I read this poem."

Teacher X tries to draw him out a little, "What exactly makes you afraid?"

"Well, umm . . . I don't know. I don't think I would want to be in a hurricane because it spins so fast."

Teacher X: "Yes, it certainly does. It can spin at more than 100 miles an hour! That's faster than the speed limit on the highway. Who else can tell us what they see?"

Let's go back to Teacher E's class as they start to work with the poem.

Building bridges: *Students need doors through which to enter new texts. Hearing a text read aloud and reading it chorally can help make a text accessible.*

Teacher E: "I'm going to read this poem to you the first time so that you can listen, close your eyes, and create some pictures in your mind," she begins. "Be alert to the way the poet uses words to help you create pictures or images."

She models the reading, attentive to proper phrasing, intonation, and speed. She pauses for a few seconds after the reading and says, "Turn to your partner and describe the picture in your mind." She listens in on student conversations to note if students are using descriptive language.

Teacher E: "Now, let's all read the poem out loud together so you can feel the words and rhythm of this text." She walks the room, helping some of the students track their way through the poem.

Keeping it comprehensible: *Dramatic enactments allow students to grasp meaning through both verbal and nonverbal expression.*

Teacher E: "Some of you may not understand what a pinwheel is, so let me show you what the poet means here. I need one volunteer to stand as the eye of the hurricane."

She calls on several students to surround the volunteer and act as the hurricane wall, and asks others to stretch their arms out wide. She models for the students how to travel in a circle, moving their arms back and forth as the "wall" of students spins. She reads the words from the poem as the students act it out. "The eye's wall/fastest spin/contrasting/the calm within/Giant pinwheel/outside arms/reaching out/causing harm." The students delight in acting this out. Teacher E reminds them, "Remember how we saw the hurricane move like this in our visual? You can see how the storm is sort of crazy, like we talked about."

Building bridges/keeping it comprehensible: *Modeling clarifies ideas and processes and makes them explicit for students.*

Teacher E: "This time, you're going to read the poem with your partner. I want you to underline words that help you picture or create an image in your mind. Let me show you what I mean."

She reads, "Thunder claps," then thinks aloud. "Hmm. . . . I can picture the thunder making a noise like two hands clapping. Can you picture that in your mind? Do you see how the poet uses the word *clap* to build an image for you? Now it's your turn. As you read with your partner, stop and discuss the images you see, underlining any key words that help you create those images."

Teacher E monitors as students read and underline, stepping in to elaborate, clarify, or question when appropriate. She notices two students underlining *circling* and *whirling*. She asks, "How does the poet use these words to create an image in your mind?"

One student answers, "We think that the winds form a whirling circle."

Teacher E encourages them to develop the idea, "So, you can picture . . ."

The student continues, "A circle of whirling air making the sea rough."

Teacher E: "In a moment, you'll get a chance to draw that picture you have in your brain." She turns to the other partner, "Do you agree with that picture?" The student nods.

Teacher E elaborates, "Both of you please repeat to me, 'When the poet uses the words *circling* and *whirling*, we can picture a whirling circle of air making the sea very rough.'" (The students echo the sentence.) "In a few minutes you can write these words down as one of your examples in your notebooks."

Teacher E stops the class briefly to reorganize their grouping structure. "I want you to share one example of your images with the partner group across from you. Be sure to read the poet's words first and then describe the image in your mind. You'll have about three minutes to share with each other."

As she listens to student discussions, Teacher E finds that some of the discussions lack a direct link between the poet's words and the students' mental images, and she realizes it would be helpful to have a few students model this process for the whole group. She brings the group back to focus and calls on a couple of students who she has either talked with or heard in discussion. She wants to ensure that she chooses a good example and sets students up for success when they're sharing in front of the whole group.

In this portion of the lesson, Teacher X's and Teacher E's classrooms read the hurricane poem. Both teachers have a similar comprehension focus: to teach students to identify and understand imagery as they read. The difference lies in the explicitness of the instruction. While preparing her students to read, Teacher E uses a chart that clearly defines the strategy of imaging and indicates when and how to use it. Teacher X

Bridging for language: Cues (such as "so you can picture . . .") give students additional language support in order to prompt a desired response and sets them up for success.

Student talk and active engagement: Build in as much focused academic student talk as possible. When students have to voice their ideas, it clarifies and cements their learning. Stay connected during this student exercise in order to pick up cues for further clarification or amplification.

communicates the focus orally by using words: "Think about how the words create pictures in your mind." Teacher X never uses terms such as *imagery* or *visualization*, although they're commonly used in academic settings, nor does she offer any examples of images pertinent to the lesson. Teacher E provides guided practice of how to use the imaging strategy by having students underline key words as they read and discuss their interpretation with their partner (and she will follow through after reading by asking students to record some of their images on a guiding template). Furthermore, Teacher E models each step of the process before asking students to work independently. *Which teacher understands how to task-analyze or design instruction so that the learner can grasp a complex strategy?* (**Energizer tips:** The more complex your lesson strategy, the more essential it is to make it comprehensible. Bridging—in this case by guided practice—helps students reach a higher level of understanding and application.)

Once Teacher X passes out the text to her students, she immediately launches them into independent reading (except for those ELL and special ed students who will have the poem read to them). Her students are on their own in applying the comprehension strategy. Teacher E recognizes that poetry should first be heard orally to establish its rhythm and cadences, so she reads the poem aloud. She asks her students to begin developing mental images while they listen, thus reducing the cognitive demand of the task. During the second reading, Teacher E has students read chorally to ensure that all students have the opportunity to read with some assistance. Not until the third reading are Teacher E's students expected to apply the comprehension strategy independently.

Teacher X seems to assume that her students will be familiar with the term *pinwheel*—a central point of comprehension. Even though one of her students asks about the word, Teacher X doesn't pick up the cue that the rest of her class may need the same information. Teacher E, on the other hand, anticipates the significance of the pinwheel image to the poem, and she chooses to have students dramatize it so that the word comes to life. *In which classroom does the teacher implement multiple methods to address a variety of learning styles and provide accessibility to the content?* (**Energizer tip:** comprehension is encouraged by repetition and reinforcement, which build familiarity and confidence for students.)

A closer look at the interactions occurring between teacher and student(s) reveals very different styles for providing feedback. Teacher X initiates questions and responds to student comments but does little to help students more fully express or develop their ideas. On the other hand, Teacher E provides additional language support and then has students rehearse the language structure so they'll experience success when writing down their examples. Teacher X frames no opportunities for students to interact or exchange ideas with one another, which limits her ability to build on student responses. Teacher E provides several formats for students to exchange ideas, and she listens alertly to student talk for opportunities to re-teach and refine students' understanding. *Which teacher is providing bridging or scaffolding to accelerate language development?* (**Energizer tip:** Providing and supporting a framework for student response enlarges students' capacity to engage the lesson material and achieve intended goals. Without bridging from the teacher to support language and meaning, students may be hampered in expressing their developing understanding.)

TEACHER **X**

Teacher X continues. "Now, everyone please take out a piece of paper. Let's think about the pictures that formed in your mind while you were reading the poem. I want you to record some of the words the author uses and write about the pictures they create in your mind. So go back over the poem and select a few ideas. Write them down and then explain what picture is in your mind."

Teacher X pairs the ELL and special ed students with partners and tells them to listen in on what their partners are thinking. She instructs the lead partners to think aloud so their ELL/special ed buddy can follow what they're doing. Several students get started immediately on the assignment, but many others are asking questions and seem unsure about what to do.

Teacher X stops the group to re-teach, "If I were recording something I was picturing as I read this poem, I might write *spinning faster and faster*, then write about how I see myself getting dizzy."

A student poses the question, "How many examples do we have to have?" Teacher X instructs the students to come up with at least three examples from the text. She allows several minutes for students to write down their examples and then concludes the lesson by having a few students who feel comfortable share their responses.

Expectations/bridging: *Teacher X's expectations are too high in regard to the assignment (no modeling) and too low in regard to her ELLs (no engagement). The assignment is a mere academic task rather than an occasion for discovery and expansion.*

Connection: *Teacher X seems more connected to her lesson plan than to her students. Their uncertainty about the assignment should have alerted her to re-teach and model.*

Now let's watch how Teacher E helps her students assimilate and demonstrate what they've learned in this lesson.

Teacher E: "Let's finish today's lesson by tracking our thinking in our reading notebooks. Please get out your notebooks, and I'll show you how to set up your page."

On an overhead projector, she draws a two-column chart:

Creating Images: "The Hurricane"	
The author's words	My picture with words

Teacher E: "You've just spent the last few minutes talking with your partner and others at your table about the images you have in your mind from the author's words. I'd like you to share at least one example in your reading notebook. You can write about your image, or draw it, or both. Let me show you my example:

Creating Images: "The Hurricane"	
The author's words	My picture with words
thunder claps	[drawing]

I can picture air currents moving together like two hands clapping.

"When you write or draw something, you have a permanent record of your learning. You can use the strategy of imaging whenever you read."

She refers to and rereads the anchor chart. "Authors choose words for very specific reasons, so look carefully at the words in the poem and think about why they are good choices to describe a hurricane." Teacher E gives students about ten minutes to complete the task. Some students provide one example, and many students provide at least two examples.

After reading, both Teacher X and Teacher E ask students to record their responses as an assessment of their learning. However, the teachers differ in how they assign the task and how they require students to demonstrate their learning. Teacher X asks her students to respond by providing three written examples of mental pictures prompted by the reading. When she realizes that a number of students are floundering, she offers an example but doesn't develop it in depth. Her inadequate guidance in regard to the poem's imagery is mirrored in her students' apparent lack of understanding and disinterest. Furthermore, Teacher X's ELL and special ed students aren't accountable for any individual response but are permitted to simply listen and follow as their English-proficient partners respond. Teacher E gives students the option of either drawing or using words when describing the images they found in the poem. Although her students are working in partner arrangements, each one is accountable for recording in his or her own notebook. Teacher E sets a time limit and accepts as many examples as students can produce during that time. Students have already rehearsed their thinking orally, so the assessment does not rest solely on their written response. *Which classroom is an example of differentiation and multilevel instruction in action?* (**Energizer tip:** Strategically leading students into the desired engagement with a lesson enables them to achieve the intended learning; inadequate leading or bridging significantly reduces engagement and learning outcomes.)

It's clear that Teacher E's instruction is more far-reaching and effective than Teacher X's. We've explored many reasons for this, but the essence is that Teacher E's teaching is *energized*. Careful attention to pertinent vocabulary and comprehensible content empowered her students. Encouraging student talk at numerous points in the lesson enhanced engagement and vigor. Building bridges that allowed students to move to new points of understanding (such as the dramatization of how a hurricane spins like a pinwheel) gave the lesson momentum. Teacher E expected all students, including her ELLs, to be active participants, and all the varied techniques she employed made this possible. She was attentively connected to her students, reading from their responses when she needed to clarify elements of the lesson. Thanks to Teacher E's energized focus and methods, this lesson worked.

ELLs maximize their learning opportunities through participation. Students become highly engaged when they are continuously and directly involved in the learning.

ELLs are better able to participate in the learning when we lead them into a lesson through modeling and guided practice. As students gain a good understanding of the learning tasks of a specific lesson, we can gradually release them to successfully fulfill independent work.

In classrooms that work for ELLs, all students are involved in the learning from beginning to end. Student achievement and highly engaged environments go hand in hand. "Student engagement is the continuous involvement of students in the learning. It is a cyclical process, planned and facilitated by the teacher, in which all students constantly move between periods of action (overt) and periods of reflection (covert)" (WestED, 2004). Teacher E begins planning for student engagement by considering how to make the content accessible to all her students in strategic ways. She's a master at facilitating the learning as she helps students negotiate meaning, using their language to discuss the content several times throughout the lesson. Her targeted feedback accelerates students' language proficiency. Her lesson has a set purpose, and the thread of instruction weaves back to that purpose before, during, and after the reading. Thus her teaching moves are cyclical in nature, as she gradually releases students to independence through constant modeling and guided practice. She returns to this cycle over and over during the stages of the lesson (in the preliminary vocabulary work, during the reading of the text, and during the student response segment at the end of the lesson). She never leaves her students aimless, unsure of what to do or how to do it.

In addition, Teacher E structures student response in a cyclical fashion, using varied modalities through which students can demonstrate their understanding of the lesson content. At times, students are in periods of reflection as they think, listen, or watch an action described by the teacher. But at frequent intervals, they respond overtly (actively) by speaking, reading, writing, or moving. Teacher E's classroom environment brims with vitality, recognizing students' contributions both cognitively and socially.

Learning inevitably occurs in classrooms where students can construct meaning through interactive, dynamic environments. Fostering such learning environments requires teachers to be closely attentive. Are we fully connected to the living interplay with students throughout our lessons, fine-tuning our teaching as we go to fit the lessons to the students? Dynamic learning also implies high expectations of our students. Do we expect our students, including our ELLs, to be capable of fast-paced learning? Perhaps not without our help. But as we learn to integrate, engage, and enrich our instruction, building bridges to language and eliminating barriers to comprehension, students naturally gain momentum.

It's amazing what energy can accomplish—and equally surprising how little can be done without it. We don't need to settle for low-energy performance from our ELLs or any students. With thoughtful attention to teaching for acceleration rather than remediation, you can teach with a confident expectation of reaching and energizing all students in your classroom.

Chapters 4 through 8 dive into the research and application of each strategic Energizer. They also point out how the Energizers and the framework intermingle, with short vignettes providing the focus and content and the Energizers supercharging the teaching and learning process. No more pedaling as fast as you can and still not achieving much momentum with your ELLs. The literacy framework and the Energizers can take you there.

• • • • • • • • • • • • • • • • •

In Brief

The ethnic and linguistic diversity in today's classrooms is challenging school systems all across the United States. Teachers must figure out how to open the doors of literacy that allow ELLs to enter the academic mainstream. The need is urgent. The answer is maximized instructional time in a highly organized reading and writing framework. This approach empowers teachers and moves ELLs forward.

♦ The literary expertise of the teacher—not the literacy program—is the determining factor for high literacy achievement. The implication is that teachers must retrofit their skills to meet the urgent challenges of linguistically diverse classrooms.

♦ Literacy is not just reading. Literacy is nothing less than proficiency in the full spectrum of reading, writing, speaking, listening, and viewing. Students can enter the structure of literacy through any of these doors. The more doorways, the better.

♦ Effective literacy instruction requires concerted effort and organization. Instructional time must be maximized (180 to 220 minutes daily), and students must be consistently engaged in authentic, literacy-promoting tasks. A high level of engagement is critical for ELLs.

♦ The comprehensive reading and writing framework presented in this chapter organizes literacy instruction throughout the day. It includes: *interactive read-alouds* (students hearing and engaging with the language of texts); *time with text* (students reading independently but with careful teacher direction); *phonics and spelling* (students learning how words are built and how they work); *guided comprehension* (students thinking about text to find meaning); and *writing* (students mirroring reading through constructing their own messages).

♦　Students should receive instruction every day in discrete skill acquisition (phonemic awareness, phonics, language conventions, etc.) and authentic experiences (lots of reading and writing with explicit instruction in vocabulary, comprehension, and writing processes). This premise is the heart of the comprehensive reading and writing framework.

♦　The comprehensive reading and writing framework is a cohesive literacy structure that can enable most students to construct solid skills. But ELLs often need an extra boost to arrive at fluent literacy. This book advances four strategic Energizers that add significant thrust to literacy instruction:

1. Keep instruction comprehensible.
2. Build bridges to language and learning.
3. Get students talking (i.e, keep them actively engaged in learning).
4. Flood instruction with vocabulary.

These strategies have increased student achievement in classrooms across the country. This book illustrates how to put them in action to energize student literacy, including that of your ELLs.

4 Energy for Learning
The Strategic Energizers—An Introduction

An enormous amount of time, thought, and effort is devoted to understanding the processes of learning and to crafting techniques and materials that will effectively engage students and help them prosper academically. School districts give conscientious attention to curriculum issues, and teachers spend countless hours in preparation. These are significant endeavors that build a framework for learning, but they aren't the learning itself. Learning happens when understanding occurs within the student.

Comprehension Is a Tremendous Source of Energy for Learning

Comprehension tends to set off a chain reaction in which the understanding of one piece of information links to another bit of meaning and then another, culminating eventually in knowledge and mastery. Conversely, when students consistently miss vital moments of understanding, there's no spark, no learning. Educators have always had to deal with various comprehension challenges, and right now we're faced with a comprehension crisis. Language is critical to comprehension because language expresses ideas and meaning. Comprehension is more or less dependent on language, and this is particularly true in school.

Language is critical to comprehension because we use language to express ideas and meaning.

The story of Helen Keller is worth reviewing because it illustrates so vividly how language enables comprehension and how comprehension tends to multiply itself and create momentum for learning. Keller was both deaf and blind from early childhood, so it was very difficult to communicate with her. But when she was nearly seven, her teacher, Anne Sullivan, began to spell the names of objects into the palm of Helen's hand, attempting to help Helen connect these letters with the objects. Helen's initial response was much like that of many ELLs in regard to decoding—she learned fairly quickly to form the letters herself and even did so in the correct order, but it was clear she didn't know she was spelling a word or that the letters and words had meaning. Then one day when Helen and Ms. Sullivan were filling a pitcher at an outdoor pump, Ms. Sullivan spelled w-a-t-e-r into Helen's hand, just as she'd done with other words on many occasions. This time something clicked for Helen: comprehension occurred. She suddenly understood that w-a-t-e-r spelled in her palm was related to the water from the pump. Touching the ground, Helen indicated that she wanted to know its name, too. By nightfall that same day she had learned thirty words and correctly associated their meanings with the objects they represented (Nielsen, 2005).

The ability to make mental connections (including language connections) is the capacity to be an active, progressive learner.

The ability to make mental connections (including language connections) is the capacity to be an active, progressive learner. This is the process and the outcome of comprehension. The attainment of meaning turns information into something that can be used for further learning. It builds mental bridges. It closes distances. It improves motivation and makes academic success more likely. Comprehension creates energy for further learning. And since comprehension builds on language, we have to learn how to address the language crisis.

The attainment of meaning turns information into something that can be used for further learning. It builds mental bridges. It closes distances. It creates energy for further learning.

Language → comprehension → learning

We all have moments when our language capabilities fall short of allowing us to fully understand something. It may be as simple as encountering a word we've never heard before. This is a minor loss of meaning we can easily compensate for. On the other hand, a significant lack of vocabulary can minimize what we understand. Few of us, for example, could readily converse about quantum physics, although we may be able to grasp the basic concepts if someone explained them to us in layman's language. Much more frustrating are the times when we simply can't express what we want to. It's not uncommon for people in moments of high emotion to exclaim, "Oh, I just can't put it into words!" Our ability to comprehend often depends on having both sufficient language and the appropriate language for the situation.

Language is our most important building material in education, and meaning is what we're building with it. Even though language skills appear to be our current crisis, we can't afford to forget that language is significant only because it leads to comprehension. It's plain that language is essentially meaningless until it's understood; we can't put language acquisition on the front burner and slide comprehension to the back one. They both need to simmer in the same pot until they blend together to generate learning.

How would a teacher handle a class that included several Helen Kellers? Even without the challenges of deafness and blindness, many students with intelligence and ability are limited by their lack of basic language skills. Like Anne Sullivan, Helen Keller's persistent teacher, we have to find ways to bring our students into language. Language leads to meaning, and meaning leads to learning (Figure 4.1). The significance of language to learning can't be overstated. Ludwig Wittgenstein (2007), a noted twentieth-century philosopher, expressed it profoundly: "The limits of my language are the limits of my mind. All I know is what I have words for."

Three arrows forming a circle, like those pictured in Figure 4.2, have become a symbol of recycling and sustainability because the cycle/circle never ends. The same is true for our circle. Language leads to meaning; meaning leads to learning;

> *Language is our most important building material in education because language leads to comprehension.*

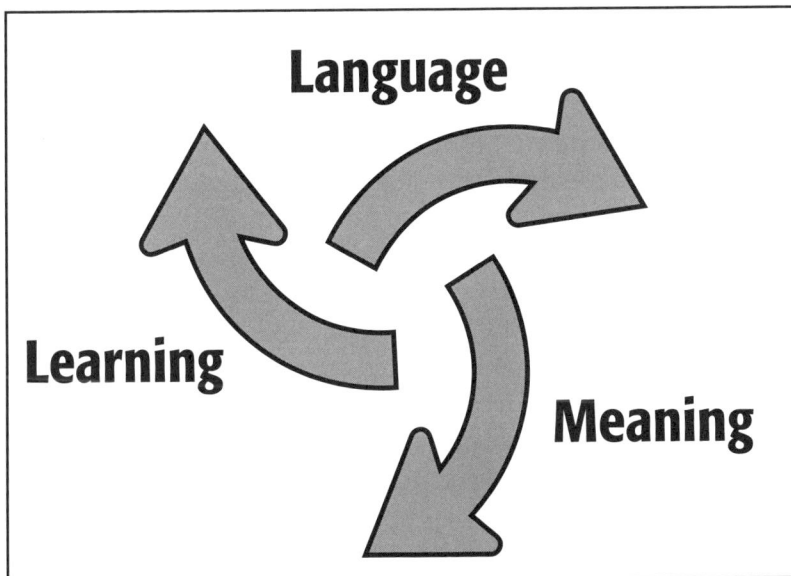

FIGURE 4.1.
A Self-Perpetuating Circle of Learning

learning leads to language. We started with language, and we ended with language. But we don't end with the same *level* of language. Every time language leads to meaning and meaning leads to learning, learning cycles right back to language with increased capacity. Every round of this cycle brings growth for each element—increased language, increased meaning, increased learning—and growth in one stimulates growth in the next. It's like a snowball rolling downhill—the more it rolls, the larger it gets. Our job is to get the language snowball rolling, to set the cycle in motion.

FIGURE 4.2.
The Snowball Effect

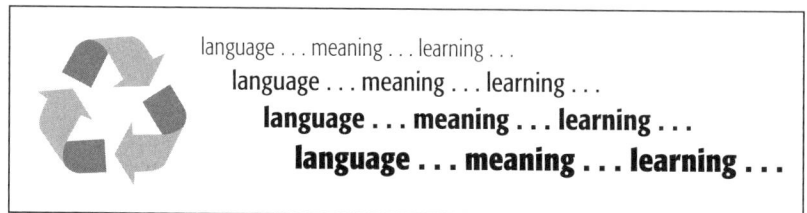

language . . . meaning . . . learning . . .
language . . . meaning . . . learning . . .
language . . . meaning . . . learning . . .
language . . . meaning . . . learning . . .

As the circle turns, its energy is self-perpetuating. The lightbulb of comprehension burns, and students increase their capacity to do work.

Experiencing this snowball of language, meaning, and learning is essential for all students. Students with solid language backgrounds can help make their own snowballs. If they've been immersed in English for several years before coming to school, they've experienced a blizzard of language that allows them to launch immediately into meaning and learning. Without this accumulation of language, it's much more challenging for ELLs to get the language-meaning-learning ball rolling.

Vigorous, systematic, explicit language stimulation throughout the school day is critical for ELLs.

Clearly, students with inadequate language skills (including ELLs) need to improve those skills as quickly as possible. They don't have the option of soaking up a good language foundation through years of casual exposure to English. Vigorous, systematic, explicit language stimulation throughout the school day is vital if these students are to catch up in knowledge and vocabulary. Because they have more ground to cover in school than their language-rich peers, our approach needs to be intensive and highly engaging. This is not merely desirable; it's indispensable.

We must transform our instruction of ELLs with instruction that is accelerated, not remedial.

"I use the term *accelerated language* to describe instruction that is fast-paced, integrated, engaging, and enriching, rather than remedial, linear, passive, or inordinately patient. . . .

Unless we transform instruction of ELLs with a more accelerated approach, we may not be able to meet the challenge of
educating these students in a timely fashion" (Mohr, 2004,
p. 19). This is a very important point of strategy—even a
turning point. Mohr characterizes it as a transformation. If we
expect our ELLs to accelerate their development of language
skills (which is the only way they can function successfully in
school and society), we cannot continue to employ teaching
methods that are "remedial, linear, passive, or inordinately
patient."

Fast-paced, *accelerated*, and *transformative* are high-energy
words. And the language skills crisis needs an infusion of
energy—a new (or renewed) passion for teaching as well as
a vigorous injection of vocabulary and strategic comprehension techniques that can boost understanding and its essential byproduct, learning. Over many years as a classroom
teacher and literacy consultant, I've identified key elements
that empower teachers and produce consistent progress for
all students—especially those students with limited language
proficiency. I call these key elements the Energizers because
they bolster in both teachers and students the capacity to
perform the needed work. With their focus on comprehension and language, they can put meaning and learning solidly
within the grasp of ELLs. They can change lack of progress
into meaningful forward movement.

> *The language skills crisis of ELLs demands an infusion of energy for both teaching and learning.*

Chapter 3 introduced four strategic Energizers and
described a teaching experience enlivened by their application.
In the next several chapters we're going to look at them in
much greater detail.

> Strategic Energizer #1: Keep instruction comprehensible.
> Strategic Energizer #2: Build bridges for language and
>   learning.
> Strategic Energizer #3: Get students talking (active
>   engagement).
> Strategic Energizer #4: Flood instruction with vocabulary.

The strategic Energizers are significant accelerators of
learning. They're research-based, drawn directly from observations of how children learn. Each of these essential strategies can enable teachers to adapt lesson content to students'
diverse levels of readiness, promoting comprehension,
participation, and eventual ownership. On the other hand,

discerning student readiness or thoughtfully considering how to best move the development of individual students forward requires more than strategic thinking. Only with attentiveness and care can our strategies be implemented to their best effect. Our awareness of our students' needs, our commitment to their growth, our motivation, and our outlook are as important as our strategic expertise. I've therefore paired the strategic Energizers with two mental Energizers, which I introduced in chapter 2:

> Mental Energizer #1: Cultivate connections:
>> Connect to kids.
>> Connect to colleagues.
>> Connect to cultures.
> Mental Energizer #2: Elevate your expectations.

The intent of the Energizers is to help us recharge in the face of new teaching demands that are likely to stretch our capabilities and challenge our courage. With their fundamental precepts and practical tools, the mental and strategic Energizers can prepare us to think and teach at higher-than-ever levels of excellence. See Figure 4.3 for a convenient reference guide to these vital Energizers.

Energizers are essential spark plugs and accelerators for teaching. But there's nothing new about them. The Energizers aren't recently hatched, nor are they a magic fix. You're unlikely to get goose bumps when you contemplate these wonder-working "trade secrets" because you've probably known about them since your college coursework. So what's the big deal?

It's a little like cooking. A great cook doesn't necessarily use extraordinary ingredients. Rather, she knows how to combine ingredients extraordinarily. We've all tasted the difference. And it *is* a big deal. If you're open to using familiar elements of teaching in more vigorous, effective ways, you and your students are sure to "taste the difference" that the Energizers can make. And that difference will be the sweet taste of success.

FIGURE 4.3. Reference Guide to the Energizers

Energy for Teaching		
Mental Energizer #1: Connect with kids, colleagues, and cultures		Plug in to new perspectives by cultivating deeper connections.
Mental Energizer #2: Elevate your expectations		High expectations lead to stronger academic demands and boost student confidence. They give lift-off to learning!
Energy for Learning		
Strategic Energizer #1: Keep instruction comprehensible		Students need numerous comprehension options. Vary your teaching strategies until the light turns on: *"I get it! I see!"*
Strategic Energizer #2: Build bridges for *learning*		Structure lessons to unfold step-by-step from initial modeling to student mastery.
Build bridges for *language*		Persist in dialogue with students, coaxing and coaching them toward greater verbal output.
Strategic Energizer #3: Get students talking		Through talking, students generate, test, and confirm ideas. Engage students in talking that promotes thinking and learning.
Strategic Energizer #4: Flood instruction with vocabulary		Vocabulary is vital—it can determine academic victory or defeat.

In Brief

♦ Learning happens when understanding occurs within the student. Comprehension is a tremendous source of energy for learning.

♦ The attainment of meaning turns information into something that can be used to further learning. It builds mental bridges. It closes distances. It creates energy for more learning.

♦ Language is our most important building material in education because language leads to comprehension.

♦ Language leads to meaning; meaning leads to learning; learning leads to language. Every time language leads to meaning and meaning leads to learning, learning cycles right back to language with increased capacity.

♦ Vigorous, systematic, explicit language stimulation throughout the school day is critical for ELLs.

♦ The language skills crisis needs an infusion of energy—a new (or renewed) passion for teaching as well as a vigorous injection of vocabulary and strategic comprehension techniques that can boost understanding and its essential byproduct, learning.

5 Energy for Learning
Keep Instruction Comprehensible

· ·

What makes comprehension so energizing in learning? This can best be answered by considering what happens when we *don't* understand something essential to our needs. Imagine yourself lost someplace where everyone speaks an unfamiliar language. You know the name of your destination but not how to get there. How will you ask for the information you need? How will you comprehend what you're being told?

You would probably communicate with local residents largely through nonverbal techniques—gestures, visuals or pictures, and body language. The locals might also slow their speech and repeat important words while employing nonverbal cues. They might draw a basic map to indicate the best route for you to take. All of you might be surprised at how well you're able to communicate with one another, even though you've had to be inventive to do so.

Let's consider this situation in more detail. You're a little lost in an unfamiliar setting, and the people around you possess information that can get you where you're going. If you had a common language, you could easily access that information just by asking a question and listening to the response. But your lack of language constitutes a lack of access. No matter how willing, eager, and helpful those around you might be, it's challenging for you to fully connect.

Communication with gestures, maps, and so on rescues you, but both you and your helpers are a little uncertain about whether you understood the intended message correctly and will be able to find your way. In other words, everyone (including you) can only hope you achieved comprehension. To varying degrees, this state of partial comprehension is the experience of ELLs throughout the school day.

Partial access leads to partial comprehension and, in turn, to partial achievement. Just as a 25-watt bulb is inadequate for bright illumination, so a student's inability to fully grasp the content and meaning of classroom interactions can leave

English language learners need multiple pathways in order to fully comprehend or grasp the content and language interactions around them.

"I see!"
"I get it!"
"I comprehend!"

Use both verbal and nonverbal methods of communication in order to reach our students and move them toward complete understanding.

him or her in the dark, unable to participate meaningfully in learning activities. Lack of understanding casts a shadow over a student's otherwise bright potential for learning.

The concepts of understanding and illumination are so commonly linked that greeting cards, comics, and advertisements commonly represent the idea of comprehension ("I see!" "I get it!") as a glowing lightbulb above someone's head.

Light and understanding are figuratively synonymous. Therefore, this symbol appears throughout the rest of this chapter when teaching approaches in support of "making it comprehensible" are discussed or illustrated.

As we've already considered, learning happens only when understanding occurs, so our interaction with our students isn't complete until they reach a point of understanding. Remember that we're teaching the student rather than just the content, so we may need to redirect our approach several times during an interaction. Comprehension isn't something we can demand. We need to coax and encourage it to emerge, using every means we can find to reach our students and move them forward.

One point of entry with our ELLs is to couple our use of language with other forms of communication that yield meaning. Pantomime and signals are examples of communication through which ideas are conveyed and meaning is achieved without spoken language. Some of our best allies in nonverbal communication are the conscious use of body language and the employment of supplementary materials (visuals, real objects, hands-on experiences, etc.). Physical gestures and postures can (and do) "speak" to our students, while supplementary materials help students relate to content.

In academic settings, making adjustments to speech so that the message is understandable to students is referred to as the use of comprehensible input (Krashen, 1985). Krashen believes that second-language acquisition results from listening to and understanding the spoken language in low-anxiety environments. To aid in language acquisition, adjust the rate at which you speak, enunciate clearly, and be aware of complex language. Teachers can also employ a variety of nonverbal techniques to make content understandable, including modeling, visuals, gestures, total physical response, and body language (Krashen & Terrell, 1983). As teachers, we constantly adapt our language to the comprehension level of students, but we need to do it more thoroughly and thoughtfully to meet the needs of our ELLs.

The comprehension techniques outlined here can be readily implemented without extensive study. They do, however, require us to be conscious of the small details of how we move and speak around our students, and of how our students are responding (e.g., are they passive or eager?). If we've taught for any length of time, some of our approaches tend to become so familiar that we may no longer think about them. But if we want to be sure we're presenting a comprehensible message, we have to think not only of the message, but of how we deliver it. Let's look at some simple but critical elements of effective delivery.

How do you know if you are presenting a comprehensible message? Observe your students carefully to see if they are responding actively or passively.

How Do Students Comprehend Nonverbal Messages?

Deciphering body language, a type of literacy at which most of us excel from a very young age, is a type of "reading" that doesn't have to be taught in school. So while you work with your students on explicit lessons, remember that they're picking up on your implicit presentation, too. They're constantly reading your unspoken messages and cues.

Research shows that up to 55 percent of any message is communicated visually, through gestures or body language (Arndt & Pesch, 1984). All of us use nonverbal communication techniques so constantly and effortlessly that we rarely think about them. But if we remain aware of them, we can use them to good advantage in our teaching—and avoid inadvertently conveying unintended messages. While students with a solid command of English will combine your verbal and nonverbal communication to assess your meaning, students with limited English proficiency will infer much of your meaning from your body language and attitude. Strategic use of nonverbal communication can allow students to access and engage in the classroom experience no matter where they are in their language development. This may include pointing to a visual as you speak a key word, using your face or body to convey a feeling, paraphrasing an idea with simpler language, or even acting out what you want students to do. Methods such as these provide a rich context from which students can draw understanding.

When you strategically employ a variety of nonverbal methods, the learning process is differentiated for your students.

To aid in becoming more conscious of your nonverbal cues and how you might intentionally employ them to enlarge your student's understanding, let's briefly review the basic elements of this unspoken but very expressive means of communication.

Are you changing your facial expressions in ways that evoke emotion and connections with your students?

1. **Facial expressions.** Our faces convey our attitudes and emotions clearly, and what students read there can either encourage or distance them.
   - An unexpressive face ("stone face") tends to communicate authority and remoteness. It's likely to be interpreted as *I'm in charge* or *Don't approach me*.
   - An open, expressive face conveys warmth and interest and encourages students to participate.
   - A smile, raised eyebrows, or comical frown can indicate *I'm interested in you* and *We're working together to understand each other* (or *our task*).

2. **Gestures.** Hand movements convey energy and enthusiasm and can tie your words to actions. Many of us nod, shrug, throw up our hands, or tilt our heads quizzically as we engage in conversation. And many words readily lend themselves to gestures or motions that elucidate their meaning (e.g., *pounding*, *writing*, *eating*, *sleeping*, *walking*, etc.). The understanding of your gestures may very well precede and enable students' comprehension of your spoken words. Gestures are not usually thought of as language, but they are at least a useful language arts tool.

A toolbox of gestures used in strategic ways will, in effect, sustain and create a language-rich environment for ELLs.

   - Encourage your students to rehearse new learning with gesture-type responses (remember the fist of three used in Ms. E's vocabulary lesson during the discussion of hurricanes in chapter 3?). You can assign any meaning you want to a gesture, and your students will enjoy selecting some of the gestures for themselves.
   - Develop consistent gestures to signify a specific word, strategy, or response, and repeat them often.

3. **Eye contact.** Eye contact says *I see you*. It also means *I'm aware of you* and *I recognize you*. It's hard for any of us to be disengaged when we're looking someone directly in the eye. On the other hand, avoiding eye contact tends to convey such messages as *I don't want to connect with you* or *You're not part of the group*. Use eye contact to hold students' attention and communicate interest.

Eye contact will help you engage your learners and maintain momentum throughout your teaching.

   - As a rule of thumb, maintain eye contact for at least three seconds.

- Be sure to make eye contact with students through-out the room. It's tempting to avoid contact with students who look bored or unmotivated—after all, they're not looking at you—but eye contact can help maintain focus and lets students know that they're noticed and important.
- **A note of caution:** Be culturally sensitive to students who may not engage through eye contact. To some, it may be a sign of disrespect.

4. **Movement.** Moving frequently around your classroom creates proximity to students that announces *We're connected, and I'm interested*. It maintains the energy flow of your lesson and keeps shy or hesitant students in the center of things. It also goes a long way toward giving you those essential eyes in the back of your head.
    - Move about the room in unpredictable patterns.
    - Use your proximity to redirect challenging students.
    - Try to remove barriers that prevent your free movement around the classroom.

Does your classroom environment promote the ability to move and remain fluid during instruction, or do you feel limited or constrained?

There's much we can do as teachers to become more conscious of our nonverbal communication with ELLs and turn it to productive use. And this fine-tuning is completely within our reach. Similarly, our verbal interactions with students can benefit from scrutiny and adjustment in order to maximize opportunities for comprehension.

How Comprehensible Are Our Verbal Messages?

We talk to our students in order to connect with them— to explain, request, direct, inform, question, encourage, and so on. But when our efforts to communicate don't result in student comprehension, we haven't really connected. And if we aren't connecting with our students, our students aren't connecting with learning. How can we make our verbal messages more comprehensible to our ELLs? Here are some basic guidelines:

- Face your students and talk directly to them.
- Vary your tone of voice and change its speed and volume to keep your message lively and engaging.

Verbal interaction is more than just speaking our intent and hoping for understanding. Utilize these strategies to achieve clarity and accessibility for all students.

Higher pitch and volume tend to convey anticipation and excitement, while lower pitch and volume express seriousness or that you're imparting a confidence. Both can work well in the classroom.

♦ Enunciate clearly but without raising your voice. Help your students connect with key words by pointing directly to objects, using meaningful gestures, or drawing pictures.

♦ Speak in simple sentences (subject-verb-object) with straightforward vocabulary. Avoid slang and idioms. Repeat information and paraphrase it frequently.

♦ Use a variety of approaches when introducing a concept so that students have several opportunities to find meaning. Utilize gestures, modeling, supplementary materials, pictures, real objects, and hands-on activities.

♦ Focus on key concepts, and provide repetition and rehearsal for essential ideas. Check often for comprehension, and have students demonstrate their learning. Restate and review throughout the lesson.

♦ Adapt lesson content to the students' comprehension level. Use a buddy system or adapt assignments for students needing further support.

♦ Begin a lesson by clearly explaining its objectives and outlining the activities involved. Write down instructions step by step (in print, not cursive). Demonstrate what you want students to do.

♦ Identify key vocabulary and help students work out its meaning. Review pertinent academic terms, and be sure they are clear to students.

♦ Pause frequently and allow some wait time. Short silences give students the opportunity to process and reflect.

♦ Ask open-ended questions. When students respond, focus on meaning rather than grammar and form. Encourage and require student interaction and participation in risk-free settings such as small student groups.

♦ Teach thinking and comprehension skills explicitly by demonstration and think-alouds.

We must not mistake the need for simple, clear speaking with the destructive notion of dumbing down. Our aim is to achieve clarity and accessibility for our students without abandoning substance and academic integrity. As with the first steps in many endeavors, the initial achievements in ELL comprehension may be a little slow and uneven, but because these students are able and intelligent, the momentum of their learning will naturally increase as we help them connect to meaning and language. We must afford ELLs numerous supports and checkpoints for comprehension, not because they are less able to understand but because this increased access to meaning will help activate their innate ability to understand.

Supplementary materials support our messages

The use of supplementary materials is yet another powerful aid in keeping instruction comprehensible. Learning opportunities for English language learners increase when teachers couple speech adjustments with nonverbal techniques on a consistent basis. According to dual coding theory, everyone stores and activates new learning by using both verbal and nonverbal (imagery) input. Using instructional techniques of both a linguistic (verbal) and nonlinguistic (visual) nature enhances the process of students' storing experiences in permanent memory (Marzano, 2004).

Supplementary materials are useful extras; they include visuals, texts, real objects, demonstrations, and hands-on activities. Their purpose is to provide multiple channels for students to learn about the topic at hand. School libraries, public libraries, and the Internet offer a wealth of resources that can add dimension to academic texts on almost any subject.

Suppose your class is studying wolves. Possible supplementary materials for such a unit might include a recording of wolves howling, a stuffed wolf toy, pictures or movies of wolves, a text about wolves in Yellowstone National Park, and a map showing where wolf populations are concentrated in the United States. Exposure to such materials will certainly broaden students' understanding of wolves. What may be less obvious is that supplementary materials often promote students' ability to access academic texts and to work out the academic tasks related to comprehension (predicting, interpreting, summarizing, etc.).

Using supplementary materials is one way to differentiate content for your students.

Jeffrey Wilhelm (2004) refers to the use of supplementary materials as "frontloading." When you frontload, you load up students' minds with background knowledge needed to access particular content. At the same time, you stir students' curiosity about the content and trigger memories of their own prior experiences related to the subject. This loading up is done "in front of" (i.e., before) approaching the academic text in order to maximize students' readiness to master the academic tasks that fulfill the lesson.

The range and variety of supplementary materials that will support your efforts to provide comprehensible input are virtually endless. The following list briefly describes some of the options.

- ♦ **Hands-on manipulatives.** Add dimension to a lesson through the use of tools or objects related to understanding a process (e.g., using counters for segmenting sounds in phonemic awareness instruction) or understanding content (e.g., referring to maps to locate the oceans and continents).
- ♦ **Realia.** Real-world three-dimensional objects provide the opportunity for students to touch and make connections with the things in their own world.
- ♦ **Visuals.** Providing any visual will help supplement and coordinate auditory and visual learning. Visuals include charts, graphic organizers, maps, and so on.
- ♦ **Pictures.** Photographs and illustrations support concept and word learning.
- ♦ **Multimedia.** Technology can be a valuable aid to learning and information retention. Its uses range from the simple to the sophisticated, such as enhancing learning with music or employing video streaming.
- ♦ **Related literature.** Students need a variety of resources to help them build the requisite background knowledge and understanding in any content area. These may include books or materials on a variety of levels.
- ♦ **Adapted text:** You'll want to modify text to ease the cognitive load when the academic content is too difficult for some students to read. This may include rewriting a piece with simpler language or finding a variety of reading material that deals with the same content but is written at different reading levels. This does not mean that we teach "down" to the students with easy materials that lack substance. All students need access to the major content concepts at any reading level (Echevarria, Vogt, & Short, 2004).

The classroom environment

The classroom environment plays a very important role in keeping learning comprehensible. A well-organized, visually stimulating environment will enhance students' understanding of academic content; a cluttered, disorganized visual environment can detract or confuse student understanding.

A visually stimulating environment should include a variety of charts and displays:

- ◆ **Word walls.** There are many types of word walls that can be presented throughout the year. When constructing a word wall, consider its placement in the room, how and when it will be used, and legibility, so that all students can access the wall from any part of the room.
  - • Only put those words on the wall that are important or key to a concept. *Less not more* is a good concept to keep in mind.
  - • Use pictures to enhance word learning and keep the learning comprehensible.
  - • Organize or group words in patterns or related concepts so that your students see how words are connected (see Figures 5.2 and 5.3).

  Tip: Word walls are only useful as a comprehensible tool when students are taught how to access and reference them.
- ◆ **Picture charts**. There are several opportunities to use pictures to enhance understanding, including teaching new vocabulary or generating topics for writing (see Figures 5.4 and 5.5).
- ◆ **Multimedia options**. A wide range of technological tools are increasingly becoming a part of everyday classroom instruction. Smart technology continues to offer tremendous potential for bringing virtual worlds to the classroom. With a click of the mouse, students can visit new places through video and pictures. Document cameras are also becoming increasingly available. They can be used in a variety of contexts but work extremely well for displaying any one- or two-dimensional visuals on a large screen. Document cameras are very useful for displaying a short piece of text for the class, or to display illustrations when reading from a picture book.

Ensure that your classroom environment enhances your instruction without introducing distractions to the learning experience.

FIGURE 5.2.
Grouped Math Concepts

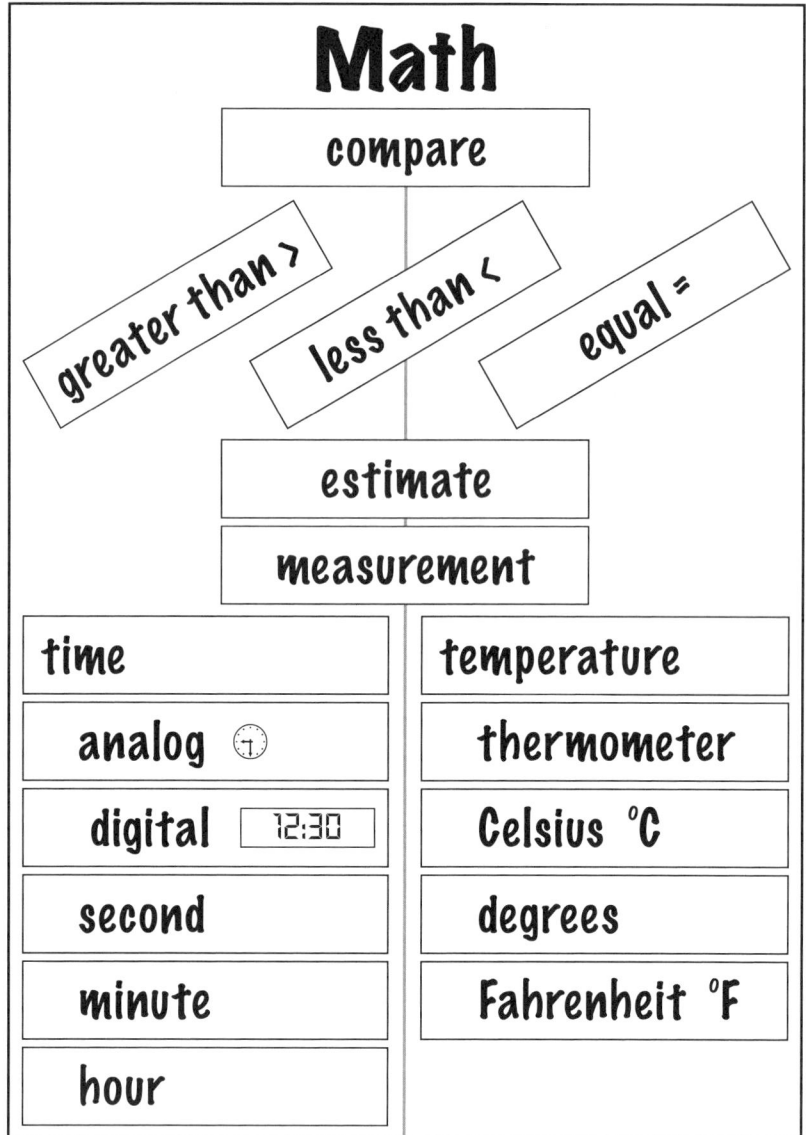

Math

compare

greater than >   less than <   equal =

estimate

measurement

time	temperature
analog 🕐	thermometer
digital 12:30	Celsius °C
second	degrees
minute	Fahrenheit °F
hour	

Keeping the Learning Comprehensible

Let's look at some brief teaching scenarios comparing Teacher E and Teacher X in their ability to keep the learning comprehensible.

Using visuals

Context of the lesson: As part of a writing lesson on developing a functional piece (step-by-step directions), students are

Math
Word Clues

+	–	x	÷
add	subtract	multiply	divide
addend	minus	factor	dividend
total	take away	product	divisible
sum	less	multiplier	divisor
both	change (money)	multiplied	mean
in all	fewer	total	quotient
plus	remain	altogether	separate
put together	count back	all	part of whole
altogether	how many more than	times	how many times
expanded	how much more	repeat	go into
perimeter	left	double	sections
combine	difference	triple	sets
increased by	discount	duplicate	distribute
lengthen	remove	reproduce	deal out
	spend		break apart
	reduced		give out
	decreased by		even
			pieces

FIGURE 5.3.
Associated Terms for
Math Operations

preparing to write about the steps involved in creating an ice cream sundae.

TEACHER E

Teacher E: Teacher E shows the students several different pictures of ice cream sundaes and generates a word bank of specific language (action verbs) that represents those actions used during the process of making a sundae. Teacher E demonstrates for students how to pull from the word bank during the drafting process, just as students will use the word bank in a similar manner when they begin their drafts.

FIGURE 5.4.
Picture Chart for
Generating Writing Ideas

Places My Family Goes

store
beach
pizza
zoo
park
movies
out to eat
parties
carnival

Teacher X: Teacher X shows the students several different pictures of ice cream sundaes and discusses the pictures with them so that they will have ideas about what to include in their own ice cream sundae. Teacher X demonstrates by writing an example of her steps in creating an ice cream sundae.

While both teachers use visuals to tap and build background knowledge, Teacher E capitalizes on the opportunity to harvest the specific language in the form of a word bank that will support students as they construct a functional writing

MAD (upset)

brother or sister bugs me

no sharing

woken up

name on the board

something breaks

lose things

getting hurt

FIGURE 5.5.
Picture Chart for
Teaching Vocabulary

piece. By showing them how to use the word bank during the drafting process, she keeps the learning comprehensible so that students will be able to imitate those writing behaviors they have just observed in the writing demonstration.

Using hand gestures

Context of the lesson: Using a read-aloud experience to introduce students to how authors use onomatopoeia, a literary language technique.

Teacher E: Throughout the text, a repetitive line occurs using prepositional terms (*over*, *under*, and *through*). Teacher E uses a repeating hand gesture to reference each prepositional term as it is encountered multiple times throughout the text. Students begin to join in, mirroring her hand gestures as the lesson progresses. Additionally, each time a sound word is referenced, Teacher E illustrates using a hand gesture, and the students rehearse the learning by saying the sound word and imitating her hand gesture (e.g., *swishy*, *swashy*—hands clasped together moving back and forth to resemble the sound of walking through tall grass).

Teacher X: Students join in a choral rhythm as Teacher X emphasizes the repetitive pattern of text. She stops after reading a sound word and provides some additional explanation to draw students' attention to how the words represent actions in the story. Teacher X also asks students to repeat the sound words so they can rehearse the oral form of each word. She does not utilize hand gestures at any point in the lesson.

Both teachers recognize the importance of choral response to keep the learners engaged and target their learning objective. Teacher E capitalizes on the opportunity to combine nonverbal (hand gestures) with verbal approaches to keep the learning comprehensible for all students and appeal to different learning styles. Teacher E is also alert to how difficult prepositional terms can be to understand, especially for English language learners. It is the constant repetition that will cement the understanding for all learners, as is evidenced as students begin to respond to the actions by repeating them involuntarily.

"Comprehensible input is any message you can understand" (SIL International, 1999).

Clear and reasonable, right? If students understand our message, then our message is comprehensible. If students are not understanding, then we need to adapt our message. A message may be clear to some students but not to others, and that requires further adaptation. The comprehension techniques outlined above can be readily implemented. They don't require extensive study. They *do* require becoming conscious of the small details of how we move and speak around our students. If we've taught for any length of time, some of our approaches tend to become so familiar we may not think about them. But if we want to be sure we're presenting a comprehensible message, we have to think not only of the message but of how we deliver it.

In the old model of education, teachers soldiered on with one-size-fits-all instruction, expecting students to keep up. The practice of comprehensible input recognizes the complexities of learning and utilizes multiform rather than uniform methods and techniques. Old-style instruction often baited a single comprehension hook, while comprehensible input weaves a net from numerous strands of comprehension techniques and casts it out to catch all students. We want to be sure this flexible and multifaceted fabric of instruction encircles all our students, drawing them steadily up to the surface of understanding.

> To differentiate *means to appropriately mediate instruction so students can process and make sense of ideas. That's what keeping learning comprehensible is all about.*

• • • • • • • • • • • • • • • • • •

In Brief

♦   In order to keep the learning comprehensible, ELLs will need multiple pathways for understanding both the language and content being presented.

♦   Strategic use of nonverbal communication allows students to access and engage in the classroom experience no matter where they are in their language development. In effect, the learning is differentiated for students.

♦   Verbal interaction is more than just speaking our intent and hoping for understanding. Utilize a variety of strategies to achieve clarity and accessibility for *all* students.

♦   Supplementary materials such as visuals, realia, and adapted text provide multiple channels to learn content in rich contexts.

♦   A well-organized, visually stimulating classroom environment provides ELLs another pathway to understanding the language and content around them.

♦   Be alert to opportunities for presenting a message in comprehensible ways. Learning happens only when understanding occurs, so our interaction with our students isn't complete until they reach a point of understanding.

6 Energy for Learning
Build Bridges for Language and Learning

. . . .

Attentive parents instinctively understand something significant about teaching: they focus on what their child can achieve *with assistance* (Rodgers & Rodgers, 2004, p.2). Think about how a mother might encourage her young child as they make cookies together. The parent would likely begin by demonstrating the process for the child, talking him through each step: "Let's be sure we have all the ingredients: flour, shortening, sugar, salt, eggs, vanilla flavoring. And your favorite—chocolate chips! We need a big bowl to mix everything together. We have to measure the flour in this little cup. See how the measuring cups come in different sizes so we can measure different amounts? This cup is the size we need for the flour. We need to fill it three times and dump it out in the bowl. . . ."

The parent shows the child each step, naming the tools and processes along the way, engaging the child interactively. The mom makes sure that the child can handle the tasks set out for him and that he knows exactly what he's expected to do. For example, rather than simply telling the child that flour has to be measured by cups, the parent is likely to show the child how to do it, counting each cup as it's filled. No doubt the child will be eager to try this on his own, and once the mom sees that the child understands the concept and can manage the process, she might ask the child to measure the sugar.

Effective teaching and parenting have much in common: the ability to successfully maximize a learning experience.

When new tasks have to be addressed, such as cracking the eggs or operating the electric mixer, the parent is likely to take charge again, modeling and discussing the new process. As the child tries a task and experiences some success with it, the parent might release that task to the child to complete independently. On the other hand, a wise parent would avoid assigning tasks that might lead to problems. For example, a parent would be unlikely to expect that a child who has never operated an electric mixer could scrape the sides of the mixing bowl without getting the spatula dangerously entangled in the beaters. But over time, as parent and child share several baking experiences, the child will probably perform more and more of the process as the mom steps back and entrusts the job to the child.

While there are several elements of cookie-making that require adult supervision (accurate measuring, inclusion of all ingredients, protection in using the hot oven, clean-up), as various tasks are modeled for the child and gradually released to him, the child's perception is *I made cookies!*

In homes where there is active parent/child interaction, children are engaged in higher order cognitive and language skills from a very young age through the daily goal-directed activities that constitute family life (grocery shopping, folding laundry, getting dressed, etc.). "In such teaching, the tasks themselves, not communication or thinking skills per se, are the subjects of direct instruction" (Tharp & Gallimore, 1991). Parents assist the child not only with the task itself but also in talking about the task. "The parents listen carefully, make guesses about the meaning of the intended communication . . . and adjust their responses to assist the child's efforts. . . . Through the instructional conversation, parents spur the child on and support the child's understanding" (Rueda, Goldenberg, & Gallimore, 1992).

It is not learning the task alone that signals success, but the ability to engage the learner in increasing his or her capacity for language or meaning to occur.

Explicit Teaching Provides a Bridge from the Known to the Unknown

We need to be sure our students know the goal of the learning experiences we introduce, and then provide the clear directions, related materials, and active guidance that will let them succeed in that learning. This is making our teaching explicit, making ourselves and our students so aware of every step of a learning process that all the mystery is taken out of it. To be fully aware of how something is done leads to understanding. It allows something that was unknown or not fully understood to become well known. To watch someone else do something, then to do it with them and to practice until we can do it well on our own is to master that skill. This is how explicit teaching works and why it's so important. If students can learn something step by step, they're likely to learn it correctly. They're more likely to be capable of using a skill on their own if they

Explicit demonstration takes the mystery out of learning something new. It is the first step in bridging for learning.

first see it modeled correctly and then practice it with coaching and feedback from a teacher and/or peers.

Bridging for learning can be compared to providing the steps that lead to a successful outcome or destination. Therefore, this symbol of steps appears throughout the rest of this chapter when teaching approaches in support of bridging for learning are being discussed or illustrated.

Explicit teaching ensures that students have as much support as they need to succeed in their learning experiences step by step. Even the pedagogical terms used to describe this mode of teaching—*scaffolding* or *bridging*—emphasize the element of support. According to various researchers

- Bridging is "a process of 'setting up' the situation to make the child's entry easy and successful and then gradually pulling back and handing the role to the child as he becomes skilled enough to manage it" (Bruner, 1983, p. 60).
- Bridging is "providing very explicit and active assistance in handing over expert knowledge that helps students to master new strategies" (Wilhelm, 2004, p. 37).
- A bridge is "the environment the teacher creates, the instructional support, and the processes and language that are leant to the student in the context of approaching a task and developing the abilities to meet it" (Wilhelm, Baker, & Dube 2001, p. 5).

"Scaffolding" or "bridging": One of your best construction tools

A scaffold is put up around a building to extend the reach of construction workers. It isn't part of the structure but rather brings workers close to the structure so they can do their jobs. In teaching, when every new lesson aims to extend students' understanding, there's a gap to bridge between what students currently know and the new learning. If we break the new learning into component parts and present it as several sequenced tasks, then walk through those tasks with our students and help them engage the process, we're making the learning accessible by giving students an instructional framework (or scaffold) they can climb. A scaffold would be of little use to construction workers if the supports they're supposed

FIGURE 6.1.
Teachers as Bridge
Designers

to stand on or grab are too few and too widely spaced for them to reach. Similarly, instructional scaffolding has to fit the specific lesson at hand, building it in detailed steps that put it within reach of students' comprehension. Another word for the same idea is *bridging*. As with scaffolding, the pedagogical meaning of bridging is very closely tied to how bridges function in the world. A physical bridge is "a structure spanning and providing passage over a gap or barrier." It's a "support . . . a thing that provides connection, contact, or transition" (Yourdictionary.com, "Bridge," 2012).

In designing physical bridges, engineers carefully consider numerous pertinent factors. They take into account the distance the bridge will span, the amount of traffic it's expected to carry, the challenges posed by terrain, and so on. Their findings determine the type of bridge and mode of support that will work best for a particular use and location. There are many different styles of bridges—arch bridges, cantilever bridges, suspension bridges, girder bridges, truss bridges, drawbridges, and more—and a single bridge often combines more than one of these styles, depending on what best meets the design criteria (SWE, n.d.).

We, too, are bridge designers, constructing pedagogical connections that encourage students to link prior knowledge to new concepts and transition from lower skill levels to more sophisticated ones. Just as engineers know the properties and strengths of various types of roadway bridges and select those that are most suitable for particular situations, so can we learn to apply an appropriate variety of bridging techniques (modeling, cueing, thinking aloud, paraphrasing, guided practice, partial solutions, etc.) to support our students in a wide range of learning experiences. "Bridging should not be seen as only one specific instructional technique. It is a broad term that encompasses many useful and thoughtful strategies" (Smith & Zygouris-Coe, 2006). "Many useful and thoughtful strategies"—this range of possibilities enables us to apply bridging to any learning terrain with strategic adaptations worthy of a skilled engineer.

Bridging for learning does not just rely on a rigid set of steps to achieve a specific outcome. It encompasses a wide range of teaching techniques responsive to the situation and students' needs in any given teaching event.

Both traffic bridges and pedagogical bridges work because of their support structures. Remove the supports and there is no bridge. And in teaching, the supports themselves actually constitute the bridge. Effective bridging is providing an appropriate sequence of supports. Thinking of bridging this way offers clear direction on how to do it. All of us employ numerous teaching supports every day. We work on motivating students, we carefully explain new skills, we provide guided practice, and so on. But a sequence of supports implies using one support after the other in an orderly flow that provides stepping stone after stepping stone to help students negotiate a particular learning experience from start to finish. It's unthinkable that a traffic bridge would take us halfway across a river and leave us suspended there because the engineers had failed to provide sufficient footings. We expect traffic bridges to cover the complete distance, carrying us from firm ground on one side to firm ground on the other. Our job in pedagogical bridging is to be sure the steps and stages of teaching carry our students all the way across a learning challenge and deliver them to the solid ground of enlarged comprehension. Also of critical importance is knowing your learners and what types of supports will be necessary.

The utilization of pre-reading, during reading, and post-reading activities is an excellent example of using a sequence of teaching supports to help students prepare for, engage with, and examine a specific text. In the pre-reading phase, one text might require more attention to building background knowledge, while another might lend itself to predicting. Students might benefit from pre-teaching vocabulary in both texts. The choice and number of teaching supports will vary from lesson to lesson depending on the learning goal, but in every case the supports must be adequate to the learning challenge and should be kept in place until students attain mastery (in other

Every literacy event requires its own set of demands that depend upon whether you're teaching something for the first time, in distributed practice opportunities over time, or with expectations for mastery.

words, the supports may need to be revisited). Good teaching and successful learning occur when an adequate number of appropriate teaching supports are employed in a progressive sequence that prepares students for a particular learning task and attentively guides them through it until they demonstrate independence.

Bridging advances students from teacher-reliance to self-reliance

A simple sequence of bridging supports is set out in Figure 6.2. It's helpful because it's easy to remember. It illustrates how expert knowledge can be handed over—literally put into the hands of students—through explicit and active assistance (Wilhelm, 2004).

This sequence can also be expressed as:

Modeled reading and writing (to students)
Shared reading and writing (with students)
Guided reading and writing (with students)
Independent reading and writing (by students)

or

Immersion ➤ Demonstration ➤ Practice ➤ Use
Source: MPS, n.d.

Design with the end in mind, knowing that ultimately you want your students to reach an independent level.

Here's one way the ideas embodied in these charts might be elaborated: "The instructional sequence in the curriculum must provide a natural order of content that for any lesson includes the prerequisite skills required prior to the specific instruction, the targeted instructional content of the lesson, and any extension skills and strategies needed to generalize

FIGURE 6.2: Bridging Supports

Teacher-Regulated (Explaining/ Modeling)	Supportive Joint Practice (Bridging)		Student-Regulated (Independence)
I DO, YOU WATCH ➤	I DO, YOU HELP ➤	YOU DO, I HELP ➤	YOU DO, I WATCH

(adapted from "Scaffolding Learning," an article from http://www.myread.org/scaffolding.htm, p. 8) the lesson. By looking back at needed prior skills, clearly explicating the skills to be learned and looking forward to extended skills, the instruction is strategically sequenced" (Arrasmith, n.d.). Although this statement isn't likely to remain in your thought as readily as "I do, you watch," it follows the same sequence and is a succinct explanation of how bridging enables students to evolve from a less developed level of skill or knowledge to a higher level.

Look back at needed prior skills ("I assess and design").
This initial phase isn't included in the charts above, but it's an indispensable precedent. No lesson can be effective unless it considers students' readiness to relate to new learning. Are students equipped with needed skills and background knowledge? Are they ready to grapple with the strategies and content of the planned lesson? In other words, is it within their zone of proximal development (ZPD)?

Revisiting prior skills and background knowledge with students helps generate motivation and confidence as you introduce them to new learning experiences. Your awareness of your students' readiness should guide you in designing a natural order of content for the lesson, including how the content will be introduced and practiced (i.e., the bridging experiences in which you and your students will collaborate through engaging in learning tasks).

Assessment and planning: two critical ingredients necessary in order to bridge for learning effectively.

Clearly explicate the skills to be learned ("I do/you watch").
This is when students should gain a clear concept of the learning task(s) and what the desired outcome looks like. As you model tasks, perform them in the same form or sequence you expect students to use in guided practice. Be sure to keep the task at the appropriate level of difficulty, as determined by your students' skills and readiness. Talk through each step to explain procedural elements and the thought processes involved. Remember to speak in the first person ("I") rather than in the second person ("you") so that students perceive that you are thinking aloud: "Now I'm going to. . . ." "I need to do this because. . . ."

Introduce academic terms that relate to the lesson and model their use as you talk through tasks. If you anticipate that certain aspects of a task may be especially challenging, let students know that and assure them you'll be working together to resolve any difficulties. Explanations and modeling

Strive for a clear, concise, targeted demonstration of learning tasks.

In this step you are providing structured opportunities to test the waters of new learning. It's a modest first step.

At this stage, grouping structures may change to differentiate students' ability to practice the learning task. We often call this the "guided practice" phase of instruction.

should be thorough enough to clarify the learning task but not so extensive that students get lost in details.

Look forward to extended skills ("I do/you help" and "You do/I help"). "I do, you help" means that teacher and students will share the new task. It gives students another opportunity to become familiar with the learning task before they engage it on their own. It's a modest first step toward the anticipated extension of skill, but for many students it provides a stronger basis for working on the task by themselves. Once again the teacher performs the task, but she invites students to name the task steps and offer their own explanations. "Who remembers what we do now?" the teacher might ask, or "Can someone think aloud for us about this?" Hints, partial solutions, and leading statements are bridging techniques that work well at this point. "Did we miss a step here? I'll show you, and then you can explain it."

"You do, I help" turns the task over to students, with active support from the teacher. Although our plan probably contemplates certain activities at this stage of instruction, not all students will be at the same point of readiness. If we truly want to mediate learning for our students, we can't rely on a single approach or activity for each of them. One teacher describes how he differentiates his support according to the need: "I might continue working with small groups of struggling students as they watch me use the strategy and then try to help me use it. Students who are getting it but still need some help work together. I'll drop in when I can to help them. And those who can use the strategy independently can work at applying it on their own, or perhaps I'll find a more complicated textual challenge for using the strategy that they can address in small groups or on their own. In this way everybody gets pushed and [bridged] appropriately to grow as far as they can" (Wilhelm, 2004, p. 37).

As students take hold of the learning task (perhaps revisiting it several times over the course of a lesson or unit), they should attempt to complete it on their own as best they can. The teacher should vary the level of assistance (bridging) offered as students progress. Students who needed suggestions and partial answers yesterday may be able to move forward today with only brief hints or leading questions. Thus the teacher gradually hands over learning to students by assisting them only with what is beyond their current ability or understanding.

"The teacher's response to student work recasts and expands upon the students' efforts without rejecting what they have accomplished on their own. The teacher's primary role is collaborative rather than evaluative" (Orey, 2001). Students' mistakes or misdirection can be sorted out through sustaining feedback, which leads students to the correct approach or concept through prompting, questioning, explaining a term, making a suggestion—or whatever approach connects with students (Cole, 2004, p. 5). Sustaining feedback mediates learning and should result in solving the problem *with* our learners, not *for* them.

It's especially important for feedback to be immediate in the "You do, I'll help" stage. If students have misunderstood or misapplied something, prompt feedback keeps an error from becoming ingrained. It also prevents students from becoming frustrated by repeatedly attempting to work out a task and being hampered by their lack of understanding. Students need to know when they're working in the right direction, too. Be generous with positive reinforcement, both for students who are progressing steadily and for those who need to renew their efforts. Our aim is "a weaning off the expert. But when we're needed, we're there—elbow to elbow, sensitively offering the boost necessary to negotiate the difficulty, to move the learner forward" (Cole, 2004, p. 2).

Mediating the learning environment through sustained feedback for the learner is bridging for language.

Release for independence ("You do, I watch"). Guided practice with appropriate mediation and collaborating should ultimately enable students to use a strategy or perform a task on their own. It's natural for students to assume responsibility for a strategy or task once they've internalized the elements involved, including language and strategies, and can apply the new learning independently. The activity or ability that was the object of the lesson enters the students' zone of actual development (ZAD), and they no longer require assistance with the task. They're also able to generalize the application of the task to other learning contexts, which greatly expands its usefulness for them (Wilhelm, Baker, & Dube, 2001, p. 4). Students have moved beyond looking forward to extended skills and are now confident in their possession. They've reached firm ground on the other side of the bridge.

Students internalize a learning task at different rates and with varying degrees of complexity. Respect the process along the way rather than focusing solely on product.

The sequence of "I do" through "you do," when infused with instructional objectives, materials, and activities pertinent to a specific learning goal, demonstrates the effectiveness of teaching by assisting, or bridging for learning.

Support should only be temporary

An effective bridging sequence always progresses from "I (teacher) do or help" to "you (learner) do," from support by the teacher to ownership by the student. But students' need for support shifts continually as they make this transition, and our provision of support should change in response. "Assistance provided should always be 'just enough' and 'just in time'" (Walqui, 2006, p. 165). In the give-and-take of instruction and learning, our aim is to find the balance between keeping too much control and releasing too soon.

We can know how much or how little support to offer by how students respond. If we give a student one form of assistance (hints, a reminder of a strategy rule, partial completion of a step, etc.), but that student is still unable to proceed with the learning task, then we must provide a more explicit directive immediately. On the other hand, if the student is able to move ahead on his or her own through our initial assistance, then the next time they ask for help we need to keep the support we provide as minimal as possible—*just enough* assistance. After sharing a helping idea or procedural step with a student, give them plenty of time to pursue the suggestion or to try a new approach before stepping in again. This is providing assistance *just in time*. As students develop ability with regard to a learning task, the frequency and obtrusiveness of assistance should decrease until the student can perform the task without prompting. "At any point in time, teachers should [bridge] students enough so that they do not give up on the task or fail at it but not [bridge] them so much that they do not have the opportunity to actively work on the problem themselves" (Clark & Graves, 2005, p. 571).

Some educators use the word *fading* to describe the progressive downshifting of support from total to partial to minimal to none (Orey, 2001). This is an apt metaphor for the gradual release of responsibility from teacher to student. The metaphors of the scaffold and bridge also convey the sense of temporary rather than permanent reliance. A scaffold erected to permit work on a building is removed when the work is complete. A bridge may be physically permanent but is not a

Never do for students what they can do for themselves. Too much hand-holding develops learned helplessness. On the other hand, too much too soon leaves students submerged in confusion and uncertainty. There is an art and science to bridging for learning.

destination in itself; it's not a place you stay but a connecting roadway you cross en route to a destination. In the practice of scaffolding/bridging, various forms of learning supports are constantly provided and removed, provided and removed, as learning tasks and the learning thresholds of students (zones of proximal development) shift and change.

The following scenarios provide a comparative study of how two teachers bridge for learning during a literacy lesson. Notice the subtle yet important differences in how Teacher E makes adjustments that provide instructional supports that impact student learning in positive ways.

Recognizing and Capitalizing on Opportunities to Bridge for Learning

Context of the lesson: During an interactive read aloud lesson, students are identifying examples of cause and effect.

Teacher E (*pointing to a picture in the text*): "When I think of cause and effect, I look for events that happen and then ask what caused that event to occur. So here I see the boy giving the dog a bath and ask, *Why is that happening?* The dog needs a bath because he is so dirty from being a stray dog for such a long time. I want you to listen once again to how I identified cause and effect: the dog needs a bath because he is so dirty from being a stray dog for such a long time." (Demonstration: *I do, you watch*). "Now talk with your partner and explain what happens and why." (Guided practice: *You do, I help.* All students rehearse what has just been demonstrated by the teacher.)

"I heard many of you say that the dog needed a bath because he was so dirty from playing outside. You are beginning to understand the cause-and-effect relationship. I'm now going to show you how to use some special words when you talk and write about cause and effect." (Reinforces *how students are approaching the target of the instruction and* communicates *the expected outcomes for the lesson. The language* I am going to show you . . . *communicates that students can expect support for what they are learning.*

Teacher E (continuing to read a few more pages, then pausing to think aloud for the students): "The author tells us that the family and their dog went for a picnic. What caused that event to happen? I am thinking *if* it is a beautiful, sunny day, *then* the family will go on a picnic with their new dog." (She writes the words *If . . . Then . . .* on a chart.) "These two words are often used to show cause and effect." (Demonstration: *I do, you watch.* Providing a chart listing the new language of cause and effect provides a concrete representation for students needing visual support.) "Let's read a bit further and then try out an example together."

Teacher E (stops at another example and elicits the students to practice all together): "Let's explain this event starting with *If. . . .*" (All students rehearse the cause-and-effect relationship as the teacher coaches them through the process.) "*Then . . .*" (Structured practice: *I do, you help.* The teacher leads the group as they practice something new.)

"Now turn to your partner and try and say it again." (Guided practice: *You do, I help.* Trying out something new with a partner.)

"Now it's your turn to try out an example with your partner." (She reads a bit farther.) "What caused the dog to run away from the family? Remember, as you talk with your partner, try to begin with (pointing to the *If . . . Then . . .* on the chart) *If . . .* is why something is about to happen and *then . . .* is what is going to happen." (Guided practice: *You do, I help.* Students are asked to apply their new learning at the next stage of learning. Bridging for language support occurs as the teacher provides the sentence stem *If . . . then . . .* to get students started.) "Begin. . . ."

Teacher E (listening in on several different sets of partners and providing language support as needed). "Wow! I am hearing many of you trying to talk about cause and effect by using *if /then* statements. Let me review a few I heard today:

"If the dog is dirty from being outside then he will need to take a bath."

"If it is a beautiful sunny day then the family will go on a picnic with their dog."

"If the dog feels scared in his new home then he will whine and cry at night."

"If the dog sees a dogcatcher coming after him with a net then he will run away from his family."

"You are learning how to identify cause and effect as you notice the different events that occur throughout a story." (Demonstration: *I do, you watch.* The teacher summarizes what students are learning and provides additional opportunities to hear the language structure.)

"Later this week we will find more examples of cause and effect in your own reading, and you will learn how to record some of those examples in your reading log." (Later in the week students will move to the independent application of the new strategy, *You do, I watch*.)

Question: *If some students aren't ready to apply this strategy independently, do you feel as though this teacher will provide additional support so that all students are successful?*

A comparison of the same lesson with Teacher X

TEACHER X

Teacher X (pointing to a picture in the text): "When I think of cause and effect, I look for events that happen and then ask what caused that event to occur. Here I see the boy giving the dog a bath and ask, *Why is that happening*?" (She calls on individual students who raise their hands. The teacher begins to demonstrate how readers identify cause and effect but gets caught in the trap of involving students in the process too soon, which, in effect, complicates her efforts to provide the explicit demonstration needed.)

Student: "The dog is dirty."

Teacher X: "Yes, that is true. But why?"

Student: "He needs a bath."

Teacher X: "Yes, but he needs a bath because . . ."

Student: "He lived outside for a long time."

Teacher X: "Yes, he is a stray dog. Now talk with your partner and explain what happens and why." (Guided practice: *You do, I help*. Will all the students be successful at rehearsing what they are learning about cause and effect when the teacher hasn't fully demonstrated the process first?)

Teacher X: "Let's remember that the dog needs a bath because he is so dirty from being a stray dog for such a long time. Now let's see if you can use some special words when you talk and write about cause and effect." (Students are reminded of how to identify cause and effect but they weren't quite ready to engage in guided practice. Teacher E communicated an expected outcome for their learning and hoped that students would be able to achieve the goal by saying, "Now, let's see. . . .")

Teacher X (pausing to think aloud for the students): "The author tells us that the family and their dog went for a picnic. What caused that event to happen? I am thinking *if* it is a beautiful, sunny day, *then* the family will go on a picnic with their new dog. These two words are often used to show cause and effect." (Demonstration:

I do, you watch. Students have heard an explicit demonstration of how to use a language structure when speaking about cause and effect. Will all students be able to grasp this learning with only an auditory example?) "Let's read a bit farther and see if you and your partner can identify another example."

Teacher X (reading a bit farther and stopping at another example): "Now it's your turn to try out an example with your partner. Start with *If . . .* to explain why something is about to happen, and continue with *then . . .* to explain what is going to happen." (Guided practice: *You do, I help.* Bridging for language support occurs as the teacher provides the sentence stem *If . . . then . . .* to get students started.)

Teacher X (repeating the correct response using the *if/then* structure): "Remember that when you begin with *if* , you start with *why* something is about to happen; *then* is *what* is happening or going to happen. Let's try it again."

Questions: *Has there been sufficient demonstration for students to apply what they are learning? Would an opportunity for structured practice first provide a more supportive context before moving to the application phase?*

Teacher X (reads a bit farther): "What caused the dog to run away from the family?" (Students raise their hands.)

Student: "The man came after the dog."

Teacher X: "That man is called a dogcatcher or warden. But why?"

Student: "He is afraid of him."

Teacher X: "But why?"

(After a few more exchanges, the teacher provides the correct model of how to explain the cause and effect using an *if/then* structure.)

Question: *Why did the teacher feel the need to call on individual students rather than partners at this stage in the lesson?*

Teacher X: Today we learned how to identify examples of cause and effect as we think about the events that occur in a story. Later this week we will find more examples of cause and effect in your own reading, and you will learn how to record some of those examples in your reading log. (Later in the week, students will move to the independent application of the new strategy: *You do, I watch.*)

Questions: *How do you know when to move to the next phase of learning in any given lesson? Is there sufficient bridging for learning in this lesson to allow students to move to an independent application of this new strategy?*

How Does Bridging for Learning Affect Student Learning?

When a teacher effectively bridges for learning, he or she maximizes students' opportunities to succeed at reaching the target objective. Teacher E provided multiple demonstrations and practice opportunities in supportive contexts so that all students could be successful. While both teachers recognized the academic demands of meeting this objective, Teacher E also understood the students' need to grasp a new language structure and provided more opportunities for rehearsal. In any lesson, there are both content and language demands; we can address both areas through the use of sufficient bridging throughout the lesson. It is always helpful to ask oneself, *What have my students learned? How do I know?* The teacher who "shows, not tells" and then expects student performance as a result of demonstrating the desired behavior will affect student learning positively.

Bridging is both structure and process

The *structure* of bridging for learning has to do with how learning tasks are constructed and carried out. It consists of a sequence of modeling and questioning activities that present a specific learning task and lead students to develop pertinent concepts and language. The structure outlines not only the content you expect to present but how you expect to present it as well. It's the choreography but not the dance, the game plan but not the game. It's intended to be "relatively stable, though easy to assemble and reassemble." The *process* of bridging for language brings the structure together with learners in the animated give-and-take of instructional conversation. The process is "interactional, . . . jointly constructed from moment to moment . . . [in] the fluid dynamics of collaborative work" (Walqui, 2006, p. 164).

The structure (plan/sequence) provides format and methodology, but the process (mediating/facilitating) invariably requires spontaneous adjustments that respond to the present moment within the scope of the structure. The challenge is that "pedagogical action is always a blend of the planned and the improvised, the predicted and the unpredictable, routine

Bridging for learning and language bring structure and process together; each supports the other to achieve a differentiated environment for all students.

and innovation." Structure and process are interdependent: we need both. Structure creates a place or context in which the process can occur. It maximizes opportunities for process. "Most importantly, then, the dynamics between the [bridging for learning] structure and the [bridging for language] process must be kept in mind." (Walqui, 2006, p. 164).

Structure, rather than process, has long dominated American classrooms. It's been customary for teachers to assign content and then evaluate learning by asking students to recite facts gleaned from that content. Recitation questioning, as this approach is called, values predictable, correct answers. A student's correct answer is the end of the interchange; there is little or no opportunity to enlarge ideas and explore broader connections. Overreliance on structure tends to value facts rather than thinking, product rather than process.

But when structure is seen as a context for the development of thought rather than as an end in itself, process (interaction, collaboration, co-construction) can flourish. Understanding that effective teaching should assist students in building their own learning, researchers have increasingly recognized the value of classroom discussion that encourages student participation in the exploration of ideas. These discussions are instructional in intent and conversational in quality, and they have come to be known as "instructional conversations" (Goldenberg, 1991).

Bridging for language can be thought of as a linguistic scaffold to bolster linguistic output. This symbol signifies the nature of interaction that increases the capacity for language output. It will appear throughout the rest of this chapter when teaching approaches in support of bridging for language are discussed or illustrated.

Instructional conversations at the heart of bridging for language

Good instructional conversations are engaging and lively, but not random. They focus on ideas or activities that students are exploring, and the theme or learning objective is maintained throughout. An important dimension of instructional conversation is bridging for language. This includes using opportunities in our moment-to-moment exchanges to clarify and enrich students' language as well as familiarizing students with academic language. When students don't

> *This rudimentary structure is commonly referred to as "assign and assess"; it is contrary to the bridging structure. Our students, in particular ELLs, will encounter difficulties on the road to academic proficiency if we use it.*

> *Facilitation is key in bridging for language. The teacher provides a supportive context so that students can attain higher levels of cognitive and language proficiency.*

understand the meaning of a phrase, an idiom, or a sentence, we can bridge that for them through paraphrasing. If they use different tenses in a single sentence or put an adjective in the wrong place, we can recast their statement to model correct usage. When they are unsure of how to express an idea, we can suggest language structure ("You might say . . ."). "Strategically, the teacher introduces provocative ideas or experiences, then questions, prods, challenges, coaxes, or keeps quiet, . . . extending discussion around ideas that matter to the participants [and] allowing them to reach new levels of understanding" (Rueda, Goldenberg, & Gallimore, 1992). Although the teacher facilitates the conversation and helps maintain its focus, she takes care not to dominate the discussion. Students talk with the teacher, but also with each other. They're encouraged to express their own ideas, which others build on or challenge. Because students are engaged and interested, there's a high level of participation.

Instructional conversations can take place with an entire class, in small groups, or just between two speakers. They can last several minutes or be very brief. Whenever we respond to student questions or comments by giving them more dimension or elaboration, we're engaging in instructional conversation that supports further development of students' language or content knowledge.

Ten elements of an instructional conversation are outlined in Figure 6.5. The teachers and researchers who collaborated on this model helpfully distinguished between instructional and conversational characteristics. Considering them separately, we can see how the instructional elements provide direction while the conversational elements enable interaction and discovery. "A skilled teacher weaves together the comments and contributions made by different students [*conversational*] with the ideas and concepts the teacher wishes to explore with them [*instructional*]" ("Instructional Conversations," 1992).

Let's look now at the types of questions or comments that keep instructional conversations flowing. The list isn't intended to be comprehensive or formulaic; it simply offers examples of how we can phrase our questions or responses to pursue a variety of learning purposes.

- ♦ Making connections between participants' comments
  - Let's rehearse what we just heard. . . .

FIGURE 6.5. Elements of the Instructional Conversation

Instructional	Conversational
1. **Thematic focus.** The teacher chooses a theme and a general plan for its development. 2. **Activation and use of background.** The teacher builds on students' prior knowledge or experience or provides pertinent background. 3. **Direct teaching.** When necessary, the teacher gives direct instruction regarding a skill or concept. 4. **Promotion of more complex language and expression.** The teacher encourages students to develop their comments in more depth by invitations to expand, questions, restatements, etc. 5. **Promotion of bases for statements of positions.** The teacher encourages students to support their statements by showing evidence in text or explaining their reasoning.	6. **Fewer known-answer questions.** Discussion explores questions that might have more than one correct answer. 7. **Responsiveness to student contributions.** While maintaining the conversational theme, the teacher responds to student remarks and uses them as opportunities to develop ideas. 8. **Connected discourse.** The discussion takes multiple, connected turns; comments build on one another. 9. **Challenging but nonthreatening atmosphere.** Students are challenged to work toward meaning, but the conversation is collaborative rather than evaluative. 10. **General participation, including self-selected turns.** The teacher doesn't always control who talks.

- Who agrees/disagrees with what [name of student] said?
- Who can add to the conversation?
- I want to add on to what I just heard. . . .
- I agree with you because . . .

Source: Wolf, Crosson, & Resnick, 2006

◆ Encouraging students to support their ideas with evidence
- How do you know that?
- Share some examples with the group. . . .
- Where did you find that information?
- Have you marked the text where it tells you that information?
- Let me show you exactly where I found some evidence. . . .

Source: Wolf et al., 2006

◆ Encouraging students to explain their thinking
- Why do you think that?

- Can you explain your thinking?
- Say more about what you are thinking. . . .
- I think because . . .

Source: Wolf et al., 2006

◆ Elaborating on correct, or partially correct, student responses

- Can you also tell me why this [concept, information] is important?
- You are thinking and explaining your ideas well. Tell me more. . . .
- What else do you know about that?
- Your ideas make sense, but that's not quite complete. Do you or anyone else have something to add?

Source: Mohr & Mohr, 2007, p. 444

◆ Elaborating on incorrect or confusing responses

- Help me understand what you mean. Tell me again.
- Tell me more so I know what you're thinking.
- Let's think through these ideas together.

Source: Mohr & Mohr, 2007, p. 444

◆ Responding to student questions

- Thank you for asking. Understanding is important. Learners ask lots of questions.
- That's an important question. Do you know anything that will help you answer that question?
- I wonder if someone else could help you answer that question. . . .

Source: Mohr & Mohr, 2007, p. 444

When instructional conversation is lacking, it can have a detrimental effect on student performance. In the following scenarios, notice how different the outcome is when instructional conversational uptake occurs during a writing conference.

Recognizing and capitalizing on opportunities to bridge for language

Context of the lesson. During a writing session, the teacher is conferencing with students about their writing pieces.

TEACHER E

Teacher E: "Tell me about your story."

Student (pointing to a drawing of a dog inside a small house): "My dog sleep in that."

Teacher E (pointing to the picture): "Oh, so your dog *sleeps* in a doghouse?" (Recasting *so the student hears the correct grammatical structure.*)

The student nods "yes."

Teacher E (pointing to the picture): "That is called a doghouse. It is a special place for dogs to sleep. It is like a little house." (Elaborating *to help the student understand a new label for a known concept.*)

Teacher E: "So you want to write, *My dog sleeps in a doghouse*?" (Clarifying.)

Student: "Yes."

Teacher E: "Say these words after me: *My dog sleeps in a doghouse.*" (Language rehearsal *for the new grammatical structure.*)

Student: "My dog sleep . . . (teacher supports and says, "sleeps") . . . sleeps in a doghouse."

Teacher E: "Say it again."

Student: "My dog sleeps in a doghouse."

Teacher E: "Let's practice one more time so you can write your words to go with your story."

Student: "My dog sleeps in a doghouse." (Multiple rehearsals *provide the auditory input necessary to complete a new mental action.*)

Teacher E: "Let me show you something that will help you as you write your words." (She draws a line for each word using length as an indicator for long or short words.) "Use your finger to point to the lines, and say your story again." (A writing technique *that temporarily assists the learner to complete the task of mapping speech to print.*)

Student (finger pointing on the lines): "My dog sleeps in a doghouse."

Teacher E: "I can't wait to hear your story after you write your words."

A comparison with Teacher X working within the same context

TEACHER X

Teacher X: "Tell me about your story."

Student (pointing to a drawing of a dog inside a small house): "My dog sleep in that."

Teacher X (pointing to the picture): "That's a doghouse."

The student nods "yes."

Teacher X: "Dogs like to sleep in doghouses. That's a great story. You are ready to write your words. Listen to the sounds and write the letters down."

Questions: *How does a teacher know when to probe further and provide further additional language support? Would this teacher's interaction be sufficient with some students?*

How does bridging for language represent the principles of differentiated instruction?

To differentiate means to appropriately mediate instruction so students can process and make sense of ideas. The bridging techniques used by Teacher E mediate the learning task so that the student can effectively engage in the complex process of writing. The question you must continually ask is: How will I mediate the instruction to maximize the opportunity for student success? Unfortunately, Teacher X falls far short of that goal. She offered some language support for learning a new label (*doghouse*) for a known concept (places where animals sleep). Yet, Teacher X does not recognize the need for additional language support necessary to encourage this young writer to apply the principles of mapping his speech to print. Over time, these missed opportunities can yield lowered expectations and a widening of the achievement gap.

Good conversation, inside and outside school, is stimulating and often revealing. It's one of the main vehicles by which people get to know one another. Instructional conversations allow teachers to know how students are progressing as learners. Student comments can reveal comprehension, reasoning capacity, meaning-making, background knowledge, and confusion, alerting teachers to needs and strengths they might not otherwise have identified. "When teachers are engaged with their students in this way, they are aware of the students' ever-changing relationships to the subject matter. They can assist because, while the learning process is alive and unfolding, they see and feel the child's progression through the zone [of proximal development], as well as the stumbles and errors that call for support" (Tharp & Gallimore, 1991).

We "see and feel the child's progression" because the learning experience (meaning-making through social interaction related to a task) is unfolding right before our eyes, and our hand is on the living pulse of it through our facilitation efforts. And as new strengths are revealed in student understanding, so are continued weaknesses, pointing the direction

The bridging process enlarges language capacity and learning possibilities for all our students. Isn't that why we teach?

for our continued assistance. Seen this way, co-constructing knowledge with our students is exciting work.

Our job description as mediators and bridge-makers could be written in just three words: *beckon, broaden, build.* What we're beckoning is student participation. What we're broadening and building is students' language and conceptual knowledge, working with and stretching their contributions as we help them reach for higher competencies (Mohr & Mohr, 2007, p. 447).

• • • • • • • • • • • • • • • •

In Brief

♦ Teaching can be compared to any other role (parent, coach, etc.) where active guidance is a critical step in achieving success in learning something new.

♦ Teachers can be compared to bridge designers, constructing pedagogical bridges that encourage students to connect prior knowledge to new concepts and transition from lower skill levels to more sophisticated development.

♦ Good teaching and successful learning occur when an adequate number of appropriate teaching supports are employed in a progressive sequence that prepares students for a particular learning task and attentively guides them through it until they demonstrate independence.

♦ The steps in bridging for learning are as follows:
   1. Look back at needed prior skills (*I assess and design*).
   2. Clearly explicate the skills to be learned (*I do, you watch*).
   3. Look forward to extended skills (*I do, you help* and *you do, I help*).
   4. Release for independence (*you do, I watch*).

♦ The structure of bridging for *learning* has to do with how learning tasks are constructed and carried out. The process of bridging for *language*, on the other hand, brings the structure together with learners in the animated give-and-take of instructional conversation.

♦ Bridging for language includes capitalizing on opportunities in our moment-to-moment exchanges to clarify and enrich students' language as well as familiarizing students with academic language. Some of the tools we might use are paraphrasing, clarifying, elaborating, recasting, and offering language support structures when needed.

♦ The bridging process enlarges language capacity and learning possibilities for all our students.

7 Energy for Learning
Get Students Talking

"There is a need to change pedagogic practices so that the dialogue that takes place in the classroom between teachers and pupils and between pupils themselves can become a powerful learning tool. . . . This may entail a reconsideration of your own role as teacher"
(Arthur & Cremin, 2010, p. 239).

"If we want children to talk to learn—as well as learn to talk—then what they say probably matters more than what teachers say"
(Alexander, 2004, p. 19)

How much do we value student talk as an important element in learning? We might discover the answer by considering which of the classrooms described below is most like our own:

♦ "The classroom where children's talk merely fills in the missing words. The teacher's agenda and lesson planning dominates the talk, and the talk delivers the content of the lesson with the occasional pause for a child to offer brief answers to questions."

♦ "The classroom where children's talk is given space and in which the child's answers actually matter. They matter because they reveal a child's thinking and understanding, or misunderstanding. The child's answer might change the focus of the lesson, either because old learning has to be revisited or because the child's response creates opportunities not anticipated in the teacher's planning" (Myhill, Jones, & Hopper, 2006, p. 80).

> *Our ELLs will thrive in language-rich environments where they not only hear conversational uptake between peers in academic settings but are encouraged to try out their new language in low-anxiety environments.*

Every teacher recognizes these scenarios. We've all delivered lessons and then used the familiar recitation script to ask a factual question, receive a student's answer, and then confirm or correct it. And certainly we've all experienced moments when students really connect with a lesson and respond with vigorous and sustained interaction, surpassing our expectations. It's clear that more teaching encounters like these would add substance and depth both to our teaching and our students' learning. Fortunately, we can learn how to set the stage for meaningful student interaction so it can become a regular and enriching feature of our classrooms.

Thinking and Talking Belong Together in Learning

One of the most energizing things we can do for our teaching is to connect (this was discussed at length in chapter 2). An arresting statement quoted there deserves to be revisited: "The interactions that take place between students and teachers and among students are more central to student success than any method for teaching literacy, or science or math" (Cummins, 1996. p. 1).

To connect means "to engage." Highly focused attention and active engagement help teachers to find teachable moments and to make strong connections with students in ways that ensure learning.

If you aren't a little taken aback by this claim, please read it again. Soak it up. Once it penetrates, you should feel a tremor in the foundation of your assumptions about teaching. Personal interactions are *central* to student success? Even student-to-student interactions? How?

For several decades now, researchers and educators have studied, applied, and verified the perceptions of Lev Vygotsky, a respected Russian educator and psychologist. His most fundamental observation was that learning takes place largely through social interaction, especially when assistance from a more knowledgeable "other" (adult or peer) enables a child to exceed his present capacity and embrace new ideas and skills. In modeling a task, it's natural for the knowledgeable other to talk through processes, respond to the learner's questions, ask leading questions, encourage, hint, and generally collaborate until the learner firms up his grasp on how to perform the work. "The child seeks to understand the actions or instructions provided by the tutor (often the parent or teacher) then internalizes the information, using it to guide or regulate their own performance" (Mcleod, 2007). This is how most of us learned to ride a bike, write our name, and master thousands of other complex details we take for granted. Vygotsky found that every step of learning occurred on the social (interactive) level first before becoming internalized. In other words, as a learner becomes secure in a task, he naturally transitions from other-assistance to self-assistance. (More details about

Vygotsky's principles are instrumental to putting into motion the language-meaning-learning cycle. Every time language leads to meaning and meaning leads to learning, learning cycles right back to language with increased capacity.

Vygotsky and the co-construction of knowledge are explored in chapter 2.)

"Vygotsky proposed that language and thought combine . . . 'children solve practical tasks with the help of their speech as well as their eyes and hands.' In focusing attention on the interaction between speech and the child's social and cultural experiences, Vygotsky provides us with a model of learning which emphasizes the role of talk and places social discourse at the center" (Corden, 2000, p. 8).

A model of learning that emphasizes student talk requires a model of teaching with the same priority. No one knows better than we teachers that student talk can be boisterous, unfocused, and hard to manage. So why do psychologists and researchers insist that talk is such an important vehicle for children's learning? What kinds of student talk have proven productive? How can we be sure student talk is really promoting learning objectives? The answers to these very natural questions are persuasive and surprising, revealing a potential for the power of student talk that most of us never imagined.

Why is talk so important to learning? Educators and researchers have spent entire careers on this question, but the bare-bones answer is very simple: thinking and talking are closely related functions—so closely related that if we want to encourage students to think, we need to allow them to talk. Consider these observations:

◆ "Language . . . is how we think. It's how we process information and remember. . . . Talk is the representation of thinking" (Fisher, Frey, & Rothenberg, 2008, p. 5).

◆ "A complex thought system requires a great deal of shared experience and conversation. It is in talking about what we have done and observed, and in arguing about what we make of our experiences, that ideas multiply, become refined, and finally produce new questions and further explorations" (Rowe, 1986, p. 43).

◆ "Having to say what you mean—thinking aloud—is a way of making your thoughts clear to yourself; having to explain and describe things to a partner is a way of developing a shared understanding of ideas. . . . This *interthinking*—the joint engagement with one another's ideas to think aloud together, solve problems, or make mutual meaning—is an invaluable use of spoken language (Mercer, 2005). Children need to learn how to do

Thinking brings about talking. Together they create meaning. If we want our students to think, them we must allow them to talk.

this and need lots of opportunities to practice" (Dawes, 2005, pp. 108–109).

"A great deal of . . . conversation" and "think[ing] aloud together [to] make mutual meaning." Do these statements describe the typical activity in your classroom? As recently as 2008, a study of 1,000 elementary school students across the United States found that 91 percent of their academic day focused on whole-class lessons or independent seatwork. They shared a learning activity with other students only 4.8 percent of the time (Pianta, Belsky, Vandergrift, Houts, & Morrison, 2008). In other words, the traditional model of the teacher owning all the speaking rights is still widespread (Cazden, 2001, p. 82).

Talking to create understanding, not to transmit knowledge

We just considered the vital linkage between learners' thinking and talking. It's equally worthwhile to scrutinize the more common patterns of classroom interaction and their impact on learning. The most obvious and well-documented aspect of traditional teaching is probably that the teacher does most of the talking. There are many reasons for this—maintaining the momentum of a lesson, curriculum coverage, class management, and so on—but the result is that students are expected to learn largely through listening. When student participation is invited, it's often merely to check comprehension. A brief, "correct" answer is solicited, and the exchange is closed when the answer is given, "each teacher utterance filling a paragraph while each child utterance barely [fills] a line" (Myhill et al., 2006, pg. 75).

The initiate- respond- evaluate discourse pattern puts ELLs' confidence and language ease to the test every time. Students must speak or recite an answer in front of their peers and are evaluated as to its correctness. Is such an anxiety- producing environment conducive to negotiating a new language?

Of course, many of us employ a range of techniques beyond the initiate-respond-evaluate (I-R-E) pattern in which the teacher asks a factual question, a student offers a response, and then the teacher validates or corrects it. The point isn't that I-R-E sequences should be entirely abandoned (sometimes they're useful or timely) but rather that such exchanges are narrow and don't allow for exploration, investigation, and the expansion of ideas. Unless a teaching approach promotes student thinking, it isn't encouraging learning.

Of even greater concern is that severe restrictions on student talk might actively *defeat* learning:

♦ "The role of the teacher as the questioner in the classroom teaches the child that their own knowledge is
subordinate to the text and the teacher" (Myhill et al.,
2006, p. 68).

♦ "Children become passive recipients and do not use
language to explore, investigate, challenge, evaluate,
and actively engage in the construction of meaning
(Corden, 2000, p. 110).

♦ "[Often] only one student has an opportunity to talk,
and . . . that talk does not require the use of even one
complete sentence, let alone extended discourse"
(Fisher et al., 2008, p. 7).

♦ "Students [may] fail to develop academic language and
discourse simply because they aren't provided opportunities to use words. They are hearing words but not
using them" (Fisher et al., 2008, p. 7).

No teacher intends to create passivity in students or
restrict the development of vocabulary and language skills.
Quite the opposite. But many of us are eager to pass along
what we know to students, which often translates into an
effort to hand over knowledge through our talk. And precisely
because our knowledge and understanding is greater than that
of our students (at least in academic terms), it's easy to slide
into the subtle notion that our students don't know enough or
aren't experienced enough to contribute meaningfully to their
own or others' learning. Another misconception we sometimes
harbor is that students are dependent almost exclusively on
their teachers for meaningful learning.

All these perceptions probably seem familiar and reasonable, but they've been disproven, and therefore we need to
undertake the mental housekeeping necessary to discard them.
The premises behind them are "predicated on a view of teaching as an act of transmission. Transmission teaching concep-
tualizes talk merely as a mechanism for information transfer, yet
contemporary learning theory asserts the impossibility of this:
however unequal the balance of knowledge between teacher
and learner, there is no way in which the knowledge of the
teacher can be transmitted directly to the learner. Talking and
learning must be used as an opportunity to create understanding rather than transmit it" (Myhill et al., 2006, p. 17).

The transfer of information through talk is impossible. Read
that statement again and ponder it for a moment. *Impossible* is a

*When we teach our
students, do we perceive
a glass half empty or a
glass half full? Do we
carry the optimistic expectation that our students
are capable of contribut-
ing and creating their
own understanding?*

hard word—a big stop sign. If it's an impossible way of learning, then we need to stop using it as a style of teaching. But it isn't talking itself that needs to stop. Rather, the purpose of talk has to be redirected. Classroom talk must be less concerned with a surface knowledge of facts and more focused on creating an understanding of ideas. This requires not only a change from lessons to discussion, but also gaining a different concept of knowledge and teaching (Cadzen, 2001, p. 5). "Talking, listening, and learning effectively does require a shift from what are often deeply routinized classroom practices and which are probably part of our professional self-image as teachers" (Myhill et al., 2006, p. 17).

Using questions that enable students to reflect, develop, and extend their thinking

Invite ELLs through questioning techniques that lead the students to negotiate meaning by using their language. Be alert to how we communicate using nonverbal techniques as a part of getting our students to talk (see chapter 5).

Where do we start? By encouraging discourse that avoids closed responses and invites mental process (evaluating, investigating, comparing, etc.). Most of us have experienced a rally in ping-pong or tennis, where keeping the ball in play as long as possible becomes an achievement in itself. To the degree that the interaction is purposeful, we want to foster the same kind of extended give-and-take with our students. We do this by how we talk to students. "The most productive talk requires not only an adult's presence and instructional skills but also an adult's skills in listening and drawing students into more even-handed exchanges. This kind of talk permits a 'negotiation' of meanings, by which is implied openness on the teacher's part" (Corden, 2000, pp. 131–132).

Productive talk involves an exchange of ideas to create understanding. This symbol represents an interchange of ideas, which can occur from teacher to student, teacher to students, student to student, student to teacher, or students to teacher. Throughout this chapter you will see this symbol for those strategies that lend to purposeful talk.

How might we convey to students our openness to ideas beyond "right" answers?

♦ Ask fewer factual questions and more higher-order questions that invite speculation, hypothesis, and analysis.
♦ Ask more questions like *How do you know that?* or *Why do you think that?*

♦ Ask provocative questions that invite disagreement and debate.

♦ Find opportunities to ask genuine questions for which the answer matters because you don't know it already.

♦ Explain what terms such as *speculate*, *reflect*, and *wonder* mean. Then plan times when you speculate or reflect together.

♦ After receiving an answer, ask your students if there were any alternative answers or different ways of considering the question.

♦ When asking a question, remember to stop and listen to the response. Listen to the children's answers before framing the next questions, and adapt your questioning if necessary.

♦ Lengthen the wait time before taking answers.

♦ Create opportunities for children to ask questions.

Source: Myhill et al., 2006, p. 83

We should also consider how student interaction (either with a teacher or other students) might be incorporated into the context of an overall lesson.

Roy Corden (2000) suggests a helpful model:

Initiate: The teacher introduces an issue, stimulates interest, and relates it to current experience.

Delegate: Pupils assume responsibility for their learning both as individuals and as a group.

Explore: Pupils investigate and interrogate.

Appraise: Pupils and teacher reflect on the learning.

Launch: Reflection operates as a launch pad to determine further initiatives (p. 137).

In this model, the teacher's management remains vital (but subtle) throughout, and students are active participants at every step. The delegation and exploration phases of the lesson focus specifically on student talk, but student input will also be an integral part of the appraisal and launching segments. Even the initiation stage is likely to invite interchange since it may well include modeling, a discussion of expected outcomes, and student questions and observations. All this oral exchange should take place within an overall framework conceived by the teacher; that structure provides a sense

Getting students talking is much more than just eliciting interaction; we must plan for talking within a structured context. Management remains vital yet subtle.

of design, direction, timing, and closure. In other words, planning for talk is as necessary as planning for content.

Helping students talk in academic settings

Clear purpose and expectations will ensure a productive talking environment to which all students—and in particular ELLs—will contribute.

"Altering the ratio of teacher-to-student talk doesn't just happen. Rather, it occurs through believing in the importance of student talk and planning with a clear purpose and expectations" (Fisher et al., 2008, p. 13). This is as true for our students as for ourselves. We want to encourage not just a good quantity of student talk but the highest possible quality. We can help achieve that goal more quickly if we introduce our students to some ground rules and expectations.

Begin by talking about talk

Although it would feel unnatural to plan a dinner conversation with friends, productive student talk requires preparation. The first step is so obvious that it's easily overlooked: we need to talk about talk. "Children who are expected to work together in a small group need to be taught how to talk to one another. They need direct instruction in the talk skills that will enable them to get the best out of their own thinking and that of all the other members of their group" (Arthur & Cremin, 2010, p. 244).

We need to let our students know that discussion isn't about right answers. We can explore the precepts that ideas are not necessarily right or wrong and that it's important to talk about many different ideas and examine them together, even if we don't always agree about them. Unless we make students understand that their answers are not being judged in a particular class interchange, they are likely to expect that "normal rules of product assessment" remain in effect (Corden, 2000 p. 144). We should explicitly teach speaking and listening skills so that our students have the tools to collaborate effectively. Begin by exploring what students know about talking, and then help them establish ground rules for talk.

Opening questions for class discussion might include the following:

- ♦ "Who thinks they are a talkative person?"
- ♦ "Who thinks they are a quiet person?"
- ♦ "Whom do you like talking to? Why?"

♦ "When are you asked not to talk? Why?"
♦ "Why is it really helpful to be able to talk?"
♦ "What sorts of things can we do by talking together?"

Source: University of Cambridge, 2012

Ask students to respond to statements such as these:

♦ "You are/are not naturally good at talking, and nothing can be done about it."
♦ "It is rude to disagree."
♦ "If you ask questions, it shows that you don't know anything."
♦ "People make fun of you if you let them know what you really think."
♦ "If you share what you know out loud, other people will do better than you."
♦ "Learning to talk and work with other people is important."

Source: University of Cambridge, 2012

Ask students what makes a good talker, a good listener, and a good discussion. Write down their ideas. After several discussions about talking and listening, students will be ready to think about ground rules for talk. These are the underlying concepts you're aiming to promote:

♦ Everyone in the group is encouraged to contribute.
♦ Contributions are treated with respect.
♦ Reasons are asked for.
♦ Everyone is prepared to accept challenges.
♦ Alternatives are discussed before a decision is made.
♦ All relevant information is shared.
♦ The group seeks to reach agreement.

Source: Arthur & Cremin, 2010, p. 245

Younger students might come up with rules like these:

♦ Don't shout.
♦ Don't all talk at the same time.
♦ Listen to each other.
♦ Give everyone a chance to say something.
♦ Help each other out.
♦ Share ideas.

◆ Take people's ideas seriously.
◆ Don't make anyone feel silly.
◆ Everyone should join in.
Source: Corden, 2000, p. 89

Generate a T-chart with your students: What discussion looks like/ sounds like. What listening looks like/sounds like. Every behavior should be modeled and revisited throughout the year.

Be sure to post the ground rules agreed on by students and revisit them prior to and even during group discussions. Ground rules can help our students consider why talking matters, their obligation to participate, and the need to respect collaborators.

Teach students how to talk about academic content

We can't take it for granted that students will know how to keep partner talk or group discussion on topic and purposeful. Like all features of classroom talk, these skills need to be explicitly outlined and practiced. Lauren Resnick and other researchers at the Institute for Learning at the University of Pittsburgh have developed an approach they call "accountable talk." Just as the ground rules for talk establish guidelines for how students should treat each other when talking together, accountable talk puts rules in place for how students should deal with the content they're going to talk about. The guiding principle is to make students accountable both to each other and to their learning (Fisher & Frey, 2007).

The basic guidelines are simple:

◆ Keep talk focused on the discussion topic.
◆ Be sure the facts or ideas introduced are accurate and pertinent to the topic.
◆ Give thoughtful attention to what other students say.
Source: Fisher & Frey, 2007

Furthermore, students can be taught specific techniques that maintain dialogue and take it to deeper levels of interpretation and meaning. These techniques include the following:

◆ "Press for clarification and explanation: 'Could you describe what you mean?'
◆ "Require justification of proposals and challenges: 'Where did you find that information?'
◆ "Recognize and challenge misconceptions: 'I don't agree because . . .'

♦ "Demand evidence for claims and arguments: 'Can you give me an example?'

♦ "Interpret and use each other's statements: 'David suggested . . .'"

Source: Fisher & Frey, 2007, p.23

These guidelines and techniques can be restated in simplified language for younger students. Like the other talking rules we've discussed, they need to remain visible to students and be employed regularly as a yardstick against which students can measure their own talk.

Accountable talk illustrates how rigorous talking can advance thinking. This is the kind of talk that "moves the conversation from task-oriented to concept-oriented learning [as] students ask one another about their thinking and build on the responses of others" (Fisher et al., 2008, p. 16).

Our ELLs will need to hear and experience multiple models of accountable talk in different settings in order to build a repertoire of these language patterns.

Familiarize students with appropriate sentence starters

Douglas Fisher, Nancy Frey, and Carol Rothenberg (2008) recommend the use of "sentence starters" to help students frame their talk in academic terms. Such opening phrases might include

♦ "The first step is . . ."
♦ "Next . . ."
♦ "Who? What? When? Where? Why?"
♦ "What do you think?"
♦ "This is important because . . ."
♦ "I agree with this because . . ."
♦ "The factors that are most important are . . ."

Source: Fisher et al., pp. 14–15

Sentence starters should address the widest possible range of cognitive skills (questioning, describing, hypothesizing, etc.). They offer students a way of framing their comments in academic language and illustrate word choices appropriate for various tasks (explaining, evaluating, instructing, questioning, etc.) (Fisher et al., p. 16). There are many possible language objectives and sentence starters; a good class exercise is to continuously enlarge the options given on this poster. Like the ground rules for talking, this kind of reference can be useful to students on an ongoing basis, especially if we bring it to their attention prior to and during discussions.

Sentence starters are one of the principles of bridging for language (discussed in chapter 6). Develop sentence stems for how to engage in academic talk in any of your content areas. This technique will provide the bridge for ELLs so they can move from oral language to academic language proficiency.

Recognize the value of exploratory or "process" talk

The purpose of dialogue is to "allow participants to create new meanings and new understandings, rather than simply reproduc[e] previously constructed understanding." Dialogue is a "process of constructing knowledge together" (Myhill et al., 2006, p. 168). We need to keep the concept of process in mind in order to fully appreciate the role of exploratory talk. "Exploratory or process talk is not for an external audience but is more concerned with working things out. Such talk is unrehearsed, untidy, and characterized by false starts, repetition, backtracking, pauses, overlaps, and interruptions" (Corden, 2000, p. 25). Exploratory talk tends to capture thinking in the act of developing an idea, as illustrated in this dialogue between second-grade students who are talking about how ants communicate:

> **Kristina:** "Well, I know they touch."
>
> **Roberto:** "But how do you know? You can't just say 'you know.'" [requesting evidence]
>
> **Kristina:** "'Cause I seen them wave their . . . their. . . . What are those pointers on their heads?"
>
> **Ting:** "Right here (points to diagram). Antennae." [offering evidence]
>
> **Alejandra:** "We're s'posed to use that word. Ms. Hirano wrote it on the board—*antennae*. They touch their antennae to see each other." [using ideas from others]
>
> **Ting:** "Do they have eyes on their antennae? Show me?" [requesting evidence]
>
> **Alejandra** (examining diagram closely): "I don't see eyes."
>
> **Roberto:** "The eyes is here" (points to label that reads 'eyes'). [giving evidence]
>
> **Kristina:** "Oh yeah, that's right! They can see. They use their eyes to see." [using ideas from others]
>
> **Ting:** "Look how teeny they are. They must not see a lot of stuff."
>
> Source: Fisher et al., 2008, pp. 99–100

It's clear that these students have had some experience with accountable talk and working together. Their conversation is on task and progresses steadily toward reasoned conclusions. The students have worked certain questions out for themselves and have thus met their own learning needs. This kind of talk may be "hesitant and incomplete, [but] it enables the speaker to try out new ideas, to hear how they sound, to see what others make of them, [and] to arrange information and ideas into different patterns" (Barnes, 1976, p. 126).

Process talk or thinking talk won't have the polish of presentational talk; take care not to devalue it on that account. Barnes (1976) differentiates between process and presentational talk in terms of whom it serves. Presentational talk is carefully prepared and practiced and can therefore give the impression that the speaker is fully in command of the content. But a smooth presentation may represent little more than good memory work that can quickly fade without having produced real learning. In contrast, process talk is concerned with coming into command, and, if engaged in until useful conclusions are reached, helps to construct understanding. Presentation talk may satisfy teachers, but process talk does far more to meet the needs of learners.

According to Corden (2000), "Successful group work in most literary activities is characterized by talk which is tentative and explorative. Interaction is dynamic and unpredictable, as children appear to go off at a tangent, leap ahead, or backtrack" (p. 91). As teachers, we need to learn not to be wary of the unpredictable nature of this kind of discussion. We can always refocus students' attention if necessary, but we can also remember that our goal is not necessarily to arrive at a foregone conclusion but rather to relish the learning possibilities of open-ended thinking.

Establish student partnerships across the day in all content areas

Talk can be more readily facilitated and managed by having students participate in partnerships that can be called into action throughout instruction. These partnerships should be prearranged by the teacher, giving consideration to students' learning styles, language proficiency, and academic development. If the classroom seating structure allows, partner combinations should differ for various content areas (see Figures 7.2, 7.3, and 7.4).

Maintaining partnerships for at least nine weeks will allow students to establish a working relationship over time. On the other hand, periodic changes of student combinations (at least every three months) can enliven partner work and initiate new learning.

Keep process—not polish—in mind when helping ELLs negotiate their new language. Students will "use but confuse" grammatical structures and proper usage while gaining command of a new language.

In certain situations, you may want to recast or respond to the student's message by restating a correct version rather than focusing on student error. Always keep your purpose in mind when deciding whether to intervene in talking situations.

FIGURE 7.2:
Student Partnerships

Peanut Butter and Jelly Partners

Briana	Kameron	
Miriam	Samahja	
Karina	Ethan	
Juan	Airy	
Robbie	Kamelah	Jordan
Abigail	Felix	
Joshua	Elijah	
Holly	Haley	

You will need to gauge a student's proficiency in and ease with language when placing him or her in group situations. Some students may need a supportive partner in group situations.

For some purposes, you may wish to have students talk in small groups (generally no larger than five). The kind of talk generated by pairs of students versus groups of students is often slightly different. Pairs tend to create a more private talk environment in which students may feel freer to talk. "Pairs seem to be more conducive to cooperation and collaboration, while groups tend to be more conducive to (friendly) disagreement and discussion. . . . In a larger group, there may be more ideas flowing, more different opinions, and a more lively discussion, though . . . some students will participate less because they are less confident or have less to say" (Jones, 2007).

WRITING PARTNERS	
Dakota	Levi
Karol	Tybloshie'
Kiera	Blanca
Adolfo	Jansen
Kayla	Jeremiah
Temekiea	Cherry
Farrah	Luz
Ms.	Jorden
Jaylan	Trenton
Shania	Todeshia

FIGURE 7.3:
Writing Partners

When more students come together to talk, each of them will have less opportunity to speak. Partners can each talk for half the time, more or less, while students in a group of four have about 25 percent of the time to talk. However, exposure to a broader range of speaking styles, ideas, and interactions has its own advantages. Partner and group talk can greatly enlarge students' opportunities to voice their own thoughts and respond to fellow learners. This is important for all students, but it has particular benefits for English language learners: "repetition of key words and phrases; functional, context-relevant speech; rich feedback; and reduced student anxiety" (Hill & Flynn, 2006, p. 56).

In many cultures, children interact and learn in peer situations. An adult may be viewed as a sign of authority, and students may be reticent to speak or look directly at the speaker. Be alert to cultural norms of behavior in your student population.

FIGURE 7.4:
Reading Partners

Let's Read!

Elephant Peanut Partners!

Manuel	Mayci
Kevin	Dylan
Alex	Adriana
Sabia	Syheede
Alexandra	Robert
Jakayla	Matthew
Samiah	Jermone
Ashton	Shaniya
Lana	Oscar

"READING IS FUN!!"

Does your classroom arrangement promote or inhibit interaction?

Arrange your classroom to promote interaction

Students can't easily see each other when their desks are arranged in rows. Talking to the back of someone's head or trying to hear someone talking across a room inhibits the natural flow of conversation. If your students sit at desks, arrange the desks in clusters so they can easily see and hear each other. Tables bring students together in a group naturally. Such an arrangement makes it easy to assign face partners (students sitting directly across from each other) or elbow partners (students sitting beside each other). It's also helpful to designate areas where small or large groups can gather. Make sure students know where you expect them to be when you call them to these areas so that they can move and settle as quickly as possible.

Help students manage noise levels and time deadlines

Student talk can sometimes generate enough noise to threaten concentration or disrupt neighboring classrooms, but it's not difficult to help students maintain a speaking volume appropriate to particular activities. Fisher et al. (2008) approach this issue by introducing vocabulary words that describe a range of sound: "*silent*, *quiet*, *moderate*, *elevated*, and *outdoor voice*" (p. 19). They help students understand the meaning of these terms and discuss which level of noise is appropriate for activities such as independent reading, partner talk, group talk, and so on. They also afford practice implementing different noise levels in class exercises. For example, the class might be asked to be silent for thirty seconds or to speak in a moderate tone for another period of time. With younger students, they sing a song, giving each line a different volume level, all the way down to a whisper. A noise meter can be useful in alerting students to the desired sound level at any given time. Such a meter can be very simply made of cardboard, with a movable arrow (like a hand on a clock) that can point to "silent," "moderate," and so on. If the noise meter is referred to consistently when undertaking different activities, students quickly become accustomed to monitoring their voices (Fisher et al., 2008, pp. 19–20.)

We very often direct students to talk with partners or work in a group for a specified amount of time. Simply announcing that time is up may terminate the talk, but it doesn't give students the opportunity to manage their discussion to allow time to reach a conclusion or complete the assignment. We can maximize the usefulness of talk time—and encourage students to take responsibility for how they use the time—by providing them with a countdown. This can be done through displaying a timer on an overhead projector or simply by writing numbers on a board that indicate time intervals, crossing them off as time passes. If you've given students 10 minutes to talk with a partner, you might write the numbers 7, 5, 3, and 1 on the board, crossing each one off as that interval passes (Fisher et al., 2008, p. 20). It's important to help students consider how to work within time intervals. What should they hope

Develop a variety of techniques that alert your students for monitoring noise levels and managing time intervals.

to have accomplished halfway through the appointed time? If they need to be prepared to share an idea at the conclusion of partner-talk time, how much time do they need to agree on that conclusion? Perhaps one-quarter of the assigned time? More? Less? As with other management skills, students will become self-governing in this arena when the concepts have been thoroughly reviewed and practiced several times.

We've talked a lot about student talk; now let's hear it in action as students and teachers work together in class.

Recognizing and capitalizing on opportunities to promote student talk

We're going to visit two classrooms. Both teachers are delivering the same lesson, but only one of them has asked students to work with a partner to accomplish the work.

Context of the lesson: As part of a word-study lesson, students are discovering how affixes (prefixes and suffixes) can work by learning how to deconstruct a word and then use this information to create meaningful sentences. This is not their first introduction to these words.

TEACHER E

Teacher E: "As you work with your elbow partner, I want you to discuss the meaning of the prefixes, suffixes, and base words as you sort them into three categories." (Teacher E walks throughout the room, checking in with groups, listening in on their discussions, and probing for clarification when needed.)

The expectation for focused student talk offers opportunities for the teacher to bridge for language when needed.

Teacher E: "I'm noticing by listening to you talk that many of you grasped our earlier discussion about how each of these word parts has some meaning, even if they aren't words by themselves. Let's name a few of these meanings together. I'm going to hold up one of the affixes, and I want you to quickly turn to your elbow buddy and share its meaning." (She goes over several examples.)

What are the many ways that the teacher can check for student understanding that have already been evidenced in this lesson?

Teacher E: "Remember that when you add a suffix to a base word it will often change its spelling, pronunciation, or meaning. Let me show you how to use this knowledge to understand words." (Teacher E builds the word *encouragement* with her word cards using a document camera to display and model for the students).

"I first think about my base word, *courage*," (pulling it apart from *en–* and *–ment*), "which means 'brave.'" The prefix *en–* means 'in or make,' so *encourage* means to make someone brave. When I add the suffix *–ment*, it means the *action* of encouraging, so I am trying to make someone feel brave when I offer them encouragement. An example of encouragement might be when I cheered on my son during a basketball game. Now I want you to build one of our words and take it apart just as I did, and discuss the meaning of the word parts with your elbow buddy." (Teacher E asks the group to deconstruct a couple more words with their partners as she moves throughout the room listening, probing, clarifying, and eliciting student talk among partners.)

Why would it be beneficial to work with one specific partner throughout the lesson instead of working with someone of the student's own choosing at the table?

Teacher E: "Before you record some meaningful sentences in your word-study notebooks, I want you to practice generating some sentences with your elbow buddy. Use what you've learned about these word parts to generate a rich, meaningful sentence. Let's try a few together."

(Students share sentences with one another. Teacher E records several different sentences from groups on the board.)

At the conclusion of the lesson, students work independently in their notebooks to deconstruct two different words and write meaningful sentences.

How does this teacher encourage interdependence as well as independent accountability?

Meanwhile, Teacher X is working with students next door:

Teacher X: "Let's begin by sorting your word parts into base words, prefixes, and suffixes. Think about the meaning of all of these word parts as you are sorting." (Teacher X walks throughout the room, checking in with individual students and clarifying misunderstanding of the task when necessary.)

How does the teacher know if students really understand the meaning of these word parts unless there is opportunity for student talk?

Teacher X: "Many of you are figuring out the difference between the prefixes and suffixes. What does *–im* mean?"

Student: "Not or in."

Teacher X: "That's right. What about . . ." (Teacher X asks individual students for a few more examples).

When a teacher asks for individual responses, how can he or she know if other students are grasping the concept?

Teacher X: "Remember that when you add a suffix to a base word, it will often change the spelling, pronunciation, or meaning. Let me show how to use this knowledge to understand words." (Teacher X builds *encouragement* with her word cards, using a document camera to display and model for the students).

Teacher X: "I first think about my base word, *courage*," (pulls it apart), "which means 'brave.' The prefix *en–* means 'in or make,' so *encourage* means to make someone brave. When I add the suffix *–ment*, it means the *action* of encouraging, so I am trying to make someone feel brave when I offer them encouragement. An example of encouragement might be when I cheered on my son during a basketball game. Who wants to come up to the doc camera and build one of our words and take it apart for the class?"

(A few students come up one at a time, and Teacher X helps each student through the process. Each student explains the meaningful parts to the group with the support of the teacher.)

What actions of the teacher either maximize or minimize student engagement?

Teacher X: "Before you record some meaningful sentences in your word-study notebooks, I want you to practice generating some sentences with someone at your table. Use what you have learned about these word parts to generate a rich, meaningful sentence. Let's try a few together."

(Students share sentences with one another. Teacher X records several sentences from different groups on the board.)

If students are asked to work together on an inconsistent basis, how will that affect student talk?

At the conclusion of the lesson, students work independently in their notebooks to deconstruct two different words and write meaningful sentences.

How do these lesson vignettes enlarge the concept of student talk in the classroom and its importance?

Both teachers elicit student talk, yet the result is quite different. Teacher E recognizes and capitalizes on opportunities to promote student talk for *all* students at the same time in peer-to-peer situations. She maximizes group interaction and minimizes individual student-to-teacher exchange unless students are expected to interact with other students at the same time.

Teacher X asks individual students to talk while others observe the teacher-student exchange. She spends more time interacting with a few individual students, who get an opportunity to talk in front of the class, while there are minimal opportunities for students to have academic-focused talk in peer situations.

The language exchange in a classroom should be balanced in regard to teacher-to-student(s), and student-to-student(s) interactions. All students, particularly ELLs, need time to negotiate the language with their peers in low-anxiety environments. They will mimic what they hear, grasping new language structures and concepts through multiple opportunities for repetition and rehearsal.

The teacher plays a vital role in achieving a low-anxiety, rich verbal environment. Teacher E sees her role as a *facilitator* of language interaction in the classroom. Several opportunities for peer interaction took place throughout Teacher E's lesson. On the other hand, Teacher X sees her role as *commander* of language interaction in the classroom. All of the student talk was filtered through the teacher and evaluated accordingly. There were few opportunities for students to interact with one another. If you were an ELL student learning a new language, which classroom would support your language development? In which environment are learners in an active rather than passive role?

If thinking matters, then talk has to matter

We've seen that talking and thinking go hand in hand. Extending talk tends to extend thinking. It seems unavoidable then to conclude that "we have to take on board the collaborative nature of meaning-making and the oral exploration of ideas" (Arthur & Cremin, 2010, p. 242). "Talk in the classroom is crucial to learning. It is where answers to puzzling questions can be found. It is where thoughtful argument and discussion make way for the understanding of new skills and difficult concepts. . . . It is where children listen to and respect the views of each other, and where everyone's learning is empowered by talking about what they have learned." (Smith, as cited in Arthur & Cremin, 2010, p. 248).

How, then, can we *not* make time for student talk?

In Brief

♦ Student talk plays a vital role in learning. It is through talking that our thinking reveals understanding. Talking allows us to process information, make sense of our thoughts, and represent new ideas.

♦ Learning takes place largely through social interaction, especially when assistance from a more knowledgeable "other"—adult or peer—enables a child to exceed his or her present capacity and embrace new ideas and skills.

♦ We must examine our patterns of discourse to discern whether our students are active or passive, confident or devalued when it comes to their contributions in a learning environment.

♦ Talking, listening, and learning require a shift from a traditional role of delivery that relies on transmission of information to a more facilitative approach that generates and accepts contributions from all involved to create meaning and understanding of ideas.

♦ Questioning techniques initiate and promote student interaction in productive ways.

♦ Clear purpose and expectations will ensure a productive talking environment in which all students—and ELLs in particular—will contribute.

♦ Learning how to engage in academic talk will require multiple models and supports (e.g., the use of sentence stems) for interaction.

♦ Recognize the value of process or exploratory talk as our students—and our ELLs in particular—negotiate a new language by practicing in different contexts as they gain command of new vocabulary and grammatical functions.

♦ Arrange for partnerships and small group interaction to encourage student talk across the day in all content areas. Establish procedures for monitoring noise levels, managing time limits, and maximizing time spent talking.

♦ Student talk matters!

8 Energy for Learning
Flood Instruction with Vocabulary

. . . .

"And the winner is . . ." Many of us hold our breath at this announcement, waiting to hear who will take home an Oscar or become the next American idol. In school, it's easy to predict who the winners will be—they're always the students with strong vocabularies. Students with in-depth word knowledge tend to be good readers, and the reading they do continually enlarges their vocabularies. Vocabulary gives them access to the sophisticated concepts and terminology of academic work, which in turn opens the door to higher education and an expansive future. Here's an equation we don't always learn in school: student + strong vocabulary = reads well with comprehension = academic success. It's an equation as reliable as 2 + 2 = 4. In contrast, students with underdeveloped vocabularies have difficulty reading and are unable to keep pace with increasingly complex academic demands. Their names are unlikely to be in the winner's envelope, at school or in the job market.

The Importance of Vocabulary

Vocabulary is often the greatest obstacle that stands between a student and academic mastery. We've already seen that students who begin school with underdeveloped vocabularies are at a disadvantage, and the gap between word-rich and word-poor students tends to grow over their years in school. We might say that vocabulary is the tuition of education. Without a substantial groundwork of words, students can never really buy into academic disciplines, nor can the educational system realize its intended investment in them.

Closing the vocabulary gap will require a committed effort to flood vocabulary, using multiple methods, throughout the day in all that we do.

Let's consider two examples of vocabulary in action. The first is a snippet of classic dialogue from the movie "The Odd Couple." As you probably recall, Oscar (Walter Matthau) is an easy-going slob with a close circle of poker-playing buddies.

Hosting a poker game at his apartment one day, Oscar offers refreshments to the guys:

Oscar: "Who wants food?"
Murray (his friend, a cop): "What do you got?"
Oscar: I got, uh, brown sandwiches and, uh, green sandwiches. Which one do you want?"
Murray: "What's the green?"
Oscar: "It's either very new cheese or very old meat."
Murray: I'll take the brown" (Simon, 1968).

Brown and green sandwiches may be laugh-out-loud funny in a movie, but they'd make a lousy restaurant menu. On a menu, in school, and in professional arenas, clear, explicit words are required for real communication about objects, concepts, and processes. And the more specialized the content, the more important it is to understand its terminology.

One afternoon I observed my son while he worked with his basketball trainer for half an hour. I wrote down all the basketball vocabulary ("academic terms") used by the coach in that short period of time. Much to my surprise, I collected over fifty terms specific to the sport. Most importantly, I noted that my son's ability to perform on the court directly correlated to how well he understood terms such as *inside pivot*, *reverse pivot*, *jab step*, and many more. When my son didn't understand a prompt from his trainer, he couldn't proceed as the trainer expected. This was a clear illustration of how a grasp of academic or technical vocabulary gives students access to learning at increasingly sophisticated levels.

"Learning, as a language-based activity, is fundamentally and profoundly dependent on vocabulary knowledge" (Simmons & Kame'enui, 1998, p. 183). "Vocabulary knowledge is fundamental to reading comprehension; one cannot understand text without knowing what most of the words mean" (Nagy, 1988, p. 1).

We're not just being told here that vocabulary is a help in learning. It's much bigger than that. "Profoundly dependent" and "fundamental" tell us that learning can't really happen without appropriate vocabulary. Learning starts with vocabulary, is continually enlarged by new and richer vocabulary, and can fail for lack of vocabulary. But since vocabulary makes learning possible (or impossible, to those without it), the emphasis is legitimate. The question is whether we're giving

Word precision is instrumental to communicating effectively.

vocabulary sufficient attention in our moment-by-moment classroom interactions. A number of studies have concluded that we're not.

Most literacy programs include vocabulary as a key component. This approach, however, can isolate vocabulary as a particular content area distinct from other content domains. If we regard vocabulary as a separate subject of study, we tend to teach it for its own sake, as if it were simply one piece of the larger instructional pie. We need to recognize instead that vocabulary is the crust on which the entire pie is constructed. Remember that learning is profoundly dependent on vocabulary and that vocabulary is fundamental to comprehension, as noted above. Therefore, vocabulary has to underlie and infuse every sphere of learning, including every element of literacy— reading, listening, discussing, and writing—as well as every content domain. Vocabulary should be ubiquitous in our instruction, "everywhere at the same time; constantly encountered" (MWCD, 2012).

Vocabulary and comprehension are so closely intertwined, it is difficult to separate the two processes. Language and thinking (meaning) work together to achieve comprehension.

At the 2005 International Reading Association conference, Michael Pressley made an urgent request to all teachers to consider "flooding" vocabulary instruction in everything they teach. It's because vocabulary does so much to stimulate academic success that it's one of our Energizers. V is for vocabulary, and the academic vigor and victory it promotes! Look for this victory symbol throughout this chapter to signal where vocabulary applications and ideas are being discussed.

Knowing a word is more like using a tool than being able to state a fact

Not so long ago, a student who could recite dictionary-style definitions of words might have been considered well-grounded in vocabulary. But knowing a word is much more complex than knowing its definition. In fact, researchers now recognize that word knowledge is not so much declarative (the capacity to declare the meaning of a word) as procedural (the ability to process a word in relation to other knowledge). "In most cases, knowing a word is more like knowing how to use a tool than it is like being able to state a fact. Word knowledge is applied knowledge: a person who knows a word can recognize and use it, in novel contexts, and uses knowledge of the word, in combination with other types of knowledge, to construct a meaning for a text" (Nagy & Scott, as cited in Kamil, Mosenthal, Pearson, & Barr, 2001). Concepts like these have revolutionized the approach to vocabulary instruction. Emphasis has shifted from traditional definition-based learning in which words were often regarded as stand-alone pieces of knowledge. Instead, effective vocabulary programs recognize the complexity of the cognitive processes through which children add words to their vocabulary.

It's helpful to be aware of these significant research findings:

- **Word knowledge is gained incrementally.** A child's initial understanding of a word is often imprecise and incomplete. Words are learned very gradually, with mature knowledge developing through many exposures over a period of years or even over a lifetime.
- **Word knowledge is multidimensional**, consisting of different types of knowledge. Some of these dimensions of knowledge include awareness of a word's verbal and written forms, its meaning, its synonyms and antonyms, how it's used in sentence structure, and how it relates to other words.
- **Many words have multiple meanings**, some of which may be associated (e.g., *The mud* made *the path slippery vs. I* made *money babysitting*), while others have no connection to each other (e.g., a *magazine* may be a storehouse for ammunition or a type of reading material). Furthermore, word meanings in general aren't rigidly fixed but take on nuances from context.
- **Word knowledge is interrelated.** What we know of one word is connected to our knowledge of other words and helps us construct meaning. For example, familiarity with the words *ocean*, *wave*, and *rhythm* can provide useful links in learning the meaning of *tide*.
- **Different words require different kinds of knowing and learning.** Our vocabularies include a wide range of words that are very different from each other in their use, interrelatedness, and level of complexity. Some words are simple function words, like conjunctions or pronouns, while others have diverse and sophisticated meanings. Clearly, knowing a word such as *she* is very different from knowing a word like *cumulonimbus* (Nagy & Scott, as cited in Kamil et al., 2001).

Our instructional approaches should mirror what research tells us about vocabulary learning.

Let's take a moment to translate these findings into the real world. The word *taco*, for example, has the potential to bring a wide range of associations to mind. You might think of the tortilla, beef, lettuce, tomato, and cheese that constitute the taco. Perhaps you would consider other kinds of Mexican food, such as quesadillas, burritos, or chile rellenos. In contrast, the image of a pizza might come to you, and perhaps your mind would wander to Italian cuisine and the time you tried to make veal parmesan from scratch. *Taco* could suggest the larger category of food, which might remind you of grocery shopping or going out to a restaurant. Going even farther afield, you might make associations with concepts that represent Mexico, such as piñatas or bullfighters, or even immigration. No doubt a number of visual images would pass through your thought as various ideas come and go.

This is just a sampling of the myriad mental connections you might make, all in a few moments and without any particular effort. It illustrates that a merely literal definition of *taco* would be inadequate to embrace all the relationships you have to the word. It shows the multidimensional, interrelated nature of word knowledge and how the word *taco* connected you to closely related as well as more remote concepts. If you were a young child, you might know only that you like tacos better than pizza and that you had tacos at a birthday party where you got to hit the piñata, but over time you would form many other connections incrementally.

My description of a taco and the various mental associations it could generate is similar to a word map or semantic map. What gives those techniques impact is that they mirror how children learn words: connections, associations, networks, webs, links, relationships, mental maps—we need to remember to think of word knowledge in these terms. If we do, we'll connect new words to students' background knowledge, chart concept associations through semantic maps and word maps, and build networks of synonyms and antonyms. The more we can tie words together for students, the broader their vocabulary network can become.

We could say that the multifaceted process of learning a new word is somewhat similar to the gradual development of social or professional relationships. For many of us, it can take several introductions over time before we can quickly and confidently address a person by his or her name. The context in which we meet them (church, sports team, office) is likely to

Visual representations such as mind maps, semantic maps, and similar tools greatly enhance vocabulary acquisition. This ties in with keeping the learning comprehensible.

impact how we relate to them, and these contexts may overlap and require that we adapt our interactions appropriately. If we know someone first in a professional capacity and later see him dancing wildly in a bar, this will most likely cause us to stretch and revise our assumptions. If we learn that he's kind to his dog but thoughtless of his grandmother, this will give us further insights into his character. Even after many years of thinking we know someone well, we may still discover new and unexpected details about him.

In the same way, there are different levels of knowing a word. Word recognition develops along a continuum from unknown (a word is completely unfamiliar), to acquainted (a student has some basic understanding of the word), to established (an understanding is firmly grounded and the student understands its use in multiple contexts) (Allen, 1999). No single learning experience or exposure will move students immediately from one level of knowledge to another; rather, students' understanding of a word tends to evolve incrementally through degrees of awareness. Our instruction must focus on moving students along the continuum from introductory encounters with a word to the ability to use it in new ways. Every time students hear or see a word, especially in varying contexts, their awareness of that word should become clearer and firmer until eventually they can hear it, speak it, read it, and write it with ease and accuracy.

Here's another way of detailing the continuum of word knowledge:

♦ Learn a basic oral vocabulary.
♦ Learn to read words already known orally.
♦ Learn new words that express concepts already known.
♦ Learn new words that express unknown concepts.
♦ Learn multiple meanings for words.
♦ Refine and enrich word meanings.
♦ Gain ownership of words not only in listening and reading but also in speaking and writing (Graves, 2006).

A student's level of language proficiency will help us determine an appropriate growth target for building a continuum of word knowledge.

This is a simple but clear outline of basic word-learning tasks, many of which come into play in any lesson in which a range of words is considered. This list illustrates the degrees of word knowledge a student experiences (all at the same time) in building his or her vocabulary. It's also a good reminder of how much multilevel teaching and learning of vocabulary should be going on at any given time.

The assimilation of word knowledge is a gradual, complex, integrated process. It doesn't happen in a single moment of learning, nor will it happen at the same pace for all students. Unlike turning on a light switch and instantly having 100 watts of illumination available, learning a word is more like the coming of dawn, with the light of understanding expanding slowly and subtly over a period of time. Our aim is to create an environment of learning that supports and encourages this steady gain.

Different types of words have different learning demands

There are three general categories of words, each of which makes its own contribution to students' vocabularies and has its own learning challenges.

- **Over-and-over words.** Also known as sight words or function words, the over-and-over words hold ideas together. They are words such as *of*, *have*, *said*, *it*, *is*, *for*, *here*, *my*, and so on. Readers must recognize these words by their appearance rather than by sounding them out or using other decoding strategies. A mere 100 of these words account for 50 percent of the vocabulary in school texts, while 300 words constitute 65 percent of the words appearing in school materials (Graves, 2006, pp. 14–15). We therefore know the basic words our students will encounter in most texts—and we must ensure that our primary school students (especially our ELLs) become thoroughly familiar with them, first orally, and then in reading. Students anchor on these words in the developing stages of reading. These words also help build the "dictionary in the brain" that students will use in writing. These are the basis of oral conversational fluency, which is the beginning of establishing a basic reading and writing vocabulary. These are the words students pick up first as ELLs, as do native speakers.
- **Meaning vocabulary** gives dimension and interest to language and thought, adding nuance, color, and distinction. These words can be very basic (*shoe*, *dinner*,

movie, *shirt*, *bad*, etc.) or less common (*attorney*, *leadership*, *fraternity*, *hospitality*, *irritation*, etc.). Meaning words are vital to listening and reading comprehension. Background knowledge, or schema, is enhanced through building meaning vocabulary because students gain more options for precise and descriptive expression. This type of vocabulary surfaces and needs attention during reading and writing instruction.

◆ **Academic vocabulary.** Unlike everyday conversation, academic language tends to be abstract and complex because it expresses cognitive processes and procedures (*evaluation*, *represent*, *hypothesis*, *assumption*, *validate*, etc.). In addition, content domains (math, science, geography, health, music, etc.) have specialized terminologies related to their distinct fields of knowledge. Academic terms embody the let's-get-down-to-business element of language, naming and describing the work of academic and professional disciplines. Knowledge of these concepts and processes is indispensable to learners performing their job as students, but English language learners can be particularly challenged by these sophisticated terms and meanings. Academic terms and processes need to be explicitly examined, reviewed, and modeled as they arise in relation to specific lessons.

Not all words require the same amount of attention. Consider how you address these three types of vocabulary throughout the day.

How Can We Flood Vocabulary Throughout the Day?

Let's step inside a classroom on a typical day. You will notice the multifaceted ways that vocabulary is addressed through daily literacy events.

Recognizing and capitalizing on opportunities to flood vocabulary

To start the day: Every day, students discuss a vocabulary word for the day. There is a word collector jar where students share interesting words that they have heard or seen. Teacher E will often select a word from the jar, write it on the board, display a meaningful sentence, and then invite a discussion about the word's meaning and connection to their lives. All students record the word, write a definition in their own words, and draw a picture in their word-study notebooks. Teacher E encourages the students to find opportunities to use the word in daily conversation.

This approach develops word consciousness, an important attribute for developing motivation and interest in learning about words.

Shared writing/morning message: At some point during the day, Teacher E writes a message with the students and invites discussion about print conventions, grammar, usage, and word meaning in context. She capitalizes on opportunities to use previously discussed vocabulary in this rich context for review and application. Today's message connected with the math lesson for the day.

> Dear boys and girls,
>
> What mathematical operations will you use today when we solve our word problems? Will you *combine* two or more *addends* together? What will you do if you need to find a *quotient*? You might need to *multiply* to find the *product*. If you are dealing with money and you spend some of it, then you will have to figure out what you have left, or the *difference*.

(As part of this shared writing experience, Teacher E provides additional support for some of the academic terms used by streaming in some short clips from the Internet that further explain the meaning of a quotient, addends, and so on. There are several sites available for math support; www.mathplayground.com has short videos to explain many different math concepts.)

A daily shared message offers opportunities to address academic words in authentic contexts.

Interactive read-aloud: There are always opportunities to discuss word meaning when reading from a rich context offered in read-aloud texts. During a read-aloud, the best opportunity to discuss a word's meaning is during the reading, when the word is mentioned in context. Today's particular lesson focused on the author's use of metaphor and how to identify and interpret the meaning. Teacher E demonstrates how the author uses a rock as a metaphor for how we should confront our problems. She discusses with the students how the author uses the attributes of a rock (still, solid, steady) to make this comparison. Students identify other examples of metaphors and discuss attributes to interpret the comparison.

The read-aloud experience offers rich opportunities to enlarge vocabulary, drawing from meaningful contexts.

Guided reading: During a small group or shared reading of a text in a large group are multiple opportunities to discuss vocabulary—before, during, and after the reading experience. Today's guided reading texts center around the concept of camouflage. Teacher E has selected three different selections from a text gradient that students will read in small groups. As part of preparing students to read the text, Teacher E displays

Direct teaching of specific words before the reading of the text is not only useful but critical to deepening students' understanding of the text.

FIGURE 8.1:
Example of a Word Bank
to Support Writers

Pleasant Feelings	*Difficult/Unpleasant Feelings*
HAPPY joyous lucky fortunate delighted overjoyed gleeful thankful thrilled **LOVE** affectionate devoted passionate admiration warm	**ANGRY** irritated disappointed discouraged annoyed upset frustrated **AFRAID** fearful terrified anxious nervous scared worried frightened timid shaky

several pictures of animals in camouflage and begins to front-load important questions to prepare students for their reading. *Why do animals need to hide from other animals? What do you notice about how animals camouflage themselves in different ways?* She links the concept of camouflage to the game hide-and-seek, a familiar connection for students. As the students discuss each photograph, the teacher writes and discusses the terms: *blend, protect, defense mechanism, predator,* and *prey*; these vocabulary terms will be important for their understanding of the text. During the reading of the text, the students' understanding of these terms will deepen as they read these words embedded in context. Teacher E will create a semantic web with the students, using these terms associated with camouflage so connections are made explicit using a visual representation.

Writing: When students write they will often rely on the vocabulary well-rehearsed and mastered from their speaking vocabulary. In order to break the cycle of "write as you speak," we must provide our learners with new labels for concepts they already know. These tools will allow the writers to be specific when making choices about what words to use in their writing. In today's lesson, students are writing about a time they spent with a pet. Students are asked to use a feeling about their pet as the entry point for their narrative. Teacher E

Anticipating specific vocabulary needed to write in a specific genre and developing word banks with your students will pay huge dividends for enlarging a writer's word choice.

provides a word bank of synonyms associated with common feelings (both positive and negative) (Figure 8.1). Students will keep this chart for future reference.

Word study: Learning about words is a complex process. Students must study the patterns that make up words, how words work in a grammatical context, and the multiple meanings associated with a word. Today's lesson focuses on developing automaticity for the spelling and usage of high-frequency words. Students work in pairs and provide clues for the retrieval of sample words to review from the word wall. Partners practice different raps or musical tunes for spelling the words and then generate meaningful sentences for how to use the word in an appropriate context. Students finish the lesson by recording two different examples of how to use five of their target words in their word-study notebooks. One student wrote

> My mom went *through* my backpack looking for my
> homework.
> I was not *through* reading my book because I had a baseball
> game last night.

How does flooding vocabulary provide a rich context for word learning?

The ability to spell a word does not always equate with understanding how the word is used across multiple contexts. Spelling instruction must be multidimensional, studying a word from multiple angles.

Our students don't acquire new vocabulary by studying words during one part of the day. Vocabulary expansion occurs through multiple exposures using multifaceted approaches. As illustrated in the vignettes above, students interact with language concepts throughout the day. Flooding vocabulary throughout the day using a variety of multifaceted approaches offers the best opportunity to significantly increase the receptive, expressive reading and writing vocabulary of ELLs.

Researchers emphasize several elements that work together to build vocabulary effectively, such as those found in the vignettes above:

- ◆ Providing rich and varied language experiences through
  - Quality teacher vocabulary
  - Reading aloud to students
  - Wide independent reading by students
  - Student discussions on academic topics
  - Writing with a purpose and for an audience

♦ Teaching individual words
♦ Teaching word-learning strategies
♦ Fostering word consciousness
Source: Graves, 2006

The teacher's vocabulary counts

Students listen to you for much of the school day. The vocabulary you use in your classroom can have a powerful impact. For ELLs, predictable routines, gestures, and physical movements; objects and pictures; and hands-on activities help connect words to meaning. When routines are established, use words that stretch students' concepts and introduce academic terms. For example, you might direct younger students to *observe* an activity rather than *watch* it, or ask older students to *articulate* rather than *explain* what an author means in a particular passage. Instead of constantly using the same phrases for classroom routines, find new and imaginative words to communicate your messages or instruction.

Reading aloud to students expands oral vocabulary

In the early primary grades, students tend to read only simple words they already know, so word-learning during these years relies almost entirely on listening and discussion. Many children's books provide engaging stories and wide-ranging vocabulary, which makes them excellent vehicles for exploring words and concepts with students. Repeated readings and explicit explanations are especially useful for ELLs or any students needing more vocabulary support. Reading nonfiction books aloud may offer opportunities to introduce basic academic terms. Michael Graves (2006) calls interactive read-alouds "the most powerful oral language activity that has been developed for use in classrooms." (The interactive read-aloud is mentioned as one of the core components of the literacy framework outlined in chapter 3.)

Wide independent reading is a cornerstone of vocabulary growth

Independent reading can be a vocabulary gold mine. Of the 2,000 to 3,500 words successful students learn every year, only a fraction are gained through explicit instruction; the great majority are learned incidentally, and independent reading delivers the mother lode. Students should read some books just for enjoyment and other books that are more challenging. The more students read, the more their vocabularies grow. The challenge

Our language usage should represent the best model in the classroom. Our students will imitate what they see, hear, and experience.

Interact means "to engage or connect." Keep this in mind during a read-aloud experience; who is doing all the talking?

is to get students to do this reading, both in and out of school. Classroom libraries, parent participation, student book clubs, and teacher encouragement can all make a difference.

Time with text is another core literacy component (also outlined in chapter 3) that promotes wide reading on a daily basis. But books whose topics and settings are culturally unfamiliar to your ELLs may present comprehension issues in independent reading. Helping ELLs to match books to their interests can encourage them to persist in reading.

There is no substitute for spending time with text when it comes to expanding vocabulary.

Teaching individual words promotes deep knowledge of key terms and concepts

Explicit instruction of specific words is important for all students, but it's particularly beneficial for students who don't yet have the comprehension and word-strategy skills to learn words through independent reading (Lehr, Osborn, & Hiebert, n.d.). How can you know which words to teach directly and in depth? As a general guideline, it's a good idea to choose a limited number of words—perhaps three to eight—that are important to understanding your lesson text. (You can give students a brief explanation of any other words in the text that they don't know.) Select words that are useful and occur often in text, such as meaning vocabulary and academic terms. Whole books are written about the explicit instruction of individual words, and this overview can offer only a brief summary of fundamental concepts.

Learning a word is much more than just knowing a definition. Get students motivated to learn new words by involving them in the process.

Here are some very basic guidelines, which can be expanded with other strategies:

♦ Begin with what children already know. Ask students to think about words they know that relate to the key word. Use these words to expand information about familiar concepts. Word maps or semantic maps are some of several effective techniques you can employ to activate prior knowledge and link it to the new learning.

♦ Support the new word with illustrations, graphics, descriptions, and real objects. Have students handle these materials and discuss them.

♦ Involve students in actively processing the word by working with synonyms and antonyms. Synonyms often help students understand a new word in context, while antonyms require them to consider a word's attributes.

- ♦ Have students rewrite definitions in their own words.
- ♦ Ask students to create sentences that use the word. This exercise demonstrates whether students understand the word's meaning. Students can also create non-examples of using the new word appropriately.
- ♦ Discuss the new word in reference to related words. Examining differences and similarities between words helps students focus on shades of word meanings.
- ♦ Be sure students are hearing and using the new word in discussion so they establish familiarity with it.
- ♦ Revisit and review the word to cement understanding. Students need multiple exposures to words over time. This requires not only seeing the word but also reviewing its meaning and using it in discussions or writing. Individual vocabulary logs can be helpful in reminding students of words they've learned.

We need to come at new words from many directions because students need to master many word-learning tasks, and different procedures are needed to address distinct tasks. The National Reading Panel (2000) recognized that no single method of instruction was comprehensive enough for all learning demands. For example, teaching a word students already know is quite different from teaching a new word that expresses an unknown concept. The panel also recognized that students at various skill levels will benefit from different kinds of instruction. Semantic mapping, for example, offers a different kind of learning from creating and discussing sample sentences. On the other hand, you don't need to master an entire catalogue of procedures. You may want to focus on five or six techniques and use them repeatedly. Also, there will be many times when it isn't time-effective to use many procedures, and one or two will be sufficient to communicate to students the knowledge they need for a particular lesson. Still, there are many varieties of charts, mapping, word play, sample sentences, and the like, and adding to your repertoire of these techniques can enliven the work for you and your students.

Word-learning strategies enable students to decipher words on their own

Learning to use context clues is essential for a reader. Context will often supply definitions, examples, or restatements of the word in question. Students should be taught to consider unknown words in the context of surrounding phrases and sentences, letting the encompassing text suggest a meaning for the new word. They can then test the possible meaning in the sentence and consider whether it makes sense or if they need to look again.

Students must also understand how to use word parts to unlock the meaning of words. Instruction in prefixes and suffixes will help students think more strategically when they meet unknown words in running text. Recognizing base and root words gives students meaningful units of language with which they can construct word meanings. According to Nagy and Anderson (1984), "For every word known by a child who is able to apply morphology and context, an additional one to three words should be understandable." Word-learning strategies are beneficial to all students, but they're particularly important to ELLs because these students need to learn such a large number of words.

Through a study of the meaningful units of the English language, we demystify the process and show our students that our language is connected to many other languages.

Fostering word consciousness encourages students to invest in language

"Kindling students' interest and engagement with words is . . . vital" (Graves, 2006, p. 120). Think about kindling. Have you ever tried to start a wood fire without it? Big logs resist catching fire unless they're fed by something smaller and more easily ignited. You might call it motivation, which is exactly what we can offer our students through word consciousness. We can help students become more word conscious by encouraging them to develop a sense of discovery and playfulness about word-learning. Individual students or the entire class might collect examples from their reading of vivid metaphors, compelling descriptions, or any kind of striking word use; these can be posted in the classroom or used as a basis for discussion about the artistry of words. Help your students become intrigued with the impact of rich language in text. You can do this by using individual sentences or an entire story, presenting one version of the text with rich language and a second version with plain language (for example, "The derelict wavered in his walk, making me skeptical of his sobriety" versus "The man staggered and I thought he must be drunk"). You can let students play with rich language to the point of exaggeration or strip sentences of all descriptive elements; the process is fun and encourages awareness of the effect of language. Idioms, clichés, puns, limericks, tongue twisters,

Let words simmer in your environment and spark your students' interest throughout the day.

metaphors, and personification are other elements of language that interest students. The history of language (how particular words or phrases evolved, including the fact that many words came into English from other languages) can be fascinating, too, and may be included as a point of interest in many lessons. When students are interested in words, they learn to understand words and word usage in many dimensions and are receptive to word-learning tasks. Promoting word consciousness can help kindle that interest and keep it burning.

Language: The lifeblood of learning

Academic language and vocabulary are "the lifeblood of learning" and are indispensable to academic progress (Zwiers, 2008, p. xv). Blood is so closely linked with sustaining life that the American Red Cross's telephone number for blood donors is 1-800-GIVE-LIFE. We might adopt the same slogan for our efforts to constantly flood vocabulary throughout all areas of instruction. We could word it this way: Give academic life— "donate" vocabulary frequently.

• • • • • • • • • • • • • • • •

In Brief
- ◆ Learning starts with vocabulary, is continually enlarged by new and richer vocabulary, and can fail for lack of vocabulary.
- ◆ Vocabulary should underlie and infuse every sphere of learning, including every element of literacy (reading, listening, discussing, and writing) and every content domain.
- ◆ Knowing a word is much more than just knowing a definition. The assimilation of word knowledge is a gradual, complex, integrated process.
- ◆ Different types of words have different learning demands. The range consists of the basic words students need for carrying on conversations and participating in early reading and writing experiences to meaning-based vocabulary that expands and enlarges a student's ability to read and comprehend at more sophisticated levels. Of particular challenge to ELLs is academic vocabulary, which tends to be abstract and complex because it expresses cognitive processes and procedures.
- ◆ Flooding vocabulary throughout the day using a variety of multifaceted approaches offers the best opportunity to signifi-

cantly increase the receptive, expressive, reading, and writing vocabulary of ELLs. These approaches include:

- Making sure that our language usage always represents the best model in the classroom. Our own vocabulary counts.
- Reading aloud to your students from a wide range of genres as much as possible.
- Wide independent reading by students, which is a cornerstone of vocabulary growth.
- Teaching individual words to promote deep knowledge of key terms and concepts.
- Teaching word-learning strategies
- Promoting word consciousness so students develop a curiosity and desire to learn new words.

◆ Closing the vocabulary gap will require a committed effort to flood vocabulary, using multiple methods, throughout the day in all that we do.

9 Energizers at Work
Transforming Teaching and Learning

Are you energized? Do you believe that you have the tools, both from a mental and strategic perspective, to reach and teach *all* of your students? Our convictions, attitudes, and expectations combined with how we shape our connections to our ELLs will transform and set into motion the energy of learning.

Julie, a teacher from Michigan, speaks of the transformation taking place in her classroom: "The Energizers have taken my teaching to a whole new level. Throughout the day—during language arts as well as content area activities, I am constantly thinking about what I need to do to make sure that my ELLs are engaged in quality instruction—using visuals, frontloading concepts, having the students turn and talk, and the like."

What teachers say about the effects of Energizers on student learning

Becky is another empowered teacher who has found ways to put new ideas into action with purpose and conviction. She comments, "Overall, the Energizers have had a huge impact on the way I plan and teach lessons in my classroom. They keep me on my toes; they have me constantly asking myself, 'Is this the best way to provide instruction to *all* of my students?' My lessons now have a clear concept, my students are able to have focused conversations, I am teaching vocabulary, and I'm always differentiating—bridging—student learning. The Energizers help me look at my lessons to ensure there is a reason they are being taught. They are not just cute or fun; my students now get an explicit point from my lessons."

"Twelve of my twenty-six students speak English as their second language and do not speak English at home. Using the vocabulary Energizer has really opened my eyes. Looking ahead into a lesson to foresee what vocabulary will need an action hook and having different ways for my students to interact with those important words has helped me lead them into comprehension. The other big Energizer for my ELLs is bridging for their learning and language. In much the same way, I am more prepared to demonstrate, paraphrase, and clarify concepts for these students, which leads to a lot less blank stares from them. They can participate with a bit of confidence—and contribute to class discussion and partner learning. All my students are now engaged in learning. They are talking more, using complete sentences, and having better quality conversations with each other."

These responses from teachers who have put the Energizers into action illustrate the power of expectation coupled with strategic implementation that gets results and puts into motion the language-meaning-learning cycle. These teacher reflections provide a snapshot of the possibilities for teaching and learning that result from energized instruction.

The Energizers revisited

Let's revisit the key principles once again. The first two Energizers are critical components of our commitment as educators. They sustain us under the continual demands of teaching.

Energizer 1: Cultivate connections.
♦   Connect to kids.
♦   Connect to colleagues.
♦   Connect to cultures.
Energizer 2: Elevate your expectations.

The next four Energizers are strategic in nature and explore ways to initiate, promote, and extend students' understanding. When used effectively, they work together to promote and sustain a rich, differentiated context for learning.

Energizer 3: Keep instruction comprehensible.

Energizer 4: Build bridges for language and learning.

Energizer 5: Get students talking.

Energizer 6: Flood instruction with vocabulary.

Strategic Energizers work together, not in isolation

The preceding chapters have provided a comprehensive view of each Energizer, the supporting research, and specifics of how to implement it effectively. The purpose for addressing each Energizer in its own chapter was to ensure a healthy grasp of each concept. However, the strategic Energizers work optimally when integrated, as each supports the others. For example, in order to effectively get students talking, teachers often bridge for language by offering the necessary academic language needed to converse in any content area. In order to flood vocabulary across the day, teachers will utilize a variety of comprehensible input techniques such as visuals and gesturing, to keep the concepts (vocabulary) accessible. Bridging for learning involves the teacher in active demonstration utilizing comprehensible techniques such as nonverbal communication, supplementary materials, and visuals. In addition, while bridging for learning, teachers will provide structured and guided practice opportunities across a lesson, which often involves getting students talking. The hurricane lesson in chapter 3 is an excellent example of all four strategic Energizers working in concert with one another. Many teachers have found the Planning Guide for the Energizers template very helpful (available as a download), particularly when the Energizers are first being implemented.

Energized Instruction = Differentiation

If differentiation crossed your mind as you read about the Energizers, you are right on track. Differentiation occurs as a result of responding to individual students' readiness, interests, and learning styles. The Energizers work toward that goal by ensuring that ELL students can grasp meaning by using a variety of comprehensible input techniques that recognize students' learning preferences and readiness for the content.

Another key principle of differentiation is recognizing the need to modify the content, process, or product in any learning event. Bridging for both language and learning is built on the premise that students process language and content in different ways and need mediated strategies in order to be successful. The use of supplementary material—or comprehensible input—provides mediation of the content. Student talk helps students process ideas and bring clarity through the use of different grouping structures (small groups and partnerships, for example).

When asked, "How do you differentiate your instruction?" you can respond with assurance that you are differentiating for your learners by putting the Energizers into action. The energy of learning will set into motion a classroom full of confident, capable learners.

Opening the Doors to Literacy and Welcoming All Students

Developing a command of a new language for both listening and speaking is a lofty goal. Yet the attainment of reading and writing proficiency in a new language is the full spectrum of literacy development that we, as educators, want every student to attain over the course of their schooling. The definition of what it means to be fully literate continues to evolve and reflects our changing societal requirements. Yet while the demands of our informational society are continually restyled, there will always exist the need to communicate, understand, and be understood through the processes of listening, speaking, reading, and writing. The literacy framework outlined in chapter 3 welcomes every student to enter the doors of literacy through a multi-method approach representative of quality components. Let's revisit the key concepts of this framework:

Every day, students develop literate behaviors by

♦ Engaging in comprehension through quality reading experiences
  • These include opportunities to interact with their peers and a teacher through an **interactive read-aloud** experience. Additionally, students need opportunities to think about and navigate text through the explicit instructional guidance offered by **guided comprehension** lessons.
♦ Engaging in real reading experiences
  • Our students need multiple, extended opportunities to spend **time with text,** reading independently at individual reading levels.

- ♦ Engaging as writers practicing the art of communicating ideas through written application
  - Students will need many opportunities to observe the **writing process** in action through explicit demonstration by the teacher and to interact through **guided practice** opportunities in authentic situations.
- ♦ Engaging in the active study of words
  - These word-study experiences provide students with an in-depth understanding of the **phonology** (aural), **orthography** (visual), and **morphology** (semantic) characteristics of words in the English language.
  - A variety of multisensory methods allow students to grasp the **phonics** and **spelling** knowledge necessary to read and write with fluency and understanding.

When students are engaged, they are connected. We don't want our students sitting on the sidelines watching how to do something from afar. The Energizers help teacher *and* students stay connected throughout any literacy event. It is not enough to teach our students; we must reach them. A powerful literacy framework coupled with energized instruction will help us reach all our students.

An upcoming companion book will provide an in-depth discussion of each component of the literacy framework, with specific strategies for implementation. Included in the text will be classroom vignettes of how the Energizers are integrated in each literacy component.

Taking Action

You may be asking yourself: *Where do I begin?* I am often asked this question after teachers have been involved in a professional learning experience such as a book study, training, collaborative inquiry, or indeed any event that promotes reflection.

Here are five ideas to consider as you ponder your next steps:

1. Identify your powerful conceptions and challenge yourself to act on them.
   - How do you show respect for children and their diversity?
   - How can you provide a safe environment in which all children will feel supported?
   - Do you hold high expectations of all children's ability to learn *and* have confidence in your own ability to teach to those high expectations?
   - How will you adapt and change to meet student needs?
   - What is reflective teaching? How will you respond to the challenges inherent in this profession?

2. Connect to your students on a variety of levels.
   - What can you find out about each child, and how can you use that information to promote cultural connections in the classroom?
   - How will you go about identifying each student's strengths, learning styles, and preferences?
   - Can you be alert and attentive enough to respond to those teachable moments?

3. Identify the strengths in your teaching style, and tap those talents for integrating the Energizers. (Use the Planning for Energizers guide to help you identify the strengths.)
   - Are you comfortable utilizing a variety of visuals and/or supplementary materials to support your instruction?
   - Are there structures you have used in the past that will help promote student talk throughout instruction?
   - Do you have a variety of methods for addressing vocabulary that you can bring to your instruction across the day?
   - Does thinking aloud or demonstration come naturally to you?

4. Seek out colleagues with whom to build collaborative discussions about teaching and student learning.
   - How can these collaborative discussions sustain you and help you grow professionally?
   - Do you see yourself as someone who can learn from and/or share with others?

5. Identify and set goals for stretching yourself professionally.
   - What particular Energizer intrigues you or stretches you beyond your comfort zone?
   - Can you remain committed to trying something new when you don't feel successful in your first few attempts?
   - What are ways to evaluate your progress? (For example, evidence of student learning, feedback from professional colleagues, feedback from parents, etc.)

References

Aaronsohn, E. (2000). Controversial literacy: A conversation with Sonia Nieto. *The Dragon Lode, 18*(2). (Spring.) Available at http://clrsig.org/dragon_lode_past.php#18_2

Alexander, R. J. (2004). *Towards dialogic teaching: Rethinking classroom talk.* Albuquerque, NM: Dialogos.

Allen, J. (1999). *Words, words, words: Teaching vocabulary in grades 4–12.* York, ME: Stenhouse.

Anderson, R. C., Hiebert, E., Scott, J., & Wilkinson, I. (1985). *Becoming a nation of readers: The report of the commission on reading.* Washington, DC: National Institute of Education.

Arndt, H., & Pesch, H. (1984). Nonverbal communication and visual teaching aids: A perceptual approach. *Modern Language Journal, 68*, 28–36.

Arrasmith, D. (n.d.). White paper: "The explicit and systematic method." Retrieved September 20, 2011, from http://www.studydog.com/SDsystematic.asp

Arthur, J., & Cremin, T. (2010). "Learning through dialogue." In *Learning to teach in the primary school* (2nd ed.). Washington, DC: Taylor & Francis.

August, D., & Shanahan, T. (2006). *Developing literacy in second-language learners: Report of the National Literacy Panel on Language Minority Children and Youth.* Mahwah, NJ: Lawrence Erlbaum.

Banks, J. A. (2006). *Race, culture, and education: The selected works of James A. Banks.* New York: Routledge.

Banks, J. A., & McGee Banks, C. A. (2010). "Culture in society and in educational practices." In *Multicultural education: Issues and perspectives* (5th ed.). Hoboken, NJ: John Wiley & Sons.

Banks, J. A., & Tucker, M. (1998). The Impact of Multicultural Education. Interview of James Banks by Michelle Tucker. Retrieved September 20, 2011, from http://theimpactofmulticulturaleducatio.weebly.com/true-multicultural-education.html

Barnes, D. R. (1976). *From communication to curriculum.* New York: Penguin Education.

Biber, B., & Snyder, A. (1948). *How do we know a good teacher?* New York: Bank Street College of Education. Available at http://www.bnkst.edu/archives/bank-street-thinkers/good-teacher/

Bierce, A. (1905). *Write it right: A little blacklist of literary faults.* Project Gutenberg Ebook (2004). Retrieved October 4, 2011, from http://www.gutenberg.org/files/12474/12474-h/12474-h.htm

Banks, J. A., Au, K. H., Nasir, N. S., Zhou, M., Ball, A. F., Bell, P., Gordon, E. W., Gutiérrez, K. D., Heath, S. B., Lee, C. L., Lee, Y., Mahiri, J., Valdés, G., Zhou, M. (2007). *Learning in and out of school in diverse environments.* Seattle: Center for Multicultural Education, University of Washington.

Block, P. (1987). *The empowered manager: Positive political skills at work.* San Francisco: Jossey-Bass.

Bondy, E., & Ross, D. D. (2008). The teacher as warm demander. *Educational Leadership, 66*(1), 54–58.

Bowman, B. T. (1994). Cultural diversity and academic achievement. Retrieved September 20, 2011, from www.ncrel.org/sdrs/areas/issues/educatrs/leadrshp/le0bow.htm

Brown University. The Education Alliance. (2006). Teaching diverse learners: Initial assessment of language, literacy, and content knowledge. Retrieved September 17, 2011, from http://www.alliance.brown.edu/tdl/assessment/initassess.shtml

Bruner, J. S. (1983). *Child's talk: Learning to use language*. New York: W.W. Norton.

Bruner, J. S. (1996). *The culture of education*. Cambridge, MA: Harvard University Press.

Campbell, D. (2006). The new majority. Retrieved September 17, 2011, from http://education.com/print/new-majority

Capps, R., Fix, M., Murray, J., Ost, J., Passel, J. S., & Herwantoro, S. (2005). *The new demography and American schools: Immigration and the No Child Left Behind Act*. Washington, DC: The Urban Institute. Retrieved January 27, 2012, from http://www.urban.org/publications/311230.html

Carlo, M. N., August, D., McLaughlin, B., Snow, C. E., Dressler, C., Lippman, D. N., Lively, T. J., & White, C. E. (2004). Closing the gap: Addressing the vocabulary needs of English language learners in bilingual and mainstream classrooms. *Reading Research Quarterly*, *39*(2), 188–215.

Cazden, C. B. (2001). *Classroom discourse: the language of teaching and learning* (2nd ed.). Portsmouth, NH: Heinemann.

Cech, S. J. (2009, January 8). Weigh proficiency, assess content. *Education Week*. Retrieved September 17, 2011, from http://www.edweek.org/ew/articles/2009/01/08/17test.h28.html

CivilRights.org. (2009, January 7). Annual *Quality Counts* education report highlights English language learners. Press release (for *Education Week* report: *Portrait of a population: How English language learners are putting schools to the test*). Retrieved January 29, 2012, from http://www.civilrights.org/archives/2009/01/005-quality-counts.htm

Clark, K. F., & Graves, M. F. (2005). Scaffolding students' comprehension of text. *The Reading Teacher*, *58*(6), 571.

Clark, W. A. V. (1999). Immigration and California communities. Washington, DC: Center for Immigration Studies. Retrieved September 17, 2011, from http://www.cis.org/print/CaliforniaImmigrantCommunities

Clements, A. (2004). Andrew Clements interview transcript. Retrieved October 4, 2011, from http://www2.scholastic.com/browse/collateral.jsp?id=10562_type=Contributor_typeId=2883

Cole, A. D. (2004). *When reading begins: The teacher's role in decoding, comprehension, and fluency*. Portsmouth, NH: Heinemann.

Corden, R. (2000). *Literacy and learning through talk: Strategies for the primary classroom*. Buckingham, UK: Open University.

Crochunis, T., Erdey, S., & Swedlow, J., eds. (2002). *The diversity kit: An introductory resource for social change in education. Part I: Human development*. Providence, RI: The Education Alliance at Brown University. Retrieved September 20, 2011, from www.alliance.brown.edu/tdl/diversitykitpdfs/diversitykit.pdf

Cummins, J. (1996). *Negotiating identities: Education for empowerment in a diverse society*. Ontario, CA: California Association For Bilingual Education.

Cunningham, A., & Stanovich, K. (1991). Tracking the unique effects of print exposure in children: Associations with vocabulary, general knowledge, and spelling. *Journal of Educational Psychology*, *83*, 264–274.

Cunningham, P. M., Cunningham, J. W., Moore, S., & Moore, D. W. (2004). *Reading and writing in elementary classrooms: Research-based K–4 instruction* (5th ed.). Needham Heights, MA: Allyn and Bacon.

Damen, L. (1987). *Culture Learning: The fifth dimension on the language classroom.* Reading, MA: Addison-Wesley. At the Center for Advanced Research on Language Acquisition [CARLA] Web site: What is culture? Retrieved September 20, 2011, from http://www.carla.umn.edu/culture/definitions.html

Dawes, L. (2005). "Speaking, listening and thinking with computers." In Grugeon, E., Dawes, L., Smith, C., & Hubbard, L. (Eds). *Teaching, speaking, and listening in the primary school* (3rd ed.). London: David Fulton.

Dennen, V. (2004). "Cognitive apprenticeship in educational practice: Research on scaffolding, modeling, mentoring and coaching as instructional strategies." In *Handbook of research on educational communications and technology* (2nd ed.), pp. 813–828. Mahwah, NJ: Lawrence Erlbaum.

Derman-Sparks, L. (1989). *Anti-bias curriculum: tools for empowering young children.* Washinton, DC: National Association for the Education of Young Children.

Derman-Sparks, L. and Olsen Edwards, J. (2010). *Anti-bias education for young children and ourselves.* Washington, DC: National Association for the Education of Young Children.

Yourdictionary.com. (2012). "Bridge." Retrieved September 20, 2011, from http://www.yourdictionary.com/bridge

Diner, H. (2008). Professor Diner discusses immigration and American diversity. Retrieved September 17, 2011, from http://www.america.gov/st/texttrans-english/2008/February/20080219165417xjsnommiS0.8737299.html

DiversityInc. (2008). Cultural competence required of today's immigrants. *eJournal USA*, *13*(2), 30–31: "Immigrants joining the mainstream." Retrieved January 28, 2012, from http://www.america.gov/publications/ejournalusa/0208.html

Echevarria, J., Vogt, M., & Short, D. (2004). *Making content comprehensible for English learners: The SIOP model* (2nd ed.). Boston: Allyn and Bacon.

Ewalt, D. M., & Rose, L. (2005). Bannister's four-minute mile named greatest athletic achievement. At Forbes.com. Retrieved September 20, 2011, from http://www.forbes.com/2005/11/18/bannister-four-minute-mile_cx_de_lr_1118bannister.html

Fielding, L. G., & Pearson, P. (1994). Reading comprehension: What works. *Educational Leadership*, *51*(5), 62–68.

Fisher, D., & Frey, N. (2007). *Checking for understanding: Formative assessment techniques for your classroom.* New York: Association for Supervision and Curriculum Development.

Fisher, D., Frey, N., & Rothenberg, C. (2008). *Content-area conversations: How to plan discussion-based lessons for diverse language learners.* New York: Association for Supervision and Curriculum Development.

Flint, A. S. (2008). *Literate lives: Teaching reading and writing in elementary classrooms.* New York: John Wiley & Sons.

Frean, A. (2009). Pupils to be taught to speak properly amid growing "word poverty." At Times Online. Retrieved September 23, 2011, from http://www.Timesonline.Co.Uk/Tol/Life_And_Style/Education/Article6174865.Ece

Freeman, M. (2003). *Teaching the youngest writers: A practical guide.* Gainesville, FL: Maupin House.

Fry, R. (2007). The changing racial and ethnic composition of U.S. public schools. At Pew Research Center/Pew Hispanic Center Web site. Retrieved September 17, 2011, from http://pewhispanic.org/reports/report.php?ReportID=79

Fry, R., & Gonzales, F. (2008). One-in-five and growing fast: A profile of Hispanic public school students. At Pew Research Center/Pew Hispanic Center Web site. Retrieved September 17, 2011, from http://pewhispanic.org/reports/report.php?ReportID=92

Fullan, M. G. (1993). Why teachers must become change agents. *Educational Leadership, 50*(6), 12–17.

Gay, G. (2010). *Culturally responsive teaching theory, research, and practice* (2nd ed.). New York: Teachers College Press.

Gill, H. (1999). Kidwatching: A naturalistic assessment technique. At Alternative approaches to assessing young children: A course companion Web site from Brooks Publishing. Retrieved September 19, 2011, from textbooks.brookespublishing.com/losardo/chapter3/links.htm

Girard, K. (2005). Lost in translation: Reaching out to English-language learners. At Edutopia Web site. Retrieved September 17, 2011, from http://www.edutopia.org/english-second-language

Goldenberg, C. (1991). Instructional conversations and their classroom applications. At eScholarship: University of California, Center for Research on Education, Diversity and Excellence, UC–Berkely Web site. Retrieved September 20, 2011, from http://escholarship.org/uc/item/6q72k3k9

Goldenberg, C. (2008). Teaching English language learners: What the research does—and does not—say. *American Educator,* Summer. At Immigration Research and Information Web site. Retrieved September 17, 2011, from http://www.immigrationresearch-info.org/report/immigrant-learning-center/teaching-english-language-learners-what-research-does-and-does-not-?page=1

Goldman, D. (2008). America 2050: Minorities in majority. At CNNMoney Web site. Retrieved September 17, 2011, from http://money.cnn.com/2008/08/13/news/economy/america_2050/index.htm

Graves, M. F. (2006). *The vocabulary book: Learning and instruction.* New York: Teachers College Press.

Grugeon, E., Dawes, L., Smith, C., & Hubbard, L. (2005). *Teaching speaking and listening in the primary school* (3rd ed.). London: David Fulton.

Hanley, M. S. (2009). School of Education at Johns Hopkins University The scope of multicultural education. At Johns Hopkins School of Education Web site. Retrieved September 20, 2011, from http://education.jhu.edu/newhorizons/strategies/topics/multicultural-education/the-scope-of-multicultural-education/index.html

Harris-Rollins, D. (n.d.). Designing powerful professional development for teachers, administrators, and school leaders. At Public Schools of North Carolina State Board of Education Department of Public Information Web site. Retrieved September 19, 2011, from http://www.ncpublicschools.org/search/?program=program&department=department&cx=01462100633343926525 2%3Asipd4jlcy9i&cof=FORID%3A11&ie=UTF-8&q=Debbie+Rollins&x=0&y=0&siteurl=www.ncpublicschools.org%2F

The Hartford. (2012). New corporate advertising campaign. Retrieved January 27, 2012, from http://www.thehartford.com/utility/about-thehartford/corporate-advertising-campaign/

Hernandez, D. J., Denton, N. A., & Macartney, S. E. (2007). Children in immigrant families—The U.S. and 50 states: National origins, language, and early education. Retrieved September 17, 2011, from http://www.eric.ed.gov:80/ERICWebPortal/search/detailmini.jsp?_nfpb=true&_&ERICExtSearch_SearchValue_0=ED496179&ERICExtSearch_SearchType_0=no&accno=ED496179

Hill, J., & Flynn, K. (2006). *Classroom instruction that works with English language learners*. New York: Association for Supervision and Curriculum Development.

Hirschman, C. (2006). The impact of immigration on American society: Looking backward to the future. From Border battles: The U.S. immigration debates. At Social Science Research Council [SSRC] Web site. Retrieved September 17, 2011, from http://borderbattles.ssrc.org/Hirschman/printable.html

Hofstede, G. (1984). "National cultures and corporate cultures." In L. A. Samovar & R. E. Porter (Eds.), *Communication Between Cultures*. Belmont, CA: Wadsworth. At the Center for Advanced Research on Language Acquisition [CARLA] Web site: What Is Culture? Retrieved September 20, 2011, from http://www.carla.umn.edu/culture/definitions.html

Howard, G. R. (1999). *We can't teach what we don't know: White teachers, multiracial schools*. New York: Teachers College Press.

"Instructional Conversations." (1992). ERIC Digest # ED347850. Retrieved January 27, 2012, from http://www.ericdigests.org/1992-2/instructional.htm

Jackson, C. D. (n.d.). QuoteWorld.org. Retrieved September 18, 2011, from http://www.quoteworld.org/quotes/7057

Jones, L. (2007). The student-centered classroom. Cambridge, UK: Cambridge University Press: Available at www.cambridge.org/us/esl/catalog/subject/project/custom/item2492501/Let's-Talk-The-Student-Centered-Classroom/?site_locale=en_US&currentSubjectID=2489423

Jordan, J. (2011). Restructuring teacher education to prepare teachers for diversity. At SEDL Web site. Retrieved September 20, 2011, from www.sedl.org/pubs/policy09/preparation.html

Kamil, M. L., Rosenthal, P. B., Pearson, P. D., & Barr, R. Eds. (2000). Vocabulary processes. In *The handbook of reading research, vol. III* (pp. 269–284). Mahwah, NJ: Lawrence Erlbaum.

Kamil, M. L., Rosenthal, P. B., Pearson, P. D., & Barr, R. (2001). Methods of literacy research: The methodology chapters from *The handbook of reading research, vol. III* (133–150). Mahwah, NJ: Lawrence Erlbaum.

Kenny, K. (2008). Irish Immigrants in the United States. At IIP Digital. Retrieved September 17, 2011, from http://iipdigital.usembassy.gov/st/english/publication/2008/03/20080307131416ebyessedo0.6800043.html#axzz1YFdyMuOl

The Knowledge Loom. (n.d.). Meeting the literacy needs of English language learners (ELLs). Retrieved September 17, 2011, from http://knowledgeloom.org/elemlit/ells_meetnds.jsp

Krashen, S. D. (1985). *The input hypothesis: Issues and implications*. London: Longman.

Krashen, S. D., & Terrell, T. D. (1983). *The natural approach: Language acquisition in the classroom*. Englewood Cliffs, NJ: Alemany Press.

Lehr, F., Osborn, J., & Hiebert, E. H. (n.d.). A focus on vocabulary. Honolulu: Pacific Resources for Education and Learning (PREL). Retrieved September 24, 2011, from http://www.prel.org/products/re_/ES0419.htm

Marzano, R. J. (2004). *Building background knowledge for academic achievement research on what works in schools*. Alexandria, VA: Association for Supervision and Curriculum Development.

Mather, M. (2009). *Children in immigrant families chart new path*. Washington: Population Reference Bureau.

Maxim, D., & Lee, C. (1997). School talk: Classroom practices that monitor and inform learning. At National Council of Teachers of English Web site. Retrieved September 18, 2011, from http://www.ncte.org/journals/st

Maxwell, L. (2008, December 31). Immigration transforms communities. *Education Week.* Retrieved September 17, 2011, from http://www.edweek.org/ew/articles/2009/01/08/17immig.h28.html

Mcleod, S. (2007). Vygotsky. At Simply Psychology. Retrieved October 9, 2011, from http://www.simplypsychology.org/vygotsky.html

Menkart, D. (1993). Multicultural education: Strategies for linguistically diverse schools and classrooms. *NCBE [National Council on Bilingual Education] Program Information Guide Series, 16, Fall.* Retrieved September 20, 2011, from http://www.ncela.gwu.edu/rcd/bibliography/BE019274/

Mercer, N. (2000). *Words and minds: How we use language to think together.* New York: Routledge.

Merriam-Webster Collegiate Dictionary [MWCD]. (2012). "Ubiquitous." Retrieved January 25, 2012, from http://www.merriam-webster.com/dictionary/ubiquitous

Minneapolis Public Schools [MPS]. (n.d.). How is balanced literacy delivered in the classroom? Retrieved September 20, 2011, from http://elementaryliteracy.mpls.k12.mn.us/balanced_literacy_approach.html

Moats, L. C. (1999). *Teaching reading is rocket science: What expert teachers of reading should know and be able to do.* New York: American Federation Of Teachers.

Mohr, K. A. (2004). English as an accelerated language: A call to action for reading teachers. *The Reading Teacher*, 58(1), 18–26.

Mohr, K. A., & Mohr, E. S. (2007). Extending English-language learner's classroom interactions using the Response Protocol. *The Reading Teacher*, 60(5), 440–450.

Myhill, D., Jones, S. M., & Hopper, R. (2006). *Talking, listening, learning: Effective talk in the primary classroom.* New York: Open University/McGrawHill.

Nagy, W. E. (1988). *Teaching vocabulary to improve reading comprehension.* Urbana, IL: ERIC Clearinghouse on Reading and Communication Skills.

Nagy, W. E., & Anderson, R. (1984). How many words are there in printed school English? *Reading Research Quarterly*, 19, 304–330.

National Center for Education Information [NCEI]. (2005). Profile of Teachers in the U.S. 2005. Retrieved January 18, 2012, from http://www.ncei.com/POT05PRESSREL3.htm

National Clearinghouse for English Language Acquisition [NCELA]. (2011). The growing numbers of English learner students, 1998/99–2008/09. Retrieved September 17, 2011, from http://www.ncela.gwu.edu/publications

National Council of Teachers of English [NCTE]. (2008). English language learners: A policy research brief produced by the National Council of Teachers of English. Retrieved September 17, 2011, from http://www.ncte.org/search?q=English+Language+Learners+A+Policy+Brief

National Reading Panel. (2000). Teaching children to read: An evidence-based assessment of the scientific research literature on reading and its implications for reading instruction. Washington, DC: National Institute of Child Health and Human Development.

Naylor, L. L. (1998). *American culture: Myth and reality of a culture of diversity.* Westport, CT: Bergin & Garvey.

Nielsen, K. E. (2005). *Helen Keller: Selected writings.* New York: New York University Press.

Nieto, S. (n.d.). Commentary. At Annenberg Learner Web site: Teaching multicultural literature: A workshop for the middle grades. Workshop 1: Engagement and dialogue. Retrieved September 20, 2011, from http://www.learner.org/workshops/tml/workshop1/commentary3.html

Nieto, S. (2002). *Language, culture, and teaching critical perspectives for a new century.* Mahwah, NJ: Lawrence Erlbaum.

Nieto, S. (2004). *Affirming diversity: The sociopolitical context of multicultural education* (4th ed.). Needham Heights, MA: Allyn and Bacon.

Noguera, P. (1999). Confronting the challenge of diversity in education: How we respond to the increase in diversity in America will be a challenge for many schools and communities, but it need not be a problem. *In Motion Magazine, April 9.* Retrieved September 17, 2011, from http://www.inmotionmagazine.com/pndivers.html

Noguera, P. (2006, October 15). School reform and second generation discrimination: Toward the development of equitable schools. *In Motion Magazine,* Retrieved September 17, 2011, from http://www.inmotionmagazine.com/er/pn_second.html

Noguera, P. (2009, April 10). Getting ready for the new majority: How schools can respond to immigration and demographic change. *In Motion Magazine.* Retrieved September 17, 2011, from http://www.inmotionmagazine.com/er/pn_newmaj09.html

Norman, S. J. (2012). The human face of school reform. *National FORUM of Educational Administration and Supervision Journal, 29*(4). Retrieved January 28, 2012, from www.nationalforum.com/Journals/National%20Forum%20of%20Educational%20Administration%20and%20Supervision/National%20Forum%20of%20Educational%20Administration%20and%20Supervision/TOCeas.htm

O'Keefe, T. (1997). The habit of kidwatching. *School Talk.* At the National Council of Teachers of English Web site. Retrieved September 18, 2011, from http://www.ncte.org/journals/st

Oregon Department of Education [Oregon DOE]. (2004). *Cultural competency summit report.* Retrieved September 20, 2011, from http://www.ode.state.or.us/news/announcements/announcement.aspx?=193

Orey, M. (Ed.). (2001). Emerging perspectives on learning, teaching and technology. Retrieved October 2, 2011, from http://projects.coe.uga.edu/epltt/

Owocki, G., & Goodman, Y. M. (2002). *Kidwatching: Documenting children's literacy development.* Portsmouth, NH: Heinemann.

Palmer, P. J. (1998). *The courage to teach: Exploring the inner landscape of a teacher's life.* San Francisco: Jossey-Bass.

Palmer, P. J. (1999). The grace of great things: Reclaiming the sacred in knowing, teaching, and learning. In *The Heart of knowing: Spirituality in education* (p. 27). New York: Jeremy P. Tarcher/Putnam.

Pappano, L. (2010). *Inside school turnarounds: Urgent hopes, unfolding stories.* Cambridge, MA: Harvard Education Press.

Pappano, L. (2011a). In school turnarounds, the human element is crucial. *Education Week,* October 9.

Pappano, L. (2011b). To improve schools, stop treating them like businesses. *The Christian Science Monitor,* January 4. Retrieved January 19, 2012, from http://www.csmonitor.com/Commentary/Opinion/2011/0104/To-improve-schools-stop-treating-them-like-businesses

Perry, T., Steele, C., & Hilliard, A. G. (2003). *Young, gifted, and Black: Promoting high achievement among African-American students.* Boston: Beacon.

Peters, J., Cornu, R. L., & Collins, J. (2003). *Towards constructivist teaching and learning: A report on research conducted in conjunction with the learning to learn project.* At Learning to Learn: A Web site of the Government of South Australia Department for Education and Child Development. Retrieved September 18, 2011, from http://www.learningtolearn.sa.edu.au/Colleagues/

Pianta, R. C., Belsky, J., Vandergrift, N., Houts, R., & Morrison, F. J. (2008). Classroom effects on children's achievement trajectories in elementary school. *American Educational Research Journal, 45*(2), 365–397.

Pressley, M. (2003, Fall). Research by Michael Pressley yields insights into the practices of effective educators. *New Educator 9*(1). Retrieved September 18, 2011, from http://www.educ.msu.edu/neweducator/fall03/pressley.htm

Principia Purpose. (2010, Summer). "Gifted coaches." *362*, 36. Available at http://content.principia.edu/document_viewer/100707_OnlineVersion_Sum10/

National Education Association (2011). *Professional development for general educators of teachers of English language learners: An NEA policy brief.* Washington, DC: Author.

Richardson, V. (1998). How teachers change: What will lead to change that most benefits student learning? *Focus on Basics, 2*(C). At the National Center for the Study of Adult Learning and Literacy [NCSALL] Web site. Retrieved September 19, 2011, from http://www.ncsall.net/index.php?id=395

Ripley, A. (2010, January/February). What makes a great teacher? The Atlantic. Retrieved September 18, 2011, from http://www.theatlantic.com/magazine/archive/2010/01/what-makes-a-great-teacher/7841/

Rodgers, A., & Rodgers, E. M. (2004). *Scaffolding literacy instruction: Strategies for K–4 classrooms.* Portsmouth, NH: Heinemann.

Rose, M., & Ayers, W. (2010). *To teach: The journey of a teacher* (3rd ed.). New York: Teachers College Press.

Rowe, M. B. (1986). Wait time: Slowing down may be a way of speeding up. *Journal of Teacher Education, 37*(1), 43.

Rubenstein, G. (2006). Vital signs: Learning is alive and well at Faubion Elementary. At Edutopia Web site. Retrieved September 20, 2011, from http://www.edutopia.org/vital-signs

Rueda, R., Goldenberg, C., & Gallimore, R. (1992). *Rating instructional conversations: A guide.* At eScholarship: University of California Web site. Retrieved September 20, 2011, from http://www.escholarship.org/uc/search?keyword=Robert+Rueda%2C+Claude+Goldenberg%2C+Ronald+Gallimore

Santa Ana, O. (2004). Foreword. *Tongue-tied: the lives of multilingual children in public education* (p. xii). Lexington, MA: Rowman & Littlefield.

Shea, M. (2000). *Taking running records: A teacher shares her experience on how to take running records and use what they tell you to assess and improve every child's reading.* Chicago: Scholastic Professional.

SIL International. (1999). What is comprehensible input? Retrieved September 24, 2011, from http://www.sil.org/lingualinks/languagelearning/otherresources/GlssryOfLnggLrnngTrms/WhatIsComprehensibleInput.htm

Simmons, D. C., & Kameenui, E. J. (Eds.). (1998). *What reading research tells us about children with diverse learning needs: Bases and basics.* Mahwah, NJ: Lawrence Erlbaum.

Simon, N. (1968). "The Odd Couple": Memorable quotes. In the Internet Movie Database (IMDb). Retrieved September 24, 2011, from http://www.imdb.com/title/tt0063374/quotes

Smith, L., & Zygouris-Coe, V. (2006). Scaffolding: FOR-PD's reading strategy of the month. Florida Department of Education and Just Read Florida! Retrieved October 2, 2011, from https://www.ocps.net/cs/services/cs/currareas/read/IR/bestpractices/SZ/scaffolding.pdf

Society of Women Engineers [SWE]. (n.d.). Bridge construction. Retrieved September 20, 2011, from http://www.swe.org/iac/lp/bridge_03b.html

South Australian Curriculum Standards and Accountability [SACSA]. (2001). South Australian Curriculum Standards and Accountability Framework. Retrieved September 18, 2011, from http://www.sacsa.sa.edu.au/index_fsrc.asp?t=About

Sparks, D. (2003, Winter). Interview with Michael Fullan: Change agent. *Journal of Staff Development, 24*(1). Retrieved September 18, 2011, from http://www.learningforward.org/news/jsd/fullan241.cfm

Stanovich, K. (1986). Matthew effects in reading: Some consequences of individual differences in the acquisition of literacy. *Reading Research Quarterly, 21*, 360–407.

Sweeney, D. (2003). Study groups. In *Learning along the way: Professional development by and for teachers* (pp. 21–22). Portland, ME: Stenhouse.

Teale, W. H. (2009, May). Students learning English and their literacy instruction in urban schools. *The Reading Teacher, 62*, 699–703.

Tharp, R. G., & Gallimore, R. (1991). The instructional conversation: Teaching and learning in social activity. At eScholarship: University of California, Center for Research on Education, Diversity and Excellence, UC–Berkely. Retrieved September 20, 2011, from http://www.escholarship.org/uc/search?keyword=Roland+G.+Tharp

Thompson, G. (2009, March 14). Where education and assimilation collide. *The New York Times.* Retrieved September 17, 2011, from http://www.nytimes.com/2009/03/15/us/15immig.html

Thomson, B. J. (1993). *Words can hurt you: Beginning a program of anti-bias education.* New York: Addison-Wesley.

University of Cambridge Faculty of Education. (2012). Thinking together: Resources for teachers. Retrieved January 25, 2012, from http://thinkingtogether.educ.cam.ac.uk/resources/downloads/Lesson1.pdf

U.S. Diplomatic Mission to Germany. (2010). About the USA: U.S. society > Hispanic Americans. Retrieved September 17, 2011, from http://usa.usembassy.de/society-hispanics.htm

Viadero, D. (2009). Research hones focus on ELLs. *Education Week.* Retrieved September 17, 2011, from http://www.edweek.org/ew/articles/2009/01/08/17research.h28.html

Vygotsky, L. S. (1962). *Thought and language.* Cambridge, MA: M.I.T. Press.

Vygotsky, L. S. (1978). *Mind and society: The development of higher mental processes.* Cambridge, MA: Harvard University Press.

Vygotsky, L. S., & Rieber, R. W. (1993). *The collected works of L. S. Vygotsky.* New York: Plenum.

Walqui, A. (2006). Scaffolding instruction for English language learners: A conceptual framework. *The International Journal of Bilingual Education and Bilingualism, 9*(2), 160.

Warren, M. (2010, October 13). They're all out: 33 miners raised safely in Chile. *Denver Post.* Retrieved September 20, 2011, from http://www.denverpost.com/breakingnews/ci_16327227

Weinstein, R. S. (2002). *Reaching higher: The power of expectations in schooling.* Cambridge, MA: Harvard University Press.

WestEd (2004). *Ways to Increase Student Engagement Before, During, and After Instruction.* San Francisco, CA: Author.

Westheimer, J. (1998). Conceptualizing community. *Journal of Research in Education, 8* (1), 9–15.

Wigginton, E. (1985). *Sometimes a shining moment: The Foxfire experience.* New York, NY: Anchor Press/Doubleday.

Wilhelm, J. (2004). *Reading is seeing: Learning to visualize scenes, characters, ideas, and text worlds to improve comprehension and reflective reading.* New York: Scholastic.

Wilhelm, J., Baker, T., & Dube, J. (2001). Scaffolding learning. At the My read Web site. Retrieved September 20, 2011, from www.myread.org/scaffolding.htm

Wilson, B. L., & Dickson, C. H. (2001). *Listening to urban kids: School reform and the teachers they want.* Albany, New York: State University of New York Press.

Wittgenstein, L. (2007). Quote. At Quotations Book Web site. Retrieved September 23, 2011, from http://quotationsbook.com/quote/40885/

Wolf, M. K., Crosson, A. C., & Resnick, L. B. (2006). Accountable talk in reading comprehension instruction. CSE Technical Report 670. Retrieved September 21, 2011, from http://www.eric.ed.gov:80/ERICWebPortal/search/detailmini.jsp?_nfpb=true&_ &ERICExtSearch_SearchValue_0=ED492865&ERICExtSearch_SearchType_0=no& accno=ED492865

Wren, S. (2001). *The cognitive foundations of learning to read: A framework.* Austin, TX: Southwest Educational Development Laboratory. Retrieved from http://www.sedl.org/ reading/framework/framework.pdf

Yen, H. (2008, June 10). U.S. minority population could be majority by mid-century census shows. *The Huffington Post.* Retrieved September 17, 2011, from http://www .huffingtonpost.com/2010/06/10/us-minority-population-co_n_607369.html

York, S. (1991). *Roots & wings: Affirming culture in early childhood programs.* St. Paul, MN: Redleaf.

Zwiers, J. (2008). *Building academic language: Essential practices for content classrooms, grades 5–12.* San Francisco: Jossey-Bass.